The Word of God for the People of God

- -

The Word of God for the People of God

An Entryway to the Theological
Interpretation of Scripture

J. TODD BILLINGS

William B. Eerdmans Publishing Company

Grand Rapids, Michigan / Cambridge, U.K.

Published 2010 by

Wm. B. Eerdmans Publishing Co.

2140 Oak Industrial Drive N.E., Grand Rapids, Michigan 49505 /
P.O. Box 163, Cambridge CB3 9PU U.K.

Printed in the United States of America

2022-05

Library of Congress Cataloging-in-Publication Data

Billings, J. Todd.
    The Word of God for the people of God : an entryway to the
    theological interpretation of Scripture / J. Todd Billings.
        p.   cm.
    ISBN 978-0-8028-6235-8 (pbk.: alk. paper)
    1. Bible — Hermeneutics.   2. Bible — Theology.   I. Title.

    BS476.B5   2010
    220.601 — dc22

                               2009030390

www.eerdmans.com

To Rachel

Contents

. . . .

Contents

Acknowledgments

·····························

I HAVE WRITTEN this book for students and pastors as well as for scholars. I am grateful to a wide range of scholars from a wide range of disciplinary perspectives for their feedback and input on this project: systematic and historical theologians, biblical scholars, and practical theologians. But I am also grateful for the many pastors and students who gave me feedback on earlier versions; they contributed greatly to the book's readability and connection to the daily ministry of the church. While I am responsible for the final form of this book (including its shortcomings), I am indebted to many for the pages within.

The origins of this work, which arises from a dual love of Scripture and Christian ministry, go back a long way. Ultimately, I give God thanks for Irenaeus, Augustine, Maurus, Calvin, and countless other saints of the church. In the growth and development of those loves in my own life, I am grateful to the everyday saints who helped to cultivate my love of Scripture together with a love for Christian ministry in a wide variety of contexts — Kansas, California, Massachusetts, Michigan, Uganda, and Ethiopia for starters. I give thanks for my many mentors and colleagues in ministry, and for the love they showed for Scripture. At Wheaton College, luminaries such as Dennis Okholm and Bruce Ellis Benson helped to develop my interest in theological and philosophical hermeneutics. My reflections were refined and expanded when I studied with Marianne Meye Thompson, James Butler, and John Thompson at Fuller Seminary, and then with Merold Westphal, Francis

Schussler Fiorenza, Sarah Coakley, and Nicholas Constas at Harvard University.

My students at Western Theological Seminary provided the initial inspiration for this book, and I am grateful to them as well. Many students displayed a love for Scripture and Christian ministry, but they had no idea why they should be interested in "the theological interpretation of Scripture." This book is a response to their conundrum — to their good questions and earnest inquiries about how and why they should bother reflecting on their theological hermeneutic for Scripture. I am particularly grateful to the students in my seminar on the Theological Interpretation of Scripture in the fall of 2007 and Systematic Theology II in the spring of 2008 for providing feedback on less refined drafts of material in this book.

A local reading group of scholars and pastors provided insightful chapter-by-chapter feedback, and to these readers I offer heartfelt thanks: Rachel M. Billings, Steven Bouma-Prediger, Timothy Brown, David Cunningham, Mark Husbands, Kristen Johnson, Trygve Johnson, and Brian Keepers. Another group of pastors provided valuable feedback from a distance, including Dan Eisnor, Travis Else, and Tim Truesdell. I am also grateful for the tireless work of my research assistant, Dustyn Keepers, who not only provided excellent feedback on chapter drafts but also accomplished many other tasks necessary for the project to move along.

Other scholars who read and commented on the book or portions of it include James V. Brownson, Jason Byassee, Matthew Levering, Michael Pasquarello III, Darren Sarisky, Kevin Vanhoozer, Francis Watson, and John Webster. Thank you for your astute responses to drafts of my manuscript.

I am also grateful to the Wabash Center for awarding me a summer research fellowship that helped to facilitate the writing of this manuscript, and to Jon Pott and the staff at Eerdmans for their support and hard work in turning a manuscript into a book.

While I have many to thank, I dedicate this book to Rachel M. Billings, my loving spouse and a brilliant Old Testament scholar. Rachel and I met as fellow doctoral students at Harvard, where I went on for a Th.D. in theology and she for a Ph.D. in Hebrew Bible/Old Testament. Our courtship developed in the midst of a "theological hermeneutics of scripture" reading group at Harvard. The topics in this book have been discussed over the dinner table, and while I speak for myself in this book, the wide-ranging exploration of the topics herein is a journey we have taken together. Perhaps our journey can give a glimpse of the possibilities of a marriage between theology and biblical studies, a marriage that can be part of the church's receptive posture in hearing God's powerful word through Scripture.

UNLESS OTHERWISE NOTED, all English translations of the Bible are taken from the New Revised Standard Version.

Introduction

....

IN RECENT YEARS, numerous books have sought to reclaim a theological approach to Scripture for the church; somewhat ironically, most
are written exclusively for a scholarly audience. In this book I seek to
widen the field of readers to students and church leaders who love
Scripture and love Christian ministry, but who are not at all sure why
they should be interested in "the theological interpretation of Scripture." In brief, the theological interpretation of Scripture is a multifac-
eted practice of a community of faith in reading the Bible as God's instrument of self-revelation and saving fellowship. It is not a single,
discrete method or discipline; rather, it is a wide range of practices we
use toward the goal of knowing God in Christ through Scripture. Reflection on our theological hermeneutic involves examining the theology
that we bring to Scripture and investigating how our theologies operate
as we read Scripture in the midst of worshiping communities. It also involves patient attention to the biblical text, various forms of biblical
criticism, and a critical engagement with the Christian tradition
through history — in a variety of cultural contexts.

For some readers, this brief description already evokes some big
questions about the theological interpretation of Scripture: Why
should I think about my theological presuppositions in approaching
Scripture? Shouldn't I just get my theology *from* Scripture? Why should
I think about Scripture in relation to questions about how we come to
know God? Why bother to hear scriptural interpretations from the

church's history, or from diverse cultural locations? Why go to the trouble of reading critical commentaries if I am interpreting the Bible for the church? There is a lively scholarly discourse on the theological interpretation of Scripture that tends to assume certain responses to these questions — rather than explicating them. In this book I seek to bridge the gap by addressing the questions directly and by presenting a constructive proposal for readers to engage as they interpret Scripture as the church.

I want to introduce readers to the practice of interpreting Scripture in the context of the triune activity of God, the God who uses Scripture to reshape the church into Christ's image by the Spirit's power. I seek to welcome readers into the *spacious* and yet *specified* place of wrestling with, chewing on, and performing Scripture. Christian readers occupy a spacious territory when they come to know the inexhaustible power of the Spirit's word through Scripture, a word that is both strangely close to us and yet always meeting us anew as a stranger. Our imaginations need rejuvenation so that we can perceive the wide, expansive drama of salvation into which God incorporates us as readers of Scripture. Yet, as Christians, we also interpret Scripture from a specified location. We are not simply modern individuals looking at an ancient text, or members of a social club looking to an instruction manual on how to make the church run more effectively. We are people who interpret Scripture "in Christ," as those united to the living Christ by the Holy Spirit's mediation and power.

This book is not an introduction in the sense of an overview of the secondary literature; it is more of an entryway through which readers can come to examine the actual theology and practice of interpreting Scripture for the church. In other words, this book does not simply talk about others who talk about God and scriptural interpretation; instead, it makes claims about God, and it enters directly into the practice of scriptural interpretation. I have placed extended exegetical examples at the end of chapters 2 through 5, each with a direct connection to Christian ministry. Through the process of making theological claims and entering into scriptural exegesis, I hope to help readers see the ways in which they inevitably occupy some kind of theological space in their reception of Scripture.

As a constructive work of theology, this is also a scholarly work that contributes to a growing body of literature on the theological interpretation of Scripture, a discourse on the reading of Scripture from a distinctly ecclesiastical location. In so doing, it engages a wide range of scholarly literature. But there are many places where I have deleted footnotes, removed technical terms, and streamlined my argument so that this book can welcome students and pastors into the practice of theological interpretation. I wish to expose readers to enough scholarly discourse to help them to know where to go to explore key issues further, through both footnotes and annotated lists ("for further reading") at the conclusion of each chapter.

The opening chapter addresses a question posed by many students and church leaders: Why bother with a theological hermeneutic at all? Shouldn't we simply derive our theology *from* the Bible, rather than bringing theological assumptions *to* the Bible? After examining some scriptural motifs about the word of God's connection to the action of God, I contrast several models for receiving Scripture theologically: we can translate Scripture into propositional building blocks to fit into a blueprint; we can pick over Scripture like food at a smorgasbord, as we choose what seems to fit our questions and needs; or we can receive Scripture as part of a Trinitarian-shaped journey of faith seeking understanding. In expositing the third position, I draw on the classical notion of reading Scripture within a "rule of faith," and then I seek to articulate a form of the rule of faith that avoids common misconstruals. In my explication, the rule of faith emerges from Scripture, and yet it provides extrabiblical guidance about the center and periphery of God's story of salvation accessed through Scripture. In light of the rule of faith, Christian scriptural interpretation takes place on the path of Jesus Christ, empowered by the Spirit to transform God's people into Christ's image, anticipating a transformative vision of the triune God.

Chapter 2 continues to develop this Trinitarian-shaped hermeneutic, but it does so with regard to a general hermeneutical question: To what extent should we read the Bible like any other book? As a working framework, I claim that, on the one hand, "all truth is God's truth," and we should use the insights from a wide range of human inquiry when we read Scripture. On the other hand, I affirm that "all truth is in Jesus Christ": we need to discern all truth claims in light of Jesus Christ as the truth, for there is no such thing as purely secular reason. With that in view, I argue that, while the church should use insights from general hermeneutics as it reads Scripture, the overall framework for interpreting the Bible as Scripture should have an unmistakably theological character: that is, the starting and ending point of scriptural interpretation should emerge from a Trinitarian hermeneutic of God's redeeming work through Scripture. On the general hermeneutics side, I seek to appropriate insights from philosophical hermeneutics about what a close reading of a text looks like, as well as point to the important role for modern critical biblical studies within a theological hermeneutic of Scripture. We can then appropriate and recontextualize these insights into a theological context for the church's reading of Scripture. Ultimately, the Bible is a book that the church cannot and should not read exactly like any other book.

In chapter 3, I extend a Trinitarian hermeneutic to three interrelated theological topics: revelation, inspiration, and canon. I argue that on the level of one's operative theology, there are two sets of either/or's that are unavoidable. Either revelation is grounded in inherent, universal human capacities or in the particularity of God's action with Israel and in Jesus Christ; second, either we function with a Deistic hermeneutic of Scripture or a Trinitarian hermeneutic of Scripture as an instrument of revelation. My argument is not one that encourages simplistic, dichotomous thinking, for there is a broad continuum of positions on revelation. Yet, along this continuum, these two theological decisions — whether they are made consciously or not — still play a decisive role. After exploring these either/or's on revelation, I give an account of how a Trinitarian theology of revelation can provide the context crucial for properly understanding the doctrines of the inspiration and canonicity of Scripture. The chapter also points to the ways in which differing theologies of revelation lie behind some significant disputes in scriptural interpretation.

All interpretation is shaped, whether we recognize it or not, by the cultural context and social location of the interpreter. In the face of this, it may be tempting to say that all (contextual) interpretations of Scripture are equally valid, or that one's interpretation of Scripture should be insulated from criticism from other cultural locations. But drawing on the Trinitarian soteriology of revelation in chapter 3, chapter 4 suggests that these are not helpful inferences to draw from the observation that all scriptural interpretation is contextual. Instead, we should hold together two theological affirmations about how the triune God works in relation to our contextual reading of Scripture. On the one hand, we should celebrate the way the Spirit works to indigenize God's word in various contexts and cultures, bringing unity in the person of Jesus Christ. Because of the Spirit's indigenizing work, scriptural interpretation from diverse contexts can be received as mutual enrichment, gifts of the Spirit. Yet there is a second side to the Spirit's work through Scripture as well. All cultures have idols that resist God's transformation in the reading of Scripture; therefore, a critique of culture is an important practice in receiving Scripture as God's word, discerning through Scripture the bounded character of the Spirit's work in Christ, which calls all cultures to continual conversion. In light of this dynamic of the Spirit's work, chapter 4 goes on to focus on discerning the Spirit: the role of experience, community, suspicion, and trust in the interpretation of Scripture as the church discerns the Spirit's indigenizing yet transforming word through Scripture.

Chapter 5 further extends our exploration of a Trinitarian, Christ-centered hermeneutic by drawing on premodern exegetes who often held such a hermeneutic in one form or another. The chapter explores the value of patristic, medieval, and Reformational approaches to Scripture with two goals in mind: first, to show why contemporary Christians need to rediscover and embrace some key premodern insights about how to approach the Bible as Scripture; second, to advocate the concrete practice of reading patristic, medieval, and Reformational exegesis when we interpret Scripture. By giving examples in the chapter and responding to common objections to premodern exegesis, I wish to give readers a taste of what reading premodern exegesis can help open up for contemporary Christians: a rich and varied feast, a renewal of the imagination to show the many ways in which the Bible can function as a word conforming believers to Christ's image by the Spirit's power. I do not advocate reading earlier exegetes to simply repeat past exegesis. Indeed, I point to ways in which we should be attentive to the shortcomings of premodern exegesis. Still, the practice of reading, singing, and engaging past exegesis can be a way to participate in the Spirit's work, seeing how the church has discerned the incarnate Word in receiving the varied and often puzzling words of Scripture.

Finally, in chapter 6, I seek to synthesize the insights of earlier chapters, as well as add further reflections on concrete reading practices of Scripture in the church. I argue that proper reading practices of Scripture should participate in the triune drama of salvation. After articulating the triune, dramatic, and soteriological context for reading practices, I try to sharpen the practical wisdom of readers by examining how particular practices do or do not participate in the triune drama. I set forth a positive vision of Scripture reading as a spiritual discipline, the role of Scripture in Christian worship, and the place of Scripture as God's instrument for mission in the world. The chapter conclusion gives a portrait for how the theological interpretation of Scripture can be used by God to renew the church and its ministries.

Through all of these chapters, I seek to integrate methods and disciplines that are often kept apart: theory and practice, biblical studies and theology, critical methods and the practices of prayer and worship. I believe that the *integration* of such practices is key for overcoming the Deistic-tending reading of Scripture among many Western Christians today. The fragmentation of these theological disciplines and practices has left church leaders, in particular, with the perplexing task of using diverse and seemingly unrelated methods for reading Scripture in the context of ministry. While Christian leaders draw on a long list of "experts," it is tempting for them to function in a compartmentalized way that implicitly assumes that God is not active through Scripture, reshaping God's people into Christ's image by the Spirit's power. Instead, all too often Scripture becomes a tool pastors use to legitimate their business-based plan for church growth, or it serves as a touchstone for sermons full of self-help advice. These are very real pressures that church leaders feel from church marketers and, at times, from the congregations themselves. The situation is exacerbated by academic training that is not integrated with theological integrity. Unfortunately, unintegrated practice can lead to an avoidance of God's powerful and transforming word through Scripture — a word that is not under our control. As inconvenient as it may be, church leaders are not called to use the Bible as though they were religious managers or religious customer service agents. They are called to read the Bible as disciples of Jesus Christ.

Scripture is the Spirit's instrument by which the living Christ speaks words of power to God's people, bringing life where there is death and hope where there is despair. My desire is that this book may help readers gain clarity about the wide and spacious yet specified way of approaching Scripture as readers who belong to Christ. I hope to welcome readers to an integrated way of reading that joyfully enters our place in the triune drama of salvation. In this way, readers of Scripture are centered in Jesus Christ, empowered and transformed by the Spirit, and sent for service into the world as a community that is continually re-formed by the word of God.

CHAPTER 1

Reading Scripture on the Journey
of Faith Seeking Understanding

W E ARE PARCHED for a word from God. As Westerners in the
twenty-first century, many of us will look under any rock, search
any trail, or explore any website in pursuit of promises of a transcendent word. We yearn for a word that will break into our lives, which are
often comfortable, yet leave us in stress and fear. We hunger for a word
that would bring a personal touch from someone other than the almighty market or the ever-just meritocracy around us. We crave something larger than what is offered by a world in which good things have
become ultimate things, in which our own interests and desires shape
what comes into our minds and what goes out. We are thirsty and hungry, hoping for more. We long for a word from God.

However, when we are honest with ourselves, we also long for a
word from God that conforms to our own plans and wishes. We want a
word from God that endorses our own decisions and priorities. We
want to be affirmed by God in what we are already doing, not confronted and called to repentance. We want God's word, but on our own
terms.

For those who bear the name of Christ, the broad contours of this
cultural situation should give us reason to pause. We do not live in
countries in which the Bible, as the written word of God, must be acquired secretly via the black market. We do not live in countries in
which preaching, as the proclaimed word of God, must be done in clandestine meetings in basements after dark. The word of God is available

1

— present around us, so it seems. It is on the shelf at home or available at the click of a mouse. Yet, if the word of God is so widely available, why is our longing for it so often unsatisfied? Why does it seem so elusive? Why is it that, in our efforts to receive God's word, we often end up speaking a word that does not seem to be from God, but a word from and controlled by us?

The word of God is commonly spoken about in the New Testament in terms of seed imagery: the seed is spread, takes root, grows, and bears fruit. There is something in the word of God that is larger than ourselves; we are correct in longing for a taste — a touch — from a reality outside of ourselves. The encounter with God's word leads to a kind of flourishing, such that "faith and love" spring up from the "hope" that comes from "the word of the gospel" bearing fruit (Col. 1:3-5). The word of God is "alive and active," a reality that saves us from our delusions and self-deceptions by penetrating "even to dividing soul and spirit, joints and marrow; it judges the thoughts and attitudes of the heart" (Heb. 4:12). The word of God takes root, grows, and flourishes in a way that gives life. Just as God spoke to give physical life to creation, so also God's word brings life through a second birth by the Spirit to those who believe (Gen. 1:11-12, 20-26; John 3:3-15).

A seed has potential to grow, flourish, and bring new life. But why doesn't it always do so? In our context, how could it be that Scripture and preaching could be ever present, but they are not always accompanied by new growth and transformation?

To address this, we will find it helpful to take a closer look at how New Testament writers use the image of seed for the word. In all three Synoptic Gospel accounts of Jesus' parable of the sower, the seed falls on different kinds of soil (cf. Matt. 13:1-23; Mark 4:1-20; Luke 8:4-15). Some falls on the path, and it is snatched by Satan. Some falls on rocky ground: it is received with joy, but it takes no root because it is not received for growth and flourishing. Other seed falls among the thorns, which choke its growth: the thorns are "the cares and riches and pleasures of this life" (Luke 8:14; the language is very similar in Mark 4:19 and Matt. 13:22). Again, the seed bears no fruit. Finally, some hear the word and accept it. For these, the word bears abundant fruit in their life (fruit that is thirtyfold, sixtyfold, or a hundredfold in the Matthew and Mark accounts).

Why does the seed of the kingdom, which the parables call the word of God, not always bear fruit? These parables suggest a few reasons. In these accounts, Jesus himself is the sower. He seems to be sowing seeds indiscriminately: throwing seed all over the place, not simply targeting the soil that appears most likely to be responsive. The word of God is proclaimed to all who can hear, but it does not always bear fruit. When asked to explain the parable of the sower, Jesus responds that some will simply "hear" the parables of the Kingdom, but "not understand." Some will "see," but "will not perceive." The word of God could be right in front of their eyes, but they would not see it, accept it, cling to it (Matt. 13:13; Mark 4:12; Luke 8:10; and parallels in John 12:37-40).

This is a stark lesson for today's Christians who want God's word to reverberate over the airwaves. The word of God does not always produce results. People may know the language, the idiom, and have high academic degrees; but they don't necessarily comprehend the word that is proclaimed. The parable does not tell us why; but it does imply that there is something more going on than simply a cognitive understanding of written or spoken words. As a theme taken up in John, we are told, "No one can see the kingdom of God without being born from above" (John 3:3). After healing a blind man who then professes faith in Christ as the Son of Man, Jesus says, "I came into this world for judgment so that those who do not see may see, and those who do see may become blind" (John 9:39). Something much bigger is going on in receiving, understanding, and believing the word of God than human linguistic understanding. Making the word available on the internet or in a mailbox is no guarantee that someone will have a transforming encounter with God's word.

Since there is nothing automatic about receiving the word of God, this event is in many ways a mystery. Yet it is not a mystery that leaves us gawking on the sidelines; rather, it is one that invites us to participate in what God is doing. Paul adapts the seed imagery in this text: "I planted, Apollos watered, but God gave the growth" (1 Cor. 3:6). Does Paul want credit for his passionate and strategic preaching of the gospel? In a word, no. "So neither the one who plants nor the one who waters is anything, but only God who gives the growth" (1 Cor. 3:7). We should not be discouraged by the fact that hearing the word of God involves much more than our own talents and strategies. We should be encouraged. God's transforming word is not so neat and tidy that we can package and market it, expecting it to sell. Its potency and fruitful-ness has more to do with God's hand than our own. We live in a world with a living God who is beyond both our hopes and our attempts to control. We need not be burdened with the task of constructing and marketing the word of God; instead, we find ourselves in the exciting yet dangerous place of being addressed by the living God, who will not leave us to ourselves.

Yet the Bible must be read, the gospel must be preached, the word must be taught. All of this happens in and through human beings like you and me. God does not bypass our human capacities, simply speaking to us by the Spirit without regard for Scripture or the work of our human faculties. Augustine says that God's voice to us "could certainly have been [given] through an angel, but the human condition would be wretched indeed if God appeared unwilling to minister his word to human beings through human agency."[1] Augustine points to an incarnational view of divine and human agency, such that attributing a work to God does not mean that human faculties are bypassed or subverted. On the other hand, we should not think that the word of God is a word under our control in such a way that if we were persuasive and savvy enough, it would always be effective. This flies in the face of how the Gospels speak about this word, which is a seed that Jesus flings freely and recklessly, knowing that not all of it will bear fruit. We receive the word of God that brings growth and life only when the Spirit enables us to see, hear, and perceive (John 3:3). Our reception of the word of God is enabled by the work of God.

Neither Building Blocks nor Smorgasbord: Scripture and the Journey of Faith

How exactly does the Bible as a book fit in with the image of the word of God as that which brings fruit to our parched and aching lives? I have suggested two aspects of a response to that question. Although Christians speak about the Bible as the "word of God" written — the inspired word of God — exposure to the contents of Scripture does not necessarily lead to a transforming encounter with God's word. Second, more pos-

1. Saint Augustine, *On Christian Teaching,* trans. R. P. H. Green (Oxford: Oxford University Press, 1997), p. 5.

itively, the contents of the Bible need the work of God the Spirit for the word to bear fruit. Although God does not bypass our human capacities, the reception of God's word is not simply a matter of human persuasion.

But these reasons do not fully answer our question. The Bible is a book; it is not the fourth member of the Trinity. It is not God. If we were to draw on a classical list of divine attributes — eternal, all-knowing, all-powerful — these words would not apply to the Bible in its capacity as a book. Yet the terms would apply to the one whom Christians have traditionally considered to be the primary author of Scripture, God himself. The book itself is not God, but it is God's instrument for transformation. How does this happen?

First, let's narrow the field by considering several examples of how the Bible is used in Christian ministry. The first two tend to resist God's transforming work through Scripture, while the third sees reading Scripture as part of a journey of transformation.

The first is the blueprint and building-block approach: people read particular passages of Scripture as if they were the concrete blocks of a building. They translate each Scripture passage into a set of propositions that can then be fit as blocks into our building's blueprint. The propositions in Scripture are facts that need organization, and the system of theology provides that organization. In a sense, we already know the extensive meaning of Scripture; our system of theology tells us that. There is thus no need to look into history, or other cultures, to see how others "hear" Scripture. Instead, the task of interpreting Scripture is to discover where in our theological system this particular Scripture passage goes. This approach to scriptural interpretation has a long history in American Christianity, and it still shows up in many Christian environments today.[2] Indeed, when topical sermons or topical Bible studies do not wrestle with the particularities of the biblical witness, biblical texts can easily become building blocks to fit into a preestablished blueprint.

The temptation with these practices is to read Scripture impressionistically. Pastor Larry needs a message on how to face temptation. The idea he would like to portray is that the key to overcoming tempta-

---

2. For a historical portrait about how this view of Scripture developed in the history of American religion such that the Bible was viewed as "a compendium of facts" that simply need classification, see George Marsden, *Fundamentalism and American Culture,* 2nd ed. (New York: Oxford University Press, 2006), pp. 56ff.

tion is taking away the source of temptation. Larry does a Scripture search until he finds a passage that fits his original idea, such as Jesus' admonition in Matthew 5:29 to "pluck out" your eye if it causes you to sin. In the sermon Larry uses this Scripture text, along with some compelling illustrations, to fit his predetermined goal for the sermon: to recommend removing the source of temptation. Notice that Larry did not go to the Scripture passage to find out how to think about temptation. He did not approach Scripture as a learner who was ready to be reshaped by God in the process of struggling with the text. Larry thought that he already had a detailed blueprint of the building. What he needed from Scripture was a tool, a block in the building to fit his original idea. Blueprint sermons often end up being like after-dinner speeches that champion a particular cultural virtue (such as "try hard to make good decisions"), peppered with biblical illustrations.

Scriptural interpretation should not be like fitting concrete blocks into a building's blueprint; but neither should it be like eating at a smorgasbord, which is a second common approach. Imagine a huge cafeteria loaded with food of many kinds for many tastes — from fried chicken to falafel, vegetable wraps to sushi. Now imagine that you are at this smorgasbord with the members of a small Bible-study group from your church. Can you imagine what some of the other members of the group would choose to eat? Would there be patterns of food on the plates that you could describe according to the age, gender, ethnicity, or socioeconomic status of the eater? I suspect that there would be certain patterns. And in the filling of these appetites at the smorgasbord, there is a direct correspondence between the identity and desires of the eaters and what they load up on their plates.

The smorgasbord approach to the Bible is, in some ways, the opposite of the blueprint approach. The smorgasbord approach dispenses with the idea that we have a detailed blueprint of what the word of God means by translating Scripture into propositions that can serve as building blocks. In contrast, the smorgasbord approach says that we don't have a "map" at all. Each of us brings something different to the Bible, and each of us gets something different out of it. Instead of trying to develop a map of Scripture, we should just keep helping ourselves to the smorgasbord of Scripture to feed our various longings.

The smorgasbord approach to the Bible takes on several different forms. It has a popular and pietistic form that scours the content of

Scripture without a map and then identifies whatever it finds there as "the word of God." Thus, the dietary laws in the Old Testament are God's key to a healthy and happy lifestyle. Examples of this approach abound in Christian publishing, as is demonstrated by titles such as *The Bible's Diet, The Bible's Seven Secrets to Healthy Eating,* and *The Maker's Diet.* Another example would be those who read the creation narrative in the first chapter of Genesis as a descriptive geological history giving us the answers to our many questions about the history of the earth. For these teachers of Scripture, the word of God is not about building a structure of systematic theology but about finding God's answers to our own particular human queries and conundrums, from how to lose weight to how to manage personal finances. There is no map, just discoveries that meet our appetites, questions, and needs.

The smorgasbord approach also has a less pietistic, more rationalist version. This approach valorizes moments like Martin Luther's stand against the tradition of the Roman Catholic church, "Here I stand." Luther is seen as the solitary individual who takes what he finds in Scripture and throws it against the map of the Catholic church's theology.[3] Tradition — and systems of theology — hide the true meaning of Scripture from us, this view declares. What we need to do is to search beneath the layers of tradition to find the true meaning of Scripture. Underneath the church's attempt to rationalize and repress the meaning of Scripture, we will find the word of God. Examples of this approach are widespread, as the number of recent titles on Jesus attests: *The Misunderstood Jew: The Church and the Scandal of the Jewish Jesus* by Amy Jill Levine; *The Secret Message of Jesus: Uncovering the Truth that Could Change Everything* by Brian McLaren; *The Five Gospels: What Did Jesus Really Say? The Search for the Authentic Words of Jesus* by Robert Funk. What do these very diverse authors have in common? They think that the real message of the Bible has somehow been "hidden" by church tradition.[4] Thus do they see tradition as something that ob-

3. This common portrait of Luther as the Reformer standing with "the Bible alone" over against the traditions of the church falls flat in the face of historical inquiry. See, e.g., the contextually sensitive portrait of Luther in Heiko Oberman, *Luther: Man Between God and the Devil* (New Haven: Yale University Press, 2006).

4. On this point, I am indebted to Marianne Meye Thompson, "Still Looking: The Ongoing Quest for Jesus," paper delivered at Western Theological Seminary, Holland, MI, May 14, 2007.

scures God's word from us rather than a Spirit-filled means of imparting the word.

In this book I wish to articulate a middle way between these two extreme approaches. I agree, along with the first approach, that Christians always bring a basic theological map to their reading of Scripture. It is impossible to leave a map behind; but the map is not a detailed blueprint. It does not tell us every stop we will make on the journey of reading Scripture; rather, it gives us the broad outline for our journey. It does not give all of the answers into which each particular text will fit. To put it differently, Scripture passages are not wholly determinative on their own, fitting seamlessly as propositions into a preestablished system of theology. The word of God in Scripture is something that encounters us again and again; it surprises, confuses, and enlightens us because through Scripture we encounter the triune God himself. Scripture interpretation is not just putting together pieces of a puzzle. Instead, it is a joyful journey of struggling with Scripture and its author, God, who calls our lives, our priorities, and our preconceptions into question. Like Jacob wrestling with the angel, we struggle with Scripture until God blesses us with it.

When we read Scripture along a path in this middle way, we enter into what some authors have called a "drama."[5] God's word is not simply an abstract set of propositions about God: God does not simply say things about God, but God "promises, commands, warns, guides," and in this way God reveals himself.[6] Through these speech-actions of God, we see how God has acted in creation, in covenant with Israel, and in Jesus Christ, incorporating us into this divine drama by the Spirit's power. As ones who are in Christ and empowered by the Spirit, we become participants in God's drama and performers of the script of Scripture. The new world into which God brings us via Scripture is wide and spacious, but it also has a specified character as a journey on the path of Jesus Christ by the power of the Spirit in anticipation of a transforming vision of the triune God.

This middle way seeks to avoid certain reductionist tendencies in

---

5. Chap. 6 will further explore the image of drama and the usefulness of speech-act theory in the interpretation of Scripture.

6. Kevin Vanhoozer, "Word of God," *Dictionary for Theological Interpretation of the Bible* (Grand Rapids: Baker, 2005), p. 853.

the smorgasbord and building-block approaches. On the other side, it does not agree with the smorgasbord approach that any kind of map or preconception for Scripture will distort our reception of God's word. There are two temptations to avoid here. The first is the failure to reflect on the theological preconceptions we bring to Scripture. Without clarifying how and why we come to Scripture, we can easily turn the Bible as the word of God into the divine answer book: it gives us answers to our own questions about diets, management techniques, financial happiness, and geology. Rather than being an instrument of divine revelation and fellowship, the Bible is thus reduced to a predictable list of answers to our felt needs and questions. The other temptation is to use the denial of our theological map as a rhetorical strategy to dismiss other interpretations of Scripture: "While other Christians are stuck in tradition, I have found the secret/hidden/real message of Jesus." This individualistic approach, which became prominent in the Enlightenment, is a way of denying the influence of communal practices and preconceptions on our reading of the Bible. This view says, "Maps distort and obscure, so let's get rid of them." But such a commitment is itself a map.

Rather than seeing biblical passages as building blocks or the entrees at a smorgasbord, I believe that we should see our encounters with Scripture texts as a journey along a path. Whatever our own personal stories are, we find a larger story of journey in the Christian faith. We do not embark on this journey of reading Scripture as an unbiased, blank slate; we embark on it with expectations about its purpose and its end. We expect and hope that God will use our reading of Scripture to bring us further down the path of knowing God in Christ. We enter as a community of Christians with shared practices, such as worshiping the triune God and celebrating baptism and the Lord's Supper. These practices and commitments will — and should — influence our interpretation of Scripture. They will make us "biased," but in a good way — a way by which the Spirit brings the word of God to fruition in our lives.[7]

Where does this journey lead us? The final end of the path is a transforming "face-to-face" encounter with our triune God, a joyful state of "knowing fully" and being "fully known" as children of God in

---

7. I will explore the dynamics of a "good bias," or preconception, toward Scripture in some depth in chap. 2.

Christ (1 Cor. 13:12; Rom. 8:15-21). Each step along the path gives us a foretaste of that final end. The path itself is Jesus Christ: it is in and through Jesus Christ that we interpret all of Scripture. Hence, the path and the journey are not completely undefined. The basic map of this path is what the church fathers call "the rule of faith." It is not a detailed map that knows all of the stops along the way. But this map is a sketch of our story, our journey: through it we know our path (Jesus Christ), our source of illumination and empowerment (the Holy Spirit), and have a foretaste of our final destination (a transforming vision of the triune God, which involves the restoration of creation and communion with God). On this path we grow in the love of God and neighbor as we grow into our identity in Christ, and we grow in the knowledge of and fellowship with God. Knowing our path means that what Scripture points to is not, first and foremost, a successful diet plan or a geological history. It is Jesus Christ, and the reading of Scripture is part of our journey, through the Spirit, to be transformed more and more into the image of Christ.[8]

This may sound like the building-block approach to some readers, but it is actually quite different. While I believe we have a sketch of what the journey is like, it does not mean that Scripture passages themselves are blocks of concrete, wholly determinate and reducible to propositional content.[9] If so, there would be no need for a transforming jour-

8. I make no claims for originality in this portrait of the rule of faith; indeed, a completely "original" rule of faith would be suspect. I draw my portrait largely from Augustine in *On Christian Teaching,* though Augustine himself is synthesizing a great deal of earlier Christian reflection in this work. As I will argue in a few pages, some key features of this rule were functioning for the New Testament writers themselves in the way in which they interpret the Old Testament in light of Jesus Christ. A theological account of Scripture like this one was operative for most Roman Catholic interpreters before the Enlightenment, and it continued in much Protestant thought into the eighteenth century. For an account of Protestant interpretation continuing in this line of thought, see Jens Zimmerman, *Recovering Theological Hermeneutics: An Incarnational-Trinitarian Theory of Interpretation* (Grand Rapids: Baker Academic, 2004), esp. chaps. 2 and 3.

9. Kevin Vanhoozer describes the role of propositions in what I am calling the blueprint/building-block approach to scriptural interpretation. "On this view, the task of theology is to systematize the information conveyed through biblical propositions." Vanhoozer, *The Drama of Doctrine: A Canonical-Linguistic Approach to Christian Theology* (Louisville: Westminster John Knox, 2005), p. 45. However, Vanhoozer correctly points out that it is unwise to fall into an opposite extreme, which sees Scripture as merely "feeling-expressing symbols" rather than "fact-stating propositions" (p. 83). In revelation

ney of faith seeking understanding. We start with faith in the triune God, a trust in Jesus Christ and the Spirit's transforming power through Scripture. In reading Scripture, we seek to know and have fellowship with God in a deeper way. Therefore, when we read Scripture in this way, we encounter a mystery. We do not know how God will speak to us and lead us into deeper love of God and neighbor until we struggle with the passage itself. It is only when we struggle with Scripture — asking hard questions, always aware of the divine address — that we lose control over it. If we treat the Bible as the bricks for a building or the food at a smorgasbord, we are in control of the process. But to enter the journey of faith seeking understanding, we need to relinquish the position of being masters over the biblical text. We are parched for a reality outside of ourselves, a word from God. To encounter this word via our reading of a book — the Bible — we need to learn how to lose our grasping and clinging control over the text.

Theology as an Inescapable Task

At this point, let me consider what some may offer as an objection to my proposal of reading Scripture on the path of Jesus Christ, by the power of the Holy Spirit, growing in love of God and neighbor on a journey of faith seeking understanding.

If we are really parched for the word of God as a reality outside of ourselves, how can we *begin* with these theological claims when we read Scripture? Shouldn't we just begin with Scripture itself, rather than bringing theological presuppositions to Scripture? Isn't it solipsistic to take refuge in our own theology rather than encountering the text in itself, the word of God as it really is? Isn't this just a strategy to keep us from hearing the words of the Bible that we don't want to hear? Isn't this a way to close ourselves off to Scripture's power to unseat our presuppositions?

These questions and objections express suspicions that are healthy

---

we encounter the self-presentation and fellowship of the triune God, a word in which God both speaks and acts. Propositions in creeds and theological discourse play an important role in our interpretation of Scripture, even as scriptural interpretation should not be reduced to "translation" into a set of propositions.

for us to think through. My claim is that Christians should not seek to come to Scripture as a blank slate, but they should be both open and self-aware about the theological lens they bring to Scripture, the assumptions that make up our theological hermeneutic. Is this, deep down, a strategy to avoid the words of Scripture? A more penetrating question underneath these questions is this: Shouldn't we just be biblical? Why do we need to do theology?

When objections like this are raised, we may find it helpful to consider the language in which the question is posed. The questioner contrasts the affirming of a theological vision with encountering "the text in itself," or the "word of God as it really is." Behind this is an assumption that a nontheological approach is, fundamentally, a more adequate approach to Scripture than one that has theological presuppositions. But is there really such a nontheological place where we can stand? What would it mean to stand in a theologically neutral place?

In my own life, I came to understand the inescapability of theology when I spent several years immersed in the writings of the philosopher Friedrich Nietzsche, an atheist. Nietzsche lived at a time when many Europeans had abandoned the Christian theology of earlier eras, and late Enlightenment thinkers were seeking a nontheological foundation for a roughly Christian morality and ethic. Nietzsche believed that that was an exercise in self-deception:

> After Buddha was dead, his shadow was still shown for centuries in a cave — a tremendous, gruesome shadow. God is dead; but given the way of men, there may still be caves for thousands of years in which his shadow will be shown. And we — we still have to vanquish his shadow, too.[10]

In some ways Nietzsche expresses ambivalence about the "death of God," a phrase by which he means that the traditional Christian God, in his view, can no longer be believed in. Given that, Nietzsche seeks to boldly vanquish the shadow of Christian belief. Nietzsche does this not only in his reflections on the history of philosophy, but first and foremost in his reflections on *human action*. For human action always has

---

10. Friedrich Nietzsche, *The Gay Science*, trans. Walter Kaufmann (New York: Vintage Books, 1974), p. 167. The following section draws on the thought of Nietzsche as expressed in various works, esp. *Thus Spoke Zarathustra*.

ontological implications: human action always points to our functional conception of the way the world is.

In his late writings, Nietzsche focuses on what it would mean to affirm and say "yes" to life in one's action. The results of his reflections are quite surprising to some: to truly affirm life, Nietzsche suggests, we must never feel guilt or remorse. Most importantly, we should never feel pity for the suffering of others. Why? Because to feel pity for a sufferer implies that this present world, with its suffering and violence, is not the way things are supposed to be. It implies that the present world is not Eden. But Nietzsche wants to affirm the "innocence" of life as we actually encounter it — thus affirming the world with all of its suffering and violence. If God is truly dead, and there is no "world of peace" that we should compare this world to, then we should not be protesting the presence of violence in the world through actions such as pity. The action of pitying a sufferer implicitly postulates a world of peace as normative (the way things should be). But such a world has never existed, Nietzsche suggests. To suggest that it does is to capitulate to a wishful-thinking world. Having pity for a sufferer, according to Nietzsche, is nihilistic rather than life-affirming: it is a world-hating activity.

What Nietzsche's analysis shows with clarity is that it is impossible to set ontological and theological issues on the shelf. For anyone who acts, there is no theology- or ontology-free space. If an atheist has pity on a sufferer, Nietzsche claims, the atheist is postulating a world of peace as normative even if the person does not officially believe in such a world. Likewise, if a Christian follows Nietzsche's advice, which is to "pass by" sufferers without engaging in any activity of pity, then this Christian is functionally denying a world of peace as a possibility. The Christian may claim to believe in Eden — a creational world of peace — as well as the world of ultimate redemption, in which there will be no more tears and suffering. But a choice to pass by rather than to protest suffering by an act of pity is a choice for functional atheism.

In light of Nietzsche's analysis, an assessment of the functional theologies and ontologies around us can never be content to hear a person's self-identification. A self-identified atheist could quite possibly be living a life that is unintelligible apart from the faith-based assumptions borrowed from one religious tradition or another. Self-identified Christians could make claims about the centrality of Jesus Christ and the Holy Spirit in their confession of faith; but functionally they would deny the centrality of Christ and the Spirit in their action. Indeed, according to the analysis of the religious lives of American teenagers by Smith and Denton in their book *Soul Searching,* a form of Deism is frequently the functional theology of American youths who self-identify as Christians.[11] In this view, humans are basically good, and God leaves them to live their own lives except in times of crisis. If you avoid doing terrible things, you go to heaven. While these teenagers may speak about Jesus Christ at times, their functional theology has no need for a mediator, no need for a sacrifice for sin, no need for the empowerment of the Holy Spirit to live the Christian life.

The fact that our functional theology can differ dramatically from our stated theology shouldn't be a surprise to the readers of the Gospels. For example, Matthew 6:24 suggests that one cannot serve both God and Mammon as "masters." Jesus is not particularly concerned here with self-identified beliefs but with functional beliefs that show up in action. As William Cavanaugh says, "If a person claims to believe in the Christian God but never gets off the couch on Sunday morning and spends the rest of the week in obsessive pursuit of profit in the bond market," then the functional master in this person's life is "probably not the Christian God."[12] Jesus' warning has potency precisely because those who consider themselves to be faithful servants of God may have a functional theology that contradicts their stated belief.

Does this mean that action is all that matters, and that our stated beliefs don't matter? No. If we are to take our cues from Scripture, what we confess is of vital importance. Positively, Paul says, "[C]onfess with your lips that Jesus is Lord and believe in your heart that God raised him from the dead, and you will be saved" (Rom. 10:9). Negatively, we are told to "test the spirits" in 1 John with the following criteria: "[E]very spirit that does not confess Jesus is not from God" (1 John 4:3). The Pastoral Epistles tell us again and again that beliefs matter, and doctrine matters. "Watch your life and doctrine closely," Paul encourages Timothy (1 Tim. 4:16). Right teaching does not come naturally, and it is not

11. For this moralistic, therapeutic Deism, see Christian Smith and Melinda Lundquist Denton, *Soul Searching: The Religious and Spiritual Lives of American Teenagers* (New York : Oxford University Press, 2005). I explore an analysis of Smith and Denton further in chap. 4.

12. "Does Religion Cause Violence?" *Harvard Divinity Bulletin* 35, no. 2/3 (Spring/ Summer 2007): 30.

always popular. "For the time will come when people will not put up with sound doctrine. Instead, to suit their own desires, they will gather around them a great number of teachers to say what their itching ears want to hear. They will turn their ears away from the truth and turn aside to myths" (2 Tim. 4:3-4 [TNIV]).

What we teach and believe matters. But our professed belief does not always sink in. Sometimes instructors teach one thing in the classroom and another thing with the rest of their lives. Moreover, as sinful human beings, our learning in Christ needs to be a transformative participation in Christ's own life by the Spirit. This involves information, but it is more than simply a body of information that we can master. We do not always absorb the messages from our worship and from Christian teaching, but we are always acting. This is where our functional beliefs are usually revealed.

Everything the church does and does not do points to its functional theology, the theology that is exposed by the actions (and omissions) in the lives of its members. When church members decide where they will invest their energies, whether into a service project, a series of potluck dinners, or a Bible study — all of these are theological decisions. How a church designs its worship service is also a theological decision. What are the elements of worship? Who, exactly, is being worshiped? What instruments, if any, do we use in worship? Where do we place announcements in a worship service? All of these decisions reflect their functional theology of who God is, what the world is like, and who they are as the church. That does not mean that there is only one theologically correct answer for how things should be done. But it does mean that all of these decisions arise from theological maps that are functioning in the community of faith. Theological reasoning and theological presuppositions are inescapable for Christians.

Note that, with all of these decisions of the church, there may be ways in which the Bible informs our theological map, but it does not do so apart from our own theological reasoning. One can find biblical support for the decision to have a Bible study, or a service project, or even a fellowship gathering at a potluck dinner. But why does one get involved in one activity rather than another? While churches as institutions may have all of these activities and more (as in the program-heavy megachurches), the church as the gathered people has to prioritize a list of biblically ordained activities. There is no way to bridge the gap between

15

hearing these particular biblical admonitions and deciding on a course of action other than thinking about how God is active in your community, what God wants from your community, and so on. In other words, the only way for us to appropriate the Bible's teaching is through a process of letting our own theological map make some connections.

Theological reasoning is inescapable because action is inescapable. As Nietzsche points out, even atheists imply something — in their actions — about the way the world is (ontology). For Christians, the key to this form of analysis is a willingness to be self-aware of one's own functional theology. I sometimes meet people who are convinced that they have no definable theological positions: to have such, they reason, would be to limit Scripture, to limit God. While there is something that is correct about this respect for mystery (which we will return to later in this chapter), the overall posture is one of denial — a denial of one's own particularity and finitude. Yet anyone who acts has a theology or an ontology. Anyone who prays has a theology. Anyone who participates in worship has a theology. One of the concrete skills of theological hermeneutics is learning how to discern the specificity of one's own theological hermeneutic.

In my personal interaction with students, this denial usually becomes obvious with a bit of annoying, yet revealing, Socratic questioning.

A: "I think Christians get too caught up in theological differences rather than just relying on the Bible. The Bible is what we can all agree on. Theology is human reasoning that divides."

B: "That's interesting. I'm curious, what makes you think that Christians should just rely on the Bible?"

A: "Second Timothy 3:16 says 'All Scripture is given by inspiration of God, and is profitable for doctrine, for reproof, for correction, for instruction in righteousness.'"

B: "Yes, that is a powerful passage of Scripture. But it does not address the question I asked: Why should Christians rely only on the Bible? I'm also curious as to why you chose that particular Scripture passage to quote. Was there a theological logic behind that decision?"

A: "Well, the Bible gives God's instructions for salvation — all that we need for our life and faith."

B: "I agree. But isn't that a theological claim?"

A: "It's supported by the Bible."

16

B: "I'm glad. That's how it should be. But why do you decide to make these Scripture passages central? Didn't you have to make a theological decision to frame the authority and scope of the Bible in that way? Aren't you sharing the theological tradition of others who have formulated a way to think about what the Bible is and does?"

A: "I would only agree with traditions if they were biblical ones."

B: "Good. But it sounds like you do have functional beliefs that give you the context for appropriating and making sense of what the Bible has to say. Right?"

Such Socratic questioning could go on and on, and sometimes it does. The goal is not to deconstruct the theological position of person "A" but to help her see that Scripture never simply comes to us in a flatly biblical way. It always comes to us within a community of shared faith and mediated by certain theological presuppositions and assumptions. We can hope that these assumptions will themselves be biblical, and that they will be open to being *reshaped* by the Bible — as it is read in light of Christ, by the Spirit's power. But until we admit that we always bring a map of faith to the biblical text, we cannot make progress in even assessing whether that map is biblical.

Reading by the Rule of Faith: A Scriptural Practice

What is the *rule of faith?* On the most basic level, it is a summary of the received teachings of the Christian church. It is not a subjective response to the gospel, such as a testimony of how one became a Christian. It is a summary of the church's confession about the basic story of the Christian faith, as informed by the Bible.[13] In early Christianity it was often used in catechesis to explain the meaning of one's baptism. Why am I baptized in the name of the Father, the Son, and the Holy Spirit? The answer frequently took the form of a threefold creed that summarized scriptural teachings about the action of the Father, Son, and Holy Spirit in salvation. Sometimes it was an oral tradition, some-

13. For a survey of the literature on the rule of faith, and an articulation of the narrative character of the rule, see Paul Blowers, "The *Regula Fidei* and the Narrative Character of Early Christian Faith," *Pro Ecclesia* 6, no. 2 (1998): 199-228.

times a fixed form such as the Nicene Creed, that made its way into the weekly worship services in some regions. While there is some variation in content, a rough summary of the content of much of the rule of faith for the early centuries of Christianity would be the Apostles' Creed:

> I believe in God, the Father Almighty,
>> the Creator of heaven and earth,
>> and in Jesus Christ, His only Son, our Lord:
>
> Who was conceived of the Holy Spirit,
>> born of the Virgin Mary,
>> suffered under Pontius Pilate,
>> was crucified, died, and was buried.
>
> He descended into hell.
>
> The third day He arose again from the dead.
>
> He ascended into heaven
>> and sits at the right hand of God the Father Almighty,
>> whence He shall come to judge the living and the dead.
>
> I believe in the Holy Spirit, the holy catholic church,
>> the communion of saints,
>> the forgiveness of sins,
>> the resurrection of the body,
>> and life everlasting. Amen.[14]

The term "rule of faith" becomes significant in the early centuries of Christianity. It was important in distinguishing Christian interpretations of Scripture from heretical alternatives. Like the word "Trinity" itself, the phrase "rule of faith" does not appear in the Bible. Yet there are good reasons to believe that something like a "rule" was functioning for the New Testament writers.

---

14. Since the Apostles' Creed was originally part of the oral tradition, a variety of versions existed in early Christianity until the creed versions congealed into the *textus receptus* in the late sixth century. As such, the fixed creed gives an indication of what was contained in a baptismal creed in early Christianity; but the rule of faith was not a completely fixed form.

Theological Presuppositions about the Event of Jesus Christ: The Old Testament in Relationship to the New

On the most basic level, all of the New Testament writers bring theological presuppositions to their interpretation of the event of Jesus Christ's life, death, and resurrection. A central presupposition is that God was active in Jesus Christ, whose ministry must be viewed in light of God's historic activity with Israel and God's vindication of Jesus' ministry and death through the resurrection. This is a key overt message in the New Testament writings; but it is also a presupposition for how they narrate the life of Christ in the Gospels, and how they interpret the Old Testament as bearing witness to Jesus Christ.

The New Testament writers interpret the Old Testament in light of the event of Jesus Christ. In a sense, the whole of the Old Testament becomes a book of prophecy to New Testament writers. The New Testament does not merely indicate that passages that were clearly messianic at the time they were written point to Christ. It is not punctiliar, that is, a connect-the-dots kind of exercise between passages such as Isaiah 7:14 and Matthew 1:18 (concerning the miraculous birth of Jesus). Rather, the New Testament appropriation of the Old Testament liberally applies nearly anything about the proper ends of Israel, even the proper ends of humanity itself, to the life of Christ.[15] In appropriating the Hebrew Scriptures christologically, the New Testament writers did not restrict the meaning of the Old Testament to something like the author's original intentions, or to how the Old Testament text would have originally been heard. Rather, they saw the event of Jesus Christ as itself shedding light on the Old Testament, revealing the "substance" of what were "shadows" in anticipation.[16]

Does this sound illogical? It is illogical if one expects to approach the Old Testament with a blank slate and develop from this a portrait of Jesus. That is not what New Testament writers ever did — or claimed to

---

15. For an exposition of the way in which Jesus Christ was seen by the New Testament writers as embodying Israel, and by extension humanity itself, see N. T. Wright, *The Climax of the Covenant: Christ and the Law in Pauline Theology* (Minneapolis: Fortress, 1992), pp. 198, 202-3; see also Wright, *What Saint Paul Really Said: Was Paul of Tarsus the Real Founder of Christianity?* (Grand Rapids: Eerdmans, 1997), p. 54.

16. I will explore this issue in more depth in chap. 5. For the language of "shadow and substance," see Col. 2:17; for "shadow," cf. Heb. 8:5; 10:1.

do. Rather, their claim was that, in light of the event of Jesus Christ, the Old Testament takes on new, unforeseen significance.[17] This depends on a very particular conviction about the identity of Jesus Christ. In the second century, Irenaeus had a nonbiblical term for it that nonetheless gets to the center of New Testament claims about Jesus: recapitulation. Jesus was not just a great teacher, nor was he just God with limbs and a mouth. In Jesus, the whole history of Israel — and through Israel, humanity — was recapitulated, or lived again. But this time the one who was true Israel and true human being did not take the path of the first Adam. As the second Adam, Christ was the righteous one, the perfect human covenant partner. But this perfect covenant partner was also the Word incarnate, the one in whom the fullness of deity dwelt. If the New Testament writers really believe claims like this about Jesus, then it is logical to apply any Old Testament passage related to the true end of Israel, humanity, and the new work of God that is hoped for in the future to one person: Jesus Christ.

If the New Testament writers saw Christ as the key to Scripture, should we as followers of Christ do any different? The idea that Jesus is the road we travel on the journey of biblical interpretation has very deep biblical and christological roots.

Traditions of Teaching Handed Down in the Church

Paul makes several references to the teaching he "received" and has "passed on to" the churches to whom he is writing (1 Cor. 11:23; 15:1-3; 2 Thess. 2:15). Some of these appear to be written, others oral. "Stand firm and hold to the teachings we passed on to you, whether by word of mouth or by letter" (2 Thess. 2:15). References to oral and written traditions that are received continue to occur from the second to the fourth century, developing into the oral and fixed forms of a rule of faith noted above (such as the Apostles' Creed). Confessions, or rules of faith, were used at times in public worship (liturgically), at times in catechesis. The

---

17. For example, when Jesus makes appeals in John's Gospel that Scripture "testifies" to him, it is not simply a matter of textual response on its own terms, but responding to the Old Testament in light of Jesus himself. "You diligently study the Scriptures because you think that by them you possess eternal life. These are the Scriptures that testify about me, yet you refuse to come to me to have life" (John 5:39).

rules became crucial for differentiating false teaching from true teaching. Why? Because a rule was not just a law; it was a measuring stick, a narrative that provided orientation about where the *center* of the Christian faith is.

Why was a rule necessary to maintain true teaching? An analogy from Irenaeus illustrates it well. Scripture is a complicated book: it can be interpreted in many different ways. It's like a mosaic that has many tiny pieces of different colors. If one properly discerns the patterns in Scripture, then the pieces of the mosaic will fit together to form a beautiful portrait of a king (Christ). But it is possible to sever the proper connections between the pieces of the mosaic, leaving one with a portrait of a dog or a fox. By distorting the inherent pattern (the rule of faith) that holds Scripture together, false (Gnostic) interpretations of Scripture miss what Scripture itself points to: Jesus Christ, as witnessed to by the Old and New Testaments. "They disregard the order and connection of the Scriptures, destroying the truth."[18] Irenaeus realizes that Scripture is simply too large and complicated a book for one to proceed in without a sense of the narrative pattern that one will find within it.

For Protestant readers, this may bring worries. Does the rule of faith threaten the idea of *sola Scriptura* (the affirmation of "scripture alone" as the final authority in theology)? It depends, of course, on how one conceives of the rule of faith. At times in early Christianity, there was an emphasis on the idea of the rule as distinct from Scripture, a pattern for organizing the narrative of Scripture even though the rule also emerges from Scripture.[19] At other times, the primary emphasis was on the rule as derivative from Scripture itself.[20]

For Reformers such as Luther and Calvin, *sola Scriptura* was not an

---

18. Irenaeus, *Against Heresies,* 1.8.1, in D. H. Williams, ed., *Tradition, Scripture, and Interpretation: A Sourcebook of the Ancient Church* (Grand Rapids: Baker, 2006), p. 69.

19. Irenaeus sometimes emphasizes the need for a tradition outside of Scripture itself (though still emerging from it) in order to refute the interpretations of Scripture by the Gnostics. See Williams, *Tradition, Scripture, and Interpretation,* pp. 68-69.

20. Consider Cyril of Jerusalem's exhortation to those preparing for baptism (ca. 350). After encouraging new converts to memorize the words of the Jerusalem Creed, he reassures them that "these articles of our faith were not composed out of human opinion, but are the principal points collected out of the whole of Scripture to complete a single doctrinal formulation of the faith." *Catechetical Lectures* 5.12, quoted in Williams, *Tradition, Scripture, and Interpretation,* p. 63.

appeal to the neutrality of readers, as if we should read the Bible without theological preunderstandings. Rather, it was an appeal to the Bible as the primary source and final authority for one's theological affirmations. Extending this trajectory, Reformation traditions consider the Bible alone to be the only infallible rule of faith. With this point, the Reformational emphasis is on the biblical character of the rule itself: in terms of its final authority, Scripture is *sui ipsius interpres,* that is, its own interpreter.

Yet this is a far cry from claiming that one should have "no creed but Christ," or that theological confessions per se should be abandoned. The Reformation and post-Reformation periods were times of prolific creed- and confession-writing for the majority of Protestants. These confessions were seen as an important aid for interpreting Scripture, yet they were subordinate to Scripture itself. They sought to give summations of the church's biblical teaching at key points, and on scriptural issues that could be easily misconstrued.

Ultimately, the rule of faith provides guidance for our functional theology: it provides a general theological framework in which the Bible is read. Yet the fact that it is functional should not lead us to think that it should be derived from experience. In the Pauline Epistles and also the patristic contexts, there is an external character to the rule: it is "received" and "passed on"; it is not an "expression" of one's own subjective response to the faith. The Apostles' Creed is not meant to be an expression of "how I came to Jesus." Rather, it is a distillation of core Christian teaching that can help unveil the inherent patterns of Scripture. This is a crucial distinction, for Paul and the patristic writers did not see themselves as the ones who developed the rule. They received it and passed it on.

Where Is the Center? Naming the Scope and Limits of Scripture

The notion of "rule" in the rule of faith may be a stumbling block to some readers. Doesn't that sound like a narrow, even arbitrary, law that tells us how to interpret Scripture?

Concerning the term "rule," it is probably best understood as rule in the sense of a rule of thumb, or in the sense of a measurement that points to the center and boundaries of a Christian interpretation of

Scripture. It points to the functional mode of operating. When we interpret Scripture, there is the possibility of many, many interpretations that can emerge within the rule of faith. But as a functional mode of operating, it points to the scope and the limits of interpretation. To interpret the Old Testament as being about a God other than the God of Jesus Christ, for example, would be a violation of the *scope* of Scripture as defined by a rule of faith such as the Apostles' Creed.

Indeed, rather than being narrow and authoritarian, many of the early creedal developments of the rule are actually wide and expansive guidelines for interpretation that seek to keep the practice of biblical interpretation itself intelligible. For example, consider a key section of the Nicene Creed, where the Son is said to be "eternally begotten" of the Father. Why does the creed use this nonbiblical language? Is it seeking to speculate about the nature of God beyond what the Bible can tell us, to give a theory of how it is possible both to be "born" as a son and "not be born" as the eternal one? The creed goes into no such speculations. Nor do the fourth-century church fathers develop speculative metaphysical theories that solve the problem of how it is possible to be "born" or "begotten" eternally. Rather, the Nicene Creed's phrase respects and retains the integrity of biblical language itself. What is it to be "eternally begotten"? Positively, I don't know; but negatively, it means that I can uphold the biblical affirmations that Christ is the Son begotten of the Father (John 3), yet the Son did not have a beginning in time, since the Son is the eternal Word who is made flesh in Jesus (John 1). The phrase "eternally begotten" does not solve the biblical paradox; it retains the paradox over against fourth-century heresies, which tended to have more of a penchant for a rationalist resolution. Phrases such as "eternally begotten" do not vanquish the mystery of God; they preserve it, and they set limits on rationalist approaches that would lead to the premature closure of biblical paradoxes.[21]

In addition to clarifying what the scope and limits of the Bible's message are, the rule of faith points to what is central in the interpretation of biblical passages. What is central when we read the Bible? The rule of faith is not the sum total of all that a particular Christian be-

21. On the way in which the Nicene-Constantinople Creed represents a defense of the mystery of God, see Lewis Ayres, *Nicaea and Its Legacy: An Approach to Fourth-Century Trinitarian Theology* (New York: Oxford University Press, 2004), chap. 11.

lieves about God; rather, it is an ecumenical teaching and practice that points us to the center. Following Augustine's general approach, I am suggesting that what is central is that we find salvation in Jesus Christ, and that we are empowered by the Holy Spirit to walk the transforming road of life in Christ, which leads to a vision of the triune God. Along the way, we are rediscovering our true selves, who we were created to be: persons who love God and neighbor. If this is our sketch of what is central, then certain things are going to come into (and out of) focus when we interpret Scripture.

For example, think for a moment about the well-known story in 1 Samuel 17 in which David faces and defeats the giant Goliath with his sling and stone. There are many possible ways that Christians preach this text, but I would suggest that they generally fall into two categories. The first sees Goliath as a metaphor for the challenges that a person of God faces in day-to-day life; David is a model of the underdog who dares to take a risk against his own inner "giants" and challenges. The sermon notes David's confidence in running "towards the battle line to meet the Philistine," even though David was being mocked and belittled by Goliath (1 Sam. 17:48). The preacher can encourage the congregation to think about the "giants" in their own lives, and then he can exhort the congregation to be like David and take risks in the face of danger. The Bible has the key to facing challenges in our personal lives. Visualize a positive outcome like David's (17:36), act with confidence in the face of challenge (17:37), and take risks (17:48-9). Who is the hero of the story? David, and more specifically, his courageous human will that we should model. The living God is not a major character in this rendering of the text.

But there is another trajectory to the preaching of 1 Samuel 17, and a wide range of historical Scripture interpreters have followed this second trajectory — from Origen to Augustine to Luther. For these thinkers, the central character in the story is God: they cannot view the David-Goliath encounter apart from God's revelation in Christ. Patristic writers usually interpret the encounter as a spiritual battle, because the New Testament teaches us that our enemies are not flesh and blood (Eph. 6:14-17).[22] Therefore, the power displayed in the story is

22. For brief selections of this interpretation, see John Franke, ed., *Joshua, Judges, Ruth, 1-2 Samuel,* Ancient Christian Commentary on Scripture (Downers Grove, IL: InterVarsity, 2005), pp. 266-76.

the power of Christ. So the defeat of Goliath comes to be about "sinners who have been converted to the faith" and hence "condemn Satan" and "renounce all his works" (Bede).[23] David's life, which is noted in the story to be one of protecting his sheep against attacking lions, is interpreted in light of Christ. Like Christ, David acts as a representative of the people of God to defeat God's enemy (Satan) on behalf of God's people (1 Sam. 17:9-10, 31, 50-51).

Other interpretations in this second trajectory also see God as the central actor, but they put more emphasis on the historical level of narrative in the Old Testament account. Here the emphasis is on God's saving action, in tandem with the faith of David, though David's faith does not deserve credit for the deliverance. The text repeatedly notes that it was not a "sword" of David that brings deliverance from the Philistines, for "the Lord does not save by sword and spear; for the battle is the Lord's and he will give you into our hand" (1 Sam. 17:47; cf. vv. 37, 50). God alone delivers Israel, and the extent to which David is ill prepared for the battle simply reinforces God's sole triumph. God does not work through David because of the latter's valiant human effort, but because of his covenantal trust that "the Lord . . . will save me from the hand of this Philistine" (17:37). For David's attempt "would have been preposterous on any other supposition than his being upheld by secret divine support."[24]

Note that the second-trajectory interpretations of 1 Samuel 17 do not simply interpret the narrative as an ancient story of battle and war. They do not dispute the historical embeddedness of this narrative; but they perceive that, for the story to be proclaimed — for the story to be treated as Scripture — one must go beyond seeing this story as simply a record of national border skirmishes in the ancient world. If Scripture is to be taught and preached in the church, a rule of faith will come into play whether we like it or not. There is no escaping a map with at least broad outlines of who God is and who we as human beings are.

This example should also help us reflect on the fact that not all

---

23. Franke, *Joshua, Judges, Ruth, 1-2 Samuel,* p. 275.

24. John Calvin, "Commentary on Psalm 144:1," Calvin Translation Society (hereafter CTS) (reprint, Grand Rapids: Baker Book House, 1999). While I quote Calvin here, my portrait of this stream of biblical interpretation is a more general one to supplement the patristic approaches noted earlier. In chap. 5, I develop further specificity about the various historical approaches to interpreting the Old Testament canonically.

maps to Scripture are equally valid. The first map is what we might roughly call a "self-help" map. It has basically Deistic assumptions about God: God created humans, and God wants humans to take risks and try hard to fulfill their potential in the face of challenges. The second map, which has a wide range of variations (I explore them further in chap. 5), is distinctly covenantal and canonical. God has given covenant promises to his people, to which the proper response is trust. God is the chief actor in the drama of saving his people. Moreover, since Christ is the fulfillment of the covenant, we should understand the story of David and Goliath in light of the overall canon of Scripture that bears witness to Christ, rather than providing instructions on self-defense or guidance for self-actualization.

"This Ain't Mapquest": Knowledge and Mystery in the Journey of Reading Scripture

So, what kind of map should we bring to the Bible? If it is not a detailed blueprint for the building blocks of a building, or a turn-by-turn guide as in computer-generated directions, or a blank agenda on which we write our own felt needs — what is it? So far I have been using the metaphor of a journey: we know the road and destination for the journey, but there are many surprises along the way. To sharpen the image of what kind of knowledge this gives us of God, let me add another biblical image for speaking about our relational knowledge of God, that of a marriage.[25] A marriage relationship involves knowledge. But, rather than being the kind of knowledge that enables mastery, it is knowledge that plays a role in continued growth and journey. I could do research on my spouse: I could memorize all the names and birthdays of her friends, the relationships and important events in her life. That might help a little in getting to know her. But the most significant knowledge of my spouse would come by living out my relationship of commitment to her in time.

---

25. In addition to OT imagery of Israel as God's spouse, the books of Ephesians and Revelation use the images of betrothal and marriage in speaking about the church's relationship to Christ, and a long tradition of interpretation of Song of Songs develops this theme as well.

I don't know what the future will hold, but for me, as a married person, the future is not a blank slate. By entering into my marriage vows, I have eliminated a wide range of possibilities: the possibility of moving around without considering my spouse's needs and interests, the possibility of dating other people — the list could go on and on. There is no way to know my spouse better apart from considering that path, and my faithfulness to that path. The knowledge of my spouse, then, is a knowledge in the context of our shared life, our shared commitment to the shape of the relationship in the marriage vows. No matter how well I get to know my spouse, even in this relationship of close fellowship, she will still be mysterious to me in many ways. If I am paying attention, I will continue to be surprised and mystified by this person whom I know so well. I have real knowledge of my spouse, but it is not the knowledge of mastery, but of fellowship. This is something like our knowledge of God: it is a knowledge tied to fellowship as we journey in faith.

Now, I could conclude that the map of my journey with my spouse is actually keeping me from real knowledge of my spouse. Perhaps I need to approach my spouse in an "unbiased" way. It is certainly true that, as her spouse, I do not know her in the same way that some of her friends or relatives know her. But to follow this path, I would simply be fooling myself by buying wholesale into an Enlightenment suspicion: the suspicion that prior commitments are incompatible with knowledge, and that maps merely bias and distort rather than enable knowledge. Trying to be unbiased in my approach to knowing my spouse would not lead me to more reliable knowledge — just a broken marriage. I should not try to escape my map of commitments and preunderstandings as I get to know my spouse better; rather, I should live into these in a way that remains open to anomaly and surprise.

Likewise, in the journey of faith, there are many routes that we could follow in pursuing and interpreting a Scripture text apart from the map of the rule of faith. We can worry that the rule of faith will bias us, but it is actually what makes knowledge in the sense of fellowship with God possible. Living in the rule of faith means that we know where the center of Scripture is, and where the limits for our journey are. As Christians, our map for the journey is that Jesus Christ is the road, the Spirit is the one who illuminates and empowers, and we are on the way to a transforming vision of the triune God. This is our journey and our story: it is the shape of our identity as the bride of Christ (Rev. 19:7-9). It is a journey that will cut off certain possibilities, such as interpretations of Scripture that do not see Christ as the center or do not draw on the Spirit as the enabler. Most importantly, just as in a marriage, the shape of this journey opens up new, exciting, and surprising possibilities in Scripture interpretation that we never could have predicted in advance. We will not see the Bible as the divine answer book for the world's perfect diet; nor will we see it simply as a literary masterpiece from the ancient world. But in the light of Christ, the Spirit uses the Bible to give us gifts of grace from the Father that evoke gratitude, thanksgiving, and service. We should not come to the Bible uncommitted. The Bible is the word of God to us precisely because we have been claimed by God in our baptism and united to Christ in his death and resurrection by the power of the Holy Spirit. As a people who have been claimed by God, we read Scripture in light of Christ, the center, by the power of the Spirit, as a gift sent from the Father to nourish our parched souls.

Conclusion: Reading Scripture as Part of the Economy of Salvation

I will develop many of the ideas in this chapter further in later chapters. But before going on, we should review where we have been. We do not access the word of God simply by understanding words on a page, words that can be reproduced, repackaged, and distributed according to our liking. We cannot access the *word* of God apart from the *work* of God: God plants the seed and nourishes it by the Spirit's power in the Christian community. Scripture is the instrument God uses for his own purposes in the redemption of creation.

In the account of the theological interpretation of Scripture that I propose, Christian readers need to come to terms with the fact that their own theological location is inescapable, and that they bring theological presuppositions to Scripture. Anyone who acts has, operative within those actions, claims about the way the world is (ontological). All actions of Christians betray their own assumptions about whether, and in what way, God is active in the world (theological). Christians need to become aware of their own functional theology and see how it influences the interpretation of Scripture.

The rule of faith is a communal, received account of the central story of Scripture that helps identify the center and the boundaries of a Christian interpretation of Scripture. It emerges from Scripture itself, but it is also a lens through which Christians receive Scripture. This is not a legalistic rule, but it is the map of a dynamic journey of transformation in Jesus Christ, by the Spirit, growing ever deeper into the knowledge and fellowship of the triune God. As Christians, we come to know the shape of this rule of faith in the community of the church: in its worship, its sacraments, its service in the world. The rule of faith points to the expansive context for the Christian interpretation of Scripture: the economy of salvation itself, in which the Spirit unites God's people to Christ and his body (the church), empowered for a surprising, dynamic journey of dying to sin and coming to life in the Spirit's new creation.[26]

As a result, the kind of knowledge of God we receive through the reading of Scripture is a Spirit-enabled, Christ-centered apprehension of a mystery. We gain real knowledge of God on this journey, but that knowledge is not reducible to propositions; it is knowledge always connected to fellowship with God, always connected with a growth of love for God and the neighbor. Becoming a better interpreter of Scripture is not about mastering the blueprint into which the propositional building blocks of Scripture fit. It is not about picking and choosing a divine answer to our own felt concerns. It is about unlearning our mastery over the biblical text and releasing it to be an instrument used by God for our transformation on the path of Jesus Christ.

For Further Reading

St. Augustine, *On Christian Teaching,* trans. R. P. H. Green (Oxford: Oxford University Press, 1997).

A classic patristic exposition of a theological hermeneutic of Scripture in which reading Scripture is a journey toward a vision of the triune God, on the path of Jesus Christ.

26. The term "economy," when joined with a prepositional phrase referring to God's work (e.g., "of salvation") refers to God's "provision," or "plan," for salvation. It is taken from the Greek word *oikonomia,* meaning literally "management of a household," or "stewardship."

James K. A. Smith, *Introducing Radical Orthodoxy: Mapping a Post-Secular Theology* (Grand Rapids: Baker Academic, 2004); John Milbank, *Theology and Social Theory: Beyond Secular Reason,* 2nd ed. (Oxford: Blackwell Publishers, 2006).

Is theology really inescapable? Is the idea of "secular" or theologically "neutral" space a dangerous myth that needs to be exposed? A recent theological movement called Radical Orthodoxy thinks so. Smith's book is an accessible introduction to this theological sensibility. The original edition of Milbank's book predates the naming of Radical Orthodoxy as a movement, but it presents a sustained interrogation of the "secular," a questioning that undergirds much later thought in Radical Orthodoxy.

Ellen F. Davis and Richard B. Hays, eds., *The Art of Reading Scripture* (Grand Rapids: Eerdmans, 2003); A. K. M. Adam, Stephen E. Fowl, Kevin J. Vanhoozer, Francis Watson, eds., *Reading Scripture with the Church: Toward a Hermeneutic for Theological Interpretation* (Grand Rapids: Baker Academic, 2006).

These two books are significant collections of essays from some of the leading contemporary advocates of the theological interpretation of Scripture.

Kevin Vanhoozer, ed., *Dictionary for Theological Interpretation of the Bible* (Grand Rapids: Baker Academic, 2005); Daniel J. Treier, *Introducing Theological Interpretation of Scripture: Recovering a Christian Practice* (Grand Rapids: Baker Academic, 2008).

The dictionary is a one-volume treasure chest of articles for Christians seeking to recover the theological interpretation of Scripture. Treier's book gives a helpful map of recent secondary literature in the theological interpretation of Scripture discourse.

D. H. Williams, *Tradition, Scripture, and Interpretation: A Sourcebook of the Ancient Church* (Grand Rapids: Baker Academic, 2006).

This is a sourcebook of helpful resources from the early church on the rule of faith, the interplay of Scripture and tradition, and the canon of Scripture.

CHAPTER 2

Learning to Read Scripture Closely

···

A Theological Perspective on General
Hermeneutics and Biblical Criticism

S ERMONS CAN BE predictable. Consider the following sermon fragments, and think about the "script" of the sermon that these
evoke.

> "Our society no longer . . ."
> "God is waiting . . ."
> ". . . the key to a happy marriage . . ."

Do these quotes call to mind sermons that you have heard? For
those of us who have heard many sermons, we can sometimes predict
the whole outcome of a sermon after hearing the first line or two. There
is the beginning of the civil religion sermon: "Our society has left its
godly roots and needs to return to God's ways." Another is the God-is-
passive-while-you-are-active sermon: "God has said yes to you in Jesus
— now what do *you* say?" And who can forget the various versions of the
self-help sermon: the key to a happy marriage, to a successful financial
future, or to managing stress. Need I say more?

At times sermons are talks in search of a biblical text. This is frequently a temptation with topical preaching, which often gives prece-
dence to the initial ideas of the preacher over what the biblical text itself
might contribute. But preachers who preach *lectio continua* (through a
particular biblical book) or along with the lectionary can be superficial
readers of the Bible as well. The practice of reading Scripture impres-

sionistically rather than closely is a practice that does not discriminate according to theological tradition or denomination.

How can we overcome this? How are we to hear Scripture as a transforming word from God? The central part of the answer is theological: how we approach the text in light of our own functional theology and the rule of faith (chap. 1), and how we think through the Bible as God's instrument of revelation (chap. 3). These features set the agenda for our reading of Scripture. But the practice of reading Scripture also draws on more general practices used in interpreting any book. It may sound simple: that is, the book has information, and we the readers absorb it. But how we think about our reading of the Bible as a book can have profound effects on how we end up interpreting the Bible as Scripture.

Reading the Bible as a Book: The Relationship of General Hermeneutics to Special Hermeneutics

What does it mean to become competent interpreters of the Bible as a collection of writings authored by human beings? This is a question that makes us consider the relationship of general hermeneutics to special hermeneutics. Hermeneutics, as I use the term, is "critical reflection on the practice of interpretation — its aims, conditions, and criteria."[1] At times the term "hermeneutics" is used to refer to the nature of all human understanding (as interpretation), but our focus here is on the interpretation of texts. Hence, "general hermeneutics" is reflection on the practice of interpreting texts in general; "special hermeneutics" is reflection on the practice of interpreting particular, special kinds of texts for a particular purpose — such as interpreting the Bible as Scripture. The Bible may be interpreted as ancient literature, or as a source for ancient history. But when the Bible is interpreted as Christian Scripture, it requires a special hermeneutic to fit with the special role and use of the Bible for Christians.[2]

For Christians, the Bible is not a book like any other. Christians

1. Charles Monroe Wood, *The Formation of Christian Understanding: An Essay in Theological Hermeneutics* (Philadelphia: Westminster Press, 1981), p. 9.

2. On the significance of focusing on "Christian uses of Christian texts" in delineating a special hermeneutic for Scripture, see Wood, *Formation of Christian Understanding*, pp. 20-26.

should reserve a special hermeneutic for the Bible that sees its diverse books and genres as one canon that functions in a particular way: that is, as I explored in chapter 1, the Bible is the Spirit's instrument for leading Christians into a knowledge of the triune God on the path of Jesus Christ. Without a notion of a biblical canon inherent in a special hermeneutic for Scripture, the books of the Bible may be read as hopelessly disparate and contradictory voices without a unifying subject matter or theme. Apart from a special hermeneutic that sees the biblical canon as God's word fulfilled in Christ, there is no reason to think that the collection of writings in the Bible are truly one book — a book with diversity, but also unity, in its witness to God in Christ.

Nevertheless, within this special hermeneutic is an important place for human history, culture, and production. God does not speak his word through Scripture in a way that bypasses human creatures, but in a way that works in and through them. In other words, on one level the Bible is a human-produced book like other human-produced books. But because God has made the Bible an instrument of divine revelation and communion, it is not merely a human-produced book in its role as Scripture. How are we to fit our hermeneutic for reading the Bible as Scripture together with our understanding of the Bible as a product of human processes? In other words, to what extent does our special hermeneutic for reading Scripture need to overlap with general hermeneutical reflection?

There are several things to note about our pursuit of this question. First, even in our general hermeneutical reflection on the practice of reading texts in general, we are not in a theology-free zone. As some scholars point out, there are biblical and theological resources that can inform our hermeneutical approach to texts in general.[3] But further, in drawing on broad, human disciplines in understanding the nature of general hermeneutics, we are affirming that the truth that we encoun-

---

3. For the purposes of the present work, I draw on figures below, such as Gadamer and Ricoeur, whose general hermeneutical reflection has implicit theological dimensions, even though it is not directly derived from Scripture. Significant works that explore distinctively Christian approaches to general hermeneutics include David L. Jeffrey, *People of the Book: Christian Identity and Literary Culture* (Grand Rapids: Eerdmans, 1996); Roger Lundin, ed. *Disciplining Hermeneutics: Interpretation in Christian Perspective* (Grand Rapids: Eerdmans, 1997); Jens Zimmerman, *Recovering Theological Hermeneutics* (Grand Rapids: Baker Academic, 2004).

ter in general hermeneutical reflection is God's truth. Given the expansive work of God's Spirit in the world, we can affirm that "all truth is God's truth," wherever it may be found. So if truth is found in philosophers such as Hans Georg Gadamer or Jürgen Habermas, Christians should celebrate it. Christians need not fear the search for truth in the liberal arts and sciences, for God is the source and owner of all truth.

The notion that all truth is God's truth has a long and venerable history in the church. Early Christian apologists, as well as many early church fathers, showed a critical appreciation for "pagan" philosophical writing. This was continued in the Reformation, when Reformers such as John Calvin had a strong appreciation for philosophers such as Seneca and Plato. These Christians were not rejecting their Christian commitments by drawing on non-Christian philosophical thought. They were honoring God by honoring his gifts in creation — and the expansive working of his Spirit. For "since the creation of the world [God's] invisible qualities — his eternal power and divine nature — have been clearly seen, being understood from what has been made" (Rom. 1:20). Human beings have been given minds to explore God's creation, and often non-Christians are better at this in practice than are Christians themselves.[4]

However, the affirmation that all truth is God's truth needs to be joined with a second, somewhat paradoxical, affirmation: all truth is in Jesus Christ.[5] Note that this is different from claiming that all truth is possessed by Christians. It refers to Jesus Christ himself, the one to whom Christians belong. The New Testament makes remarkable claims about Jesus Christ that lead to this second affirmation. Jesus Christ is the Word, who was in the beginning with God (John 1). All things are created in and through Jesus Christ (Col. 1:16). "He is before all things, and in him all things hold together" (Col. 1:17). If Jesus Christ is truly "Lord" — and not simply Lord over Christians but Lord over the whole earth, over the whole universe — then there cannot be

---

4. To say that non-Christians know some truths that Christians do not is not to say that non-Christians have experienced salvation in Jesus Christ. Paul ends Romans 1:20 with the conclusion that, since God has granted knowledge of God in the creation, people "are without excuse" when they deny God. What it does mean is that Christians should be open yet discerning in searching out truth wherever it may be found.

5. The two sides of the paradox here have a rough correspondence to a part of Karl Barth's thought about "parables of the Kingdom" that can be found outside the walls of the church. See chap. 3 below for further exploration of this theme.

any truth that is outside of Jesus Christ.[6] This is not simply saying, "All truth is in the historical Jesus," as if we could deduce our philosophical, psychological, and other truths from an analysis of Jesus as the first-century Galilean. Rather, it claims that through Scripture we have access to a revelatory history of God's work in Jesus Christ: in this first-century Galilean the eternal Word of God was made flesh, presenting to us the words and action of the Father in his person. "Whoever has seen me has seen the Father" (John 14:9). Jesus Christ is the Alpha and the Omega, the beginning and the end. There is no "truth" that is a blip on the screen outside of Christ. The truth that is in Christ is spacious. It is like a land where we could have a thousand new insights and discoveries, wide open for exploring. However, it is also a land that is specified: it is an "in Christ" land, a land where Jesus Christ is Lord.

While it is important to affirm that all truth is God's truth and that all truth is in Jesus Christ, we should also recognize that, as finite sinners, we will not always be able to see clearly exactly how these two hold together. At times, affirming that all truth is God's truth may seem to be in tension with affirming that all truth is in Jesus Christ. Why not simply affirm the first statement if the two statements can appear to be in tension? Because it is important that we exercise discernment in our claims about truth being God's truth. To put it differently, all truth claims occupy a theological location, whether their advocates openly admit it or not. Christians should not expect a naked form of reason to always lead to God's truth. There is no such thing as reason that is truly secular; ontological and theological assumptions about reality are embedded in all areas of human inquiry.[7] Therefore, it should not surprise us that in our pluralistic environment there are many — often incompatible — claims to "truth." Not all of these truths are in Christ. For example, while most scientists who are Christian would affirm an evolutionary account of the earth's geological history, affirming a philosophical naturalism that de-

6. For a helpful account of how confessing the lordship of Christ relates to all truth being in Christ, see " 'The Crucified One is Lord': Confessing the Uniqueness of Christ in a Pluralist Society," in *The Church Speaks: Papers of the Commission on Theology, Reformed Church in America, 1985-2000,* ed. James I. Cook (Grand Rapids: Eerdmans, 2002), pp. 129-53.

7. For an account of the theological location of ostensibly "secular" social sciences, see John Milbank, *Theology and Social Theory: Beyond Secular Reason,* 2nd ed. (Oxford: Blackwell, 2006).

nies the existence of the Creator would be a truth that is not in Christ. If God is the Creator, and all creation is through Christ, then Christians must distinguish the truth claims about how the earth came to be from truth claims about whether this process has a transcendent author and sustainer.

LET US APPLY our two affirmations to the question of how to be competent interpreters of the Bible as a book. In reading the Bible, we need to understand the words on the page or read aloud from the pulpit. We need to understand sentences and paragraphs, and we need to understand something about genres, such as poetry, apocalyptic writing, law, wisdom, and so forth. None of these areas of knowledge comes from the Bible itself: the Bible does not teach us how to read books. These issues are in the realm of general hermeneutics, that is, the processes involved in the reading of any book. Since the Bible is a book, reading the Bible involves a broad range of disciplines — from grammar to history, from textual criticism to sociology. This has had a wide-ranging effect in the history of Christian mission, as basic education often receives a major boost in areas where a community has turned to the Christian faith. Why? Because the community wants to be able to read so that the people can read the Bible.

Yet Christians should not read Scripture exactly as they read any other book. An agnostic expert in ancient literature may have finely honed skills in reading texts. That scholar can provide very helpful insights into the history, context, and textual features in a passage of Scripture. But this is not enough for the Christian. For Christians, the Bible is the written word of God, the Spirit's instrument for transforming God's people into Christ's image. As I observed in chapter 1, the parable of the sower and other biblical passages suggest that receiving this word of God involves much more than simply apprehending information or understanding words and sentences. Instead, it requires the working of the Spirit in the Christian community: the Spirit illuminates the words as they point to Christ on the journey of faith. This process is not something that general hermeneutics can manufacture. Insights from general hermeneutics must be taken up and sanctified in this triune drama of revelation. The reception of the word of God is not produced merely by human effort.

For Christians, reading Scripture involves nothing less than entering into the triune God's activity of redeeming fallen creation through the instrument of Scripture. This is an "in Christ" truth that we should be clear about. But participating in the Spirit's work through Scripture does not bypass human processes either. In the preface to his classic work on biblical hermeneutics and proclamation, *On Christian Teaching,* Augustine responds to potential critics who think that they have no need for linguistics, rhetorical philosophy, and other "pagan" disciplines because "all worthwhile illumination of the difficulties of these [Scripture] texts can come by a special gift of God."[8] In other words, these critics think that you should not spend too much time working with secular disciplines to inform your preaching and teaching of Scripture, because God just illuminates the human mind directly. Don't prepare too much for preaching a sermon, they say. It will quench the Spirit!

Augustine grants that, on the one hand, these critics have a point: God is free. God can speak through a donkey, as in the case of Balaam (Num. 22–24). God does not need human agency or human disciplines to communicate his word. But, though God could have chosen to present his word through an angel, God chooses to use human beings and human agency.[9] Augustine points to a profound truth about the working of God's Spirit: the Spirit enables, empowers, and sanctifies human agency rather than bypassing it. This truth is shown in fullness in Jesus Christ himself, who did not become less human by being fully divine, but was fully human in his perfect union with God. For those who are in Christ, then, God does not simply zap his word into their heads by the Spirit, though God would be free to do so. God's Spirit works in and through human means, human disciplines, human understandings of linguistics, texts, and rhetoric.

In light of the way the Spirit works in and through human processes, general hermeneutics should be used by Christians in an ad hoc manner, for the purpose of the journey of faith seeking understanding. General hermeneutics should not set the starting point nor the ending point for a Christian reading of Scripture.[10] Doing so would be an act of

8. Augustine, *On Christian Teaching,* trans. R. P. Green (Oxford: Oxford University Press, 1997), p. 3.

9. Augustine, *On Christian Teaching,* p. 5.

10. On the danger of subscribing to a general "theory of meaning" to set the agenda for a Christian interpretation of Scripture, see Stephen Fowl, *Engaging Scripture: A Model for Theological Interpretation* (Malden, MA: Blackwell Publishers, 1998), chap. 1.

idolatry: deciding on our own terms when and where God can appear in the process of biblical interpretation. Nevertheless, general hermeneutics does point us to some competencies and methods that are important in reading the Bible, that is, how to understand the human, historical, creaturely means by which God has chosen to communicate his life-giving word. God uses Scripture as a word of fellowship *through* these human means of understanding and interpretation, not apart from them.

"Understanding" and "Explanation" of the Biblical Text within the Triune Drama of Salvation

Christians should read Scripture in a way that goes beyond an impressionistic reading (as displayed in the examples opening this chapter), in which they avoid the surprises and challenges of the text. Instead, they should encounter the text in a way that is open to learning, listening, and transformation. But what does this look like in terms of the process of reading Scripture as a text? I explore this below under two categories: *understanding* and *explanation*. I use these words in a specialized sense, a sense influenced by the hermeneutical thought of Hans Georg Gadamer and Paul Ricoeur. In the section on "understanding," I offer a brief description of what a close, transformative reading of a text looks like, and how this relates to the horizon of possible meanings of the contemporary reader. I explore an example of what the process of understanding looks like by examining the process of reading a novel, and then I adapt this description to the special case of reading Scripture.

Yet texts do not fall from the sky as catalysts for transformation; rather, they emerge through a process of creaturely production. Texts arise at a particular point in time, from a particular cultural context. In the second section below, the one on "explanation," I explore the important practice of explaining the contextually located features of the text — in various forms of linguistic and historical analysis. In that section I argue that we should use a wide range of methods to examine the historical, cultural, and linguistic location of the biblical text. While there is a danger in this process of seeking to become masters over the biblical text rather than hearers, historical and critical approaches should be drawn on in a way that nurtures rather than subverts a transformative reading of the Bible as Scripture. Why should "explanation" be done in a receptive and theological mode? Because, for Christians, the Bible is not just like other books. While explaining contextually located features of the text is important, the Bible ultimately consists of creaturely texts that are produced and sanctified by the Spirit of God to be God's own transforming word in Christ. I conclude this chapter with an exegetical example to show how some of these dynamics operate in the practice of biblical interpretation in Christian ministry.

The Process of Understanding in Reading

Let's begin our look at the process of understanding in reading a text by considering the reading of a fantasy novel. Imagine that you have decided to read the Ring trilogy by J. R. R. Tolkien. There could be a variety of reasons why you might choose to do this: perhaps you have enjoyed previous novels in the genres of fantasy or science fiction; or perhaps you have seen *The Lord of the Rings* movies, and you want to experience the books on which the films were based. At any rate, you come with certain expectations about what the books will contain. You may expect certain features because of the fantasy genre. From reading the jacket copy, you may expect certain twists of plot. You may expect the book to be exciting or relaxing — that is, to produce certain effects on you as a reader. You do not come to the book as a blank slate. And while your background, past experience with novels, and expectations about this book will certainly bias your reading of the novel, these features of your preconceptions actually help facilitate your understanding of the book. If you knew nothing about the genre of fantasy, you might think that the book was ancient history; if you were unfamiliar with fiction, you might think that the story of Frodo was a story of your past life (if you believed in past lives). Your own preconceptions — with their attendant cultural influences, beliefs, and expectations about books, novels, fantasy, and Tolkien — will shape your reading of the novel. You will need to refine some of these preconceptions, but your preconceptions are what caused you to pick up the book in the first place.

As you read the book, you find yourself imaginatively entering into the world of Middle Earth. Perhaps you identify with Frodo at points, or with Frodo's companion Sam at other moments. Perhaps you lose yourself in the drama as Frodo leaves his small village in the Shire. You may have had similar experiences of leaving what is comfortable and familiar to face the threatening world beyond. As you experience these things in reading *The Lord of the Rings,* you are not leaving behind your past, your context, or your preconceptions. Rather, those experiences are helping you enter into the novel as something bigger than yourself. You do not decide whether Frodo leaves the Shire; he does so whether you will it to be so or not. He leaves the Shire even if you came to the book with the idea that all three novels are set in the Shire. That preconception needs to be revised. Yet surprises like that contribute to your joy of reading the novel.

Even if this is your second time through *The Lord of the Rings,* there will be details that you had not remembered: the light on the mountain, the fear of Pippin, and hundreds of other details that make the novel imaginatively compelling. You can learn the basic features of the plot from *Cliff's Notes,* but you won't be able to enter into the story — its atmosphere, its texture, its ironies — without reading, and even rereading, the book. Each time you read it will be different, because each time you bring a different set of preconceptions to the book. And if you are a good reader, you will not just skim the book to make sure it has all the basic features that you remember. You will actually read the book, allowing yourself to enter into the Shire and Middle Earth and Mordor. In doing so, you allow your preconceptions to be changed, so that the set of experiences, expectations, and interests that you bring to the novel are different from the ones you had when you first read it.

Now let's make some hermeneutical observations about our reading of *The Lord of the Rings.* We will explore four levels of observations: first, the role of *preparation* for understanding the text; second, a description of the process of reading in terms of *play;* third, a description of the process of reading in terms of *narrative and metaphor;* finally, in light of our reflections on the role of preunderstandings in the process of reading, we will examine the notion of reading a text within a *tradition.*

Preparation

Reading a book is not a mechanistic process of internalizing information. Rather, we begin with our interests, our preconceptions, our questions, those things that led us to pick up the book in the first place. In general terms, these interests are not the enemy of good interpretation. In the example above, one's previous experience with the genre of fantasy or interest in the plot of *The Lord of the Rings* are assets that make a deeper understanding of the book possible. As long as one is open to surprises and anomalies that reshape our presuppositions, the preunderstandings themselves are not roadblocks; they are bridges that help make an understanding of the book possible.

But how does one become a reader who is open to surprise, open to the "otherness" of a text? For Gadamer, there is not a particular method that can be used to ensure this quality in readers. Instead, the classical study of the humanities cultivates traits that help develop and form these virtues in readers. Such a reader can be distanced from the "immediacy of desire, of personal need and private interest" so that one can "keep oneself open to what is other."[11] Ideally prepared readers open themselves to hearing even what they do not want to hear from a text when they are addressed by the text. When readers have developed this virtue, they can move beyond knee-jerk reactions and be open to new images or ideas in their encounter with the text.

Gadamer's emphasis on preparation for reading has analogues in what premodern Christians frequently taught about reading Scripture. One needs the spiritual preparation of involvement in the Christian community, prayer, worship, and discipleship to understand Scripture correctly. This broad Christian tradition believes that our Sunday worship liturgy — and our moral behavior on Monday morning — shapes how we read Scripture. Like Gadamer, they believed that these preparations were not simply a rational method we could do in our head. There is no "E-Z as 1-2-3" guide to prepare us to read Scripture. Why? Because reading Scripture is part of the process of discipleship in the context of the Christian community. Moreover, we bring our whole lives to our reading of Scripture, so that the whole of our lives may be addressed by God through Scripture.

11. Hans Georg Gadamer, *Truth and Method,* 2nd ed., trans. Joel Weinsheimer and Donald G. Marshall (New York: Continuum, 1993), pp. 13, 17.

Reading as Play

When we seek to understand a text, we should not just treat it as an object over which we exercise control (in a subject-object relation). Instead, reading a text is more like a healthy conversation, a subject-subject relationship in which we do not treat the other person as an object to be understood and thus dominated. In a healthy conversation we display an openness toward the person's claim on us: it is a genuine listening.[12]

Gadamer has a compelling image for what takes place in the process of understanding: play. This is not careless or silly play. It is more like a game that is played and taken seriously as such. Imagine that you are playing a game of tennis. What's going on in your head? Are you observing the game as a spectator would? Not if you are serious about the game: that would be treating the game as an object. Instead, you keep your eyes and mind on the ball, on the court, on the other player. You don't know how the other player will play. You cannot control the game or predict in advance where the ball will go. Instead, you respond to what your opponent does — point by point, volley by volley. If it is a subject-to-subject relationship as in a serious game, you cannot force the game into your mold. You cannot wish your hits to be inbounds, and then they will be. You have to face what the game gives you, face what is "other" about it, and respond.

Likewise, a good reader of the *Ring* trilogy will not simply treat her preconceptions about the book as matters of fact. Whether it is her first or fiftieth time reading the book, she needs to reshape her preconceptions. She cannot do that simply by distancing herself from the novel, declaring what it can and cannot be saying. Or, in the tennis analogy, you cannot do it by leaving the tennis game to watch as a spectator. You can do it via a careful, close reading of the text, a reading that is open to surprises, open to anomalies, open to the point-by-point action of the text as an "other." It is not a process of rational control, for, as Gadamer says, there is a *"primacy of play over the consciousness of the player."*[13] In other words, all playing is a being-played. The text has a "givenness" that plays

12. For a helpful exposition of this point in Gadamer, see Andrew Louth, *Discerning the Mystery: An Essay on the Nature of Theology* (Oxford: Oxford University Press, 1983), pp. 39-41.

13. Gadamer, *Truth and Method*, p. 104 (italics in original).

you, exerts a kind of noncoercive force over your preunderstandings. In the act of reading as play, you allow yourself to be played by the game itself, by entering into the to-and-fro movement of the game rather than trying to exercise rational control over the game.

Play requires vulnerability and trust. Certain parts of our view of reality will be called into question, even changed, as we allow ourselves to be addressed by the text. In being "played" by an ancient text, for example, we see that it does not merely address ancient readers. Or our neighbor. Our own field of meaning, our horizon, is expanded when we are played by the text.

With regard to the reading of Scripture, a reader should enter into play with the biblical text such that he is surprised, called into question, and addressed by the text. Reading Romans 5 as Scripture is not reducible to an intellectual specification of Paul's intended meaning in writing the chapter to Christians in Rome, but it involves allowing oneself to be addressed by God through a text that implicates the reader as a sinner reconciled to God through Jesus Christ. What exactly does this mean? It means that we must return to the text and become open to surprises, and to being played by the text through the Spirit's power. Some readings of Scripture are better than others. But the image of being played by the text can help show how the act of reading an ancient text is not simply about identifying an ancient meaning and making a correlate application to contemporary reality (in which *we* are in charge of the correlation). A good reader allows herself to be addressed about the subject matter on which the text speaks. Play requires that she lose her control over the game as she enters into it — and in losing control allows her life to be addressed.

The Imaginative Power of Narratives

Metaphors and narratives are not an inferior way to present a "literal truth."[14] Rather, they function in ways that direct discourse forms of

---

14. This section draws on important themes in Paul Ricoeur's hermeneutics. For an account of how Ricoeur relates imagination and entering into a possible "world" to the reading of Scripture, see esp. "The Bible and the Imagination," in *Figuring the Sacred: Religion, Narrative, and Imagination* (Minneapolis: Fortress, 1995), pp. 144-66.

writing cannot: they present an imaginative world to inhabit, often with a shock value that calls the reader's world into question. For example, as the good reader enters imaginatively into the virtual world of Middle Earth through the narrative of *The Lord of the Rings,* that world functions as a pair of sunglasses do for seeing reality. Evil comes to be associated with the hunger for power and control, as those who seek after the ring of power. The narrative provides a lens through which to view the story of Frodo, but also a lens that implicates the appearance of evil on the reader's own horizon. By presenting a possible world, narrative and metaphor lead to new insights and perspective on the reader's own world: new features come into focus, and others become peripheral.

With respect to the reading of Scripture, the power of metaphor has powerful implications for narrative portions of Scripture, wherein the reader can imaginatively enter into the world revealed by the text. As readers identify with the Israelites eating manna in the wilderness (they are tempted to hoard it against God's commands), that lens can shed light on our own context: the temptation to cling to wealth as a right rather than to act as stewards of goods according to God's commands (Exod. 16). In Matthew's Gospel, Jesus tells the parable of the generous employer who pays his employees a full day's wage even though they come to work late and work only one hour. In this parable of "the kingdom of heaven," the other workers complain to the employer that he is unjust in his generosity to the latecomers (Matt. 20:1-15), which provides a lens through which current readers can see their own meager theology of grace. In these examples, the narrative discloses a reality that is more dynamic than simply the discursive claims that "God provides for his people" or "God is free to show mercy, so do not begrudge God's generosity." These narratives are not inferior attempts at declarative sentences, but they provide a possible world for readers to inhabit: the narrative lens makes the readers' own contexts appear in a different light. Narratives do not simply present us with new information, but with a new way to perceive the world around us.

In addition, the power of metaphor and narrative has implications for the reading of the nonnarrative genres of Scripture as well. In the Bible's poetry, apocalyptic literature, and wisdom literature, biblical texts frequently use metaphor and simile. In the genre of law, the giving of the law is set within a narrative framework within the biblical books themselves. Furthermore, since Christian readers read Scripture through a rule of faith (chap. 1), which has a narrative shape, all genres of Scripture are taken up into this larger "story" of the biblical canon. A portion of the law, or an individual proverb, is seen in light of the canon's story of God's creating, judging, and redeeming work that finds its fulfillment in Jesus Christ. Whether or not narrative is a prominent feature in the biblical genre, the passage becomes a moment in the tri-une drama of salvation when read in light of the canonical story of Scripture, a story summarized in the rule of faith.

Overcoming the Prejudice Against Preunderstandings

A common inclination in contemporary Western societies is to think that preunderstandings are the sorts of things we need to move beyond, so that we can deal with "the thing itself." Some biblical scholars, while admitting that we always come to the Bible with preunderstandings, think that the goal of biblical studies is to get beyond the preunderstandings we bring to the text. We may be Christian — and, even more specifically, Pentecostal or Lutheran or Reformed — when we approach the biblical text, but we need to overcome these broadly Christian and specific confessional preunderstandings when we read the biblical text.

There is a descriptive issue here that is closely tied to a normative one. These biblical scholars contend that, normatively speaking, we *should* overcome our preunderstandings. But this depends on a descriptive account of the hermeneutical process in which preunderstandings distort our understanding of texts. But is that descriptive account persuasive?

As I noted above in the example of reading from the *Ring* trilogy, the reader's expectations and preunderstandings need not block textual understanding; they may actually open up possibilities for it. If one is a prepared, "ideal" reader, some preconceptions will be legitimated and others will be eliminated as the reader engages the text with its surprises and anomalies. But even when this happens, readers do not leave their preunderstandings behind: their preunderstandings are shaped by a close reading of — their play with — the text. Even if you have read the novels of Tolkien five or ten times, your preunderstandings about them will never be perfect: you will not know "the book in itself," as op-

45

posed to others who merely have biased ideas about the book. You will have a concept of what the book is about, and it will most likely be a better one than that of most people who have only read the book once, because it is informed by the shape and details of the text.

This process is often called the "hermeneutical circle": we always move back and forth between understanding particular parts of a text and our understanding of the text as a whole. While some interpretations are shaped by the text more than others are — and thus some interpretations are, in fact, stronger than others — there is no point at which we have arrived at "the final meaning" of the text. Texts are simply much more rich and multivalent than that.

Thus, if preunderstandings are simply inescapable, and if they can actually help the process of understanding emerge from the text, then we should not make the normative move of trying to get beyond those preunderstandings. There is no advantage in trying to be neutral in coming to the text. Nor should we see the final goal of interpretation as being able to leap out of our horizon into the minds of the text's original audience. Either denying our horizons' lens or projecting our identities as readers can be ways of avoiding the address of the text.

As applied to the reading of Scripture, a key feature of the horizon for Christian readers relates to the Christian practices in which readers participate. Christians pray, sing praise, and perform acts of service. More than that, Christians do not do these acts in a merely generic way, but with a certain specificity: Christians worship the love and majesty of God, they worship Jesus Christ as their saving Lord, and they speak about the communal working of the Holy Spirit. These things will help shape our reading of the Bible. They will influence the horizon that we bring to Scripture. When the worshiping Christian reads about Jesus, she will not see him as simply a distant historical figure. This is the Jesus that Christians know, the one to whom they have been united by the Holy Spirit. These practices will bias, or shape, the Christians' reading of Scripture. But is that necessarily a bad thing?

For instance, consider the following verse from John 15:5: "I am the vine, you are the branches. Those who abide in me and I in them bear much fruit, because apart from me you can do nothing." Christians will read this in a biased way. It is likely that they will think about their own Christian lives and whether they have been abiding in Christ's power or their own. There is nothing objective about this approach. A more objective approach might consider the historical question of what would lead the Gospel writer to include a Jesus teaching that involves the images of vine and branches. This line of inquiry can be fruitful for Christians as well, as we will explore in the next section. But the question that comes from one formed by Christian worship opens up interpretive possibilities that the second question ignores. Christian readers should read Scripture closely, which involves being open to the surprises and otherness of the text. But that does not mean that a Christian encounter with the subject matter of the text (such as God, Jesus Christ, the Holy Spirit) becomes a liability; rather, it is an asset that opens new doors of understanding.

Overcoming the Prejudice against Tradition

Part of the Enlightenment prejudice against preunderstandings is based on its protest against the authority of traditions. One should not accept truths from authorities (such as the church or state) but from "thinking for oneself," by reason alone. But if Gadamer is right about how preunderstandings can enable rather than simply block understanding, then this critique of tradition does not hold water. Gadamer's view profoundly calls into question the Enlightenment prejudice against tradition.

For Gadamer, the idea of understanding in a tradition has nothing to do with coercion, that is, a tradition's forcing one to think in a particular way. Belonging to a tradition is not about blind obedience to its norms; it is about making use of legitimate preunderstandings that have shown themselves useful and productive over time. For example, a tradition that thinks Tolkien's novels are about space adventures is not going to last very long. But traditions that emerge from — yet go beyond — the text are much more likely to last through time. For example, the Roman Catholic tradition of natural law has been alive for centuries, because it opens windows into the biblical text itself. This tradition can lead to understandings of the text that go beyond the text, yet it can push the readers back to the logic and details of the text.

Ultimately, we read with the lens of tradition (whether we realize it or not) because we are not the only readers to read this book. We are not solitary individuals who are alone in our quest for what is right and true about the subject matter of the text. Instead, we are interested in the text's subject matter, and we participate in traditions as we join others with similar interests.

Gadamer notes that some particular texts, the "classic" ones, have shown themselves to have the power to speak to many generations: they are books that address us in "a timeless present that is contemporaneous with every other present."[15] They address our lives even as the horizons of readers have changed dramatically through time; even so, many generations have interest in the subject matter of these classic books. These generations are addressed by the text in different ways because of their context, for one understands in "a different way" if one is to understand at all. But that is the beauty of traditions: they open up deeper, more penetrating possibilities for textual understandings than we could have on our own. In addition, in terms of reading Scripture, traditions join us together with the "cloud of witnesses" (Heb. 12:1) and the work of the Spirit through the centuries.

Take, for example, the tradition of reading the Bible in light of the Nicene Creed. Does this practice simply force the Nicene Christian to read in a certain way? While one certainly must decide whether to be a Nicene Christian (thus there is an element of the will involved), in terms of the interpretation of Scripture, it functions as a preconception that opens up hundreds of possibilities we might otherwise have missed. Should Jesus Christ be worshiped? Nicene Christianity says yes, while Arian Christianity says that Christ should not be the direct object of worship.[16] If one believes that Christ should be worshiped, one will read John 15:5 and many other passages in a dramatically different way than if Jesus Christ were simply a steppingstone to the Father, the real God. Yet Nicene Christianity is a tradition. From a purely exegetical perspective, there are arguments for and against the Nicene tradition. But there is no neutral way to establish Nicene Christianity as the only way to read the biblical texts.

This is not to say, of course, that Nicene and Arian traditions of biblical interpretation are equally valid. It is possible that one interpretation is better than the other (I would suggest that this is, in fact, the case

---

15. Gadamer, *Truth and Method,* p. 288.

16. See Frank C. Senn, *Christian Liturgy: Catholic and Evangelical* (Minneapolis: Fortress, 1997), pp. 36-40.

for Nicene Christianity). Yet there is no neutral or purely biblical ground on which to make such a judgment. The evaluation must be made from within the hermeneutical circle. In our practice of reading Scripture, we cannot sit on the sidelines and be neutral. We either use a Nicene preconception in interpreting Scripture (which you probably do if your church worships Jesus Christ as the Son, as well as the Spirit) or we don't. When interpreting passages such as Philippians 2:9-11, where Jesus Christ appears to receive adoration, all readers inhabit a Nicene or non-Nicene tradition of reading Scripture, whether they recognize it or not.

All Christians, in fact, read the Bible from within particular traditions. The question is, what traditions are operative? I grew up in a Baptist church where any talk of "tradition" was greeted with great suspicion. To us, Christians who talked about tradition were focusing on the nonessentials; by contrast, we were simply biblical. Yet, if we become aware of the inescapability of tradition, we can see my Baptist practice in a different light. We had traditions about how the worship service would be run. Our "spontaneous prayers" had distinct and undeniable patterns. We had a shared theology, and we would certainly recognize it when someone diverged from that shared theology. While the questions would be raised in terms of whether the teaching was "biblical" or not, the functional reality was that my Baptist church had doctrinal traditions, worship traditions, orthopraxy traditions, and so on. It just didn't want to name them as such.

Sometimes this failure to recognize the operative traditions of one's own teaching leads to deeply ironic consequences. For example, for much of the twentieth century various forms of dispensationalism have been widespread in American Christianity. The popular forms of this approach would correlate contemporary events in the Middle East or Russia with a scientistic reading of the prophetic works of Scripture. Thus, for example, even President Ronald Reagan considered Armageddon imminent because of his assessment of contemporary political affairs. Later, a similar version of dispensationalism was popularized in the *Left Behind* series of books and movie.

Dispensationalism, prominent in conservative evangelical circles, considers itself to be a theologically conservative movement. Why? Ostensibly because it has based its conclusions on Scripture. But what *traditional* (or theological) preunderstandings did dispensationalists bring to their reading of Scripture to come to these conclusions? This reading of Scripture claims to recover an early (or "primitive") strand of thought from the Bible itself; as such, it is a form of primitivism that emerged from the Enlightenment: "Primitivism retains the most minimal commitment to God's action in history (in the life of Christ and usually in the first century of apostolic activity) and then seeks to make only this first-century 'New Testament church' normative for contemporary practice."[17] This approach misconstrues the Reformation cry of *sola Scriptura* as a way to dismiss the Spirit's work in the church through the ages. It also denies the embodied, historical character of Christian knowledge; hence its inevitable connection to "tradition." Instead, readers attempt to leap outside of their own historical and cultural context to recover the hidden, primitive meaning of the biblical text. In the case of this kind of dispensational hermeneutic, the "primitive" meaning is a prophetic one that predicts particular twentieth- and twenty-first-century events.

The central irony of dispensationalism is that this conservative Christian movement actually uses an Enlightenment hermeneutic in interpreting Scripture. This primitivist hermeneutic emerges from the Enlightenment in its attempt to overcome the located, contextual, traditional character of all understanding. Although parts of dispensationalist eschatology involve a significant departure from church tradition, the movement considers itself "conservative" simply by claiming to be "biblical."[18]

On the other side, the ironies of denying one's own functional tradition run just as deep among strands of self-identified "progressive" or "liberal" Christians. The Jesus Seminar is an example of a group involved in another form of primitivism. The seminar is made up of a group of scholars who have courted media coverage and captured the imagination of many progressive Christians. The titles of the books by Jesus Seminar authors give a clue to their attitude toward their own project: Robert Funk's *The Five Gospels: What Did Jesus Really Say? The Search for the Authentic Words of Jesus;* Funk's *The Acts of Jesus: What Did*

---

17. James K. A. Smith, *Who's Afraid of Postmodernism? Taking Derrida, Lyotard and Foucault to Church* (Grand Rapids: Baker Academic, 2006), pp. 128-29.

18. For a helpful historical account of the emergence of dispensationalist eschatology, see Larry V. Crutchfield, *The Origins of Dispensationalism* (Lanham, MD: University Press of America, 1992).

Jesus Really Do? Marcus Borg's *Meeting Jesus Again for the First Time;* and John Dominic Crossan's *Jesus: A Revolutionary Biography.* What all of these titles have in common is the implicit claim that their portraits of Jesus get behind all of the traditions about Jesus, traditions that give a false account of what Jesus said and did. These books assume that traditions distort the reality about Jesus. Rather than rely on traditions and the Gospel accounts of Jesus, we need to meet Jesus again "for the first time," adopt a "revolutionary" approach that dispenses with false traditions, and engage in an unbiased assessment of what Jesus actually said and did. We need to uncover the "primitive" strand of tradition behind the biblical texts themselves.

While titles may result from the spin of publishers who want to sell books, the Jesus Seminar's own account of its methods has a scientistic tone that makes its participation in the tradition of Enlightenment prejudice against preunderstanding quite clear. Funk describes the way his method makes it possible, "on purely objective grounds," to isolate older, more authentic sayings of Jesus.[19] Crossan shows his Enlightenment approach with his frequent reference to the "historical Jesus" as the "real Jesus." One must go "behind" the interpretations of our earliest manuscripts, the Gospels, in order to reconstruct the real, and historical Jesus. Crossan implies that he is not influenced by the likes and dislikes of his own horizon.

> It is very important to me — *to be honest in my search for the historical Jesus.* I have tried to reconstruct the historical Jesus as accurately as possible. It was never my purpose to find a Jesus whom I liked or disliked, a Jesus with whom I agreed or disagreed. I do not pretend that I have the final picture of Jesus, but I do offer my portrait as an honest one.[20]

The implication is that, while other reconstructions are shaped by the horizon of the interpreter, Crossan has overcome this by an act of the will — an act of being "honest." Yet the shaping force of Crossan's preunderstandings are all too apparent: he equates the "reality" of Je-

19. Robert W. Funk, *The Five Gospels: What Did Jesus Really Say? The Search for the Authentic Words of Jesus* (New York: HarperCollins, 1997), p. 26.

20. John Dominic Crossan, *Who Is Jesus? Answers to Your Questions about the Historical Jesus* (Louisville: Westminster John Knox, 1999), p. 7.

sus with his "historicity," and the "traditions" of the Gospels are something the historian must get "behind" to find the real Jesus. While New Testament scholars may debate the merits of such claims, we should note, for the purpose of our discussion, that Crossan gives us no bare honesty in his portrait of Jesus; rather, he gives us a set of Enlightenment preconceptions about what is real, what is historical, what is reliable, and what an impartial historian may honestly discover.

Even though one of the above movements self-identifies as conservative and the other as liberal, these divergent movements do share one particular Enlightenment prejudice: the prejudice against preunderstanding and a desire to uncover the most "primitive" traditions that have been obscured by later interpreters. In other words, despite their differences, they share an Enlightenment tradition that eschews tradition.[21] This is a case in which a general hermeneutic — where what counts is the meaning of a text — subverts two theological dimensions of how premodern Christians have interpreted Scripture: both the role of the Holy Spirit through history and the doctrine of the church.

As I observed in the preceding chapter, early Christians interpreted Scripture in light of a rule of faith that summarized the Christian message and provided orientation concerning the center and boundaries for a Christian interpretation of Scripture. While the rule of faith itself emerges from Scripture, it is important to recognize that early Christians did not attempt to interpret Scripture from a neutral theological standpoint; nor did they seek to eschew later tradition (such as the rule of faith itself) to uncover the most primitive strand of scriptural meaning. Why not? There are theological reasons to call such a hermeneutic into question. First, as persons reading Scripture as the story of God's action with creation and Israel that culminates in Jesus Christ, Christians read Scripture by the Spirit, for the Spirit is promised to "testify" on behalf of Jesus and "guide you into all truth." The Spirit "will glorify me [Jesus], because he will take what is mine and declare it to you" (John 16:13, 15).

This does not mean that Christians always interpret Scripture cor-

---

21. While both movements share an Enlightenment prejudice against tradition, the primitive strand to be discovered does differ: while dispensationalism seeks to uncover a primitive biblical tradition apart from the interpretation of the later church, the Jesus Seminar wishes to separate and isolate a particular primitive strand *within* the biblical materials itself.

rectly; but it does mean that as a result of the Spirit's work, scriptural interpretation takes place in the sphere of the Spirit, bearing witness to Jesus Christ. But this leads us to our second theological reason: the church. The Spirit does not just pop into the heads of individuals; rather, the Spirit acts as an agent who unifies Christians in Christ, across the barriers of history and culture.[22] Therefore, the Christian tradition is not merely a human realm of activity, but a sphere in which the Spirit has been at work. The Spirit's work in the church is among sinners; as such, the tradition of the church is not above being reformed through further engagement with Scripture. But all of this reading and struggling with Scripture takes place within the context of the rule of faith, a doctrinal vision of the journey that Christians make as they read Scripture in light of the incarnation, life, death, and resurrection of Jesus Christ.

Thus, while premodern authors were not seeking to give a hermeneutical description of the process of understanding, their theological convictions were incompatible with the Enlightenment prejudice against preunderstanding and tradition per se. The church was often in need of reform, and many premodern Christians looked to Scripture as a source to guide reform, as well as to criticize particular traditions that they considered incompatible with Scripture. But these critics often argued that moving away from an aberrant tradition could be a way to rejoin another, more biblical Christian tradition. The goal was not to be the first to correctly understand a passage of Scripture because it was written by the prophets or the apostles (in a "primitivist" mode). Rather, the goal was to read Scripture in such a way that the church's teaching and practice could be realigned with the Spirit's work in the past.[23]

In summary, on the side of *understanding*, we have seen how there are parallels between a general description of textual understanding

---

22. We will explore the exegetical basis for this claim in chap. 4.

23. When it comes to the Reformation era, this account applies to many Roman Catholics who sought reform, as well as the Lutheran and Reformed parts of the Reformation in particular. For all of these groups, there was an emphasis on a "return to the sources" and often Scripture in particular, but not in a way that eschewed earlier tradition. On the contrary, Roman Catholic, Lutheran, and Reformed authors all argued that their teachings maintained continuity with key dimensions of the earlier church tradition, even as they argued for the reform of some of that tradition.

(inspired by Gadamer and Ricoeur) and premodern assumptions about interpreting the Bible as Scripture. The two are not identical, and the general hermeneutic needs to be adapted and reshaped for the special task of interpreting Scripture. But since the close reading of texts does not come automatically, it is helpful to draw on these insights from general hermeneutics on the importance of preparation, imagination, preunderstanding, and tradition in reading. For the reading of Scripture, the decisive issue relates to the role of the Spirit and the church. I believe that these convictions should lead us to reject the Enlightenment prejudice against tradition. This is not so that we can pretend that we live in the twelfth or sixteenth century. Rather, it frees us to embrace a hermeneutic that has overcome its infatuation with the Enlightenment and restores our sense of hearing the Spirit's continuing testimony to the Word in the church's scriptural interpretation. With that said, let us move to the second part of the dialectic, on *explanation,* which recontextualizes and yet draws deeply on the work of modern critical biblical scholarship.

The Place of Biblical Criticism in a Transformative Reading of Scripture

As I have described above, good readers are open to surprises, to the expansion of their horizons through engagement with the text. In the overall process of reading, readers should allow themselves to be addressed by the text rather than treating it as an object to be mastered. These insights from general hermeneutics serve within a special hermeneutic of Scripture as pointers to help Christians give a "close" rather than an "impressionistic" reading of the Bible, a creaturely word produced and appropriated by the Spirit as God's own word.

However, there is a second side to the task of giving a close reading of the biblical text: it involves not only preparation, preunderstandings, and tradition, but also methods. On the one hand, there is no magic method to acquire that will give us "the final meaning" of a text; on the other hand, since all writing involves the use of particular words, forms, and genres, a text does have a structure that is, in some sense, open to various forms of analysis. This may seem to contradict the first side of the dialectic above, which claims that an ideal reader will not simply treat a text as an object to be mastered. However, the use of literary and textual methods can analyze texts as human products in such a way that the reader stays open and receptive to the text's address. In addition to the above insights about the process of understanding a text, there is a wide range of critical methods that Christian readers of Scripture should use in their receptive encounter with the biblical text.

Although holding together these two sides of interpretation may seem incompatible to some, these sides were held together tightly in much Christian interpretation of Scripture before the Enlightenment. For example, in *On Christian Teaching,* Augustine's scriptural hermeneutic seamlessly holds together commitments on both sides of the dialectic:

all interpretation leads to love of God and neighbor	ideal readers display a knowledge of Greek and Hebrew, and a facility for textual criticism
readers should orient themselves toward God and a life of holiness	readers should have broad competencies in history, logic, and rhetoric
readers should be able to discern the Spirit's word that extends beyond the literal sense of the text	readers should display an anthropological awareness of the cultural differences between one's own time and the period when the text was written[24]

Even though the list of tasks in the second column has been severed from the first in modernity, the task for theological exegetes of Scripture is to bring these two sides of the dialectic back together.

Why is this critical or analytical task necessary for scriptural interpretation? It is necessary because there is no access to the scriptural texts apart from historical and linguistic analysis. All translations of Scripture are, to some extent, interpretations based on historical and linguistic inquiry. Every entry in a Bible dictionary draws on the critical

24. This list emerges from Augustine's *On Christian Teaching,* but its form is adapted from Francis Watson, in A. K. M. Adam, Stephen Fowl, Kevin Vanhoozer, and Francis Watson, *Reading Scripture with the Church* (Grand Rapids: Baker Academic), p. 122.

55

analysis of ancient texts and cultures. The revelation of God in Scripture takes place at particular times, in particular places, in particular cultures, and thus a close reading of a text will involve an analysis of its linguistic and historical features.

In fact, taken within the broader framework of reading a text within a tradition, the insights of critical textual analysis can play a crucial role in recovering true play with a text. They can highlight the otherness of the text at points, showing ways in which we have too quickly domesticated the biblical text with preunderstandings that need revision. At other points, critical insights can increase the potency and relevance of texts as they clarify certain commonalities between the ancient and contemporary horizons.

For example, consider the passages in the Gospels that refer to the Pharisees. Because they were the ones concerned with maintaining Jewish law, it is easy for us to write them off as fanatical legalists who occupy a space opposite that of Jesus. If we don't consider ourselves to be Judaizing legalists, we consider ourselves off the hook when Jesus rebukes the Pharisees. Jesus' rebuke does not apply to us. But historical-critical study shows that, in the context of Judaism at the time of Jesus, his ministry and message has some common points with that of the Pharisees, who were not all simply legalists seeking to earn their salvation. The Pharisees sought a renewal of obedience to covenant law from within the framework of God's covenantal promises to Israel. They certainly did differ from Jesus and from the early Christian movement, but there was common ground as well.[25] The insight that Pharisees were covenantal thinkers rather than stereotypical legalists has implications for our reading of the Gospels. Just when we thought we were safe from the implications of Jesus' words directed at the Pharisees because we have nothing in common with them, this historical insight can put us back in the game so that our lives are vulnerable once again to the piercing and healing word of God in the Gospels.

Scholars acquired these insights about the larger context of the Pharisees by reading sources outside the Bible. This behind-the-text in-

---

25. For an overview of the change in scholarship on the Pharisees, see James Dunn, *Jesus Remembered* (Grand Rapids: Eerdmans, 2003), pp. 266-70. It is important to note that while extrabiblical sources have enhanced our understanding of the Pharisees, there are still significant ongoing scholarly disputes about the identity of the Pharisees.

quiry contributes to our understanding of the biblical text itself. Both Old Testament and New Testament studies have been enriched by the many ancient texts that have become available since the nineteenth century from cultures and peoples surrounding Israel and the early church. By reading the Old Testament in the light of the literature of the Ancient Near East, and reading the New Testament in light of Second Temple Judaism, we can sharpen our understanding of the genres and literary conventions within the biblical writings. This often comes by noticing areas of both commonality and difference between biblical writings and other ancient writings. For example, the Old Testament creation story in Genesis shares some commonalities with the Babylonian *Enuma Elish;* the Exodus law with the Babylonian Code of Hammurabi; the Old Testament Proverbs with the Egyptian *Instruction of Amenemope;* the New Testament writings with extracanonical, intertestamental Jewish writings of the period (such as The Wisdom of Solomon, Jubilees, etc.) and the writings of the Qumran community (found in the Dead Sea Scrolls). The canonical biblical writings, of course, have differences from these other pieces of ancient literature; but they also share certain cultural and literary conventions, and a study of these other writings enables us to clarify the various genres within the Bible.

For some historical critics, these extracanonical writings confirm their sense that the biblical writings are not divinely inspired, since the biblical materials share literary conventions with the writings of some of the surrounding pagan cultures. But even the critical moment of examining the Bible occupies a theological space. To assume that writings cannot be divinely inspired if they share cultural and literary conventions with surrounding cultures is both a Deistic and Gnostic claim. First, it is Deistic in that it assumes that where we see signs of the human origins of the biblical texts, it means that God was not actively working in and through the writers and redactors of the Bible. Closely allied with this assumption is a Gnostic one: that for God to speak through Scripture, God must bypass the embodied, historical, culturally embedded life of human beings.

We need not see the commonalities between biblical and extrabiblical genres and conventions as a reason to despair of God's action in and through Scripture. Instead, we should remember that Christian teaching itself claims that God reveals himself in history to particular people at particular times. The writings of Scripture are human writings (and thus historically and culturally embedded) that God produces and uses in his outworking of salvation. Commonality with other literature is not, in itself, a theological problem; rather, it points to the extent to which God has lovingly chosen to work through human means even though God could have freely bypassed such means.[26]

Instead, when we approach behind-the-text contextual issues theologically, using them to direct our attention back to the biblical text, they can become part of a transforming theological reading of Scripture. At times this can come by way of clarifying the genre of a work. For example, the imaginative (and confusing) use of images and numbers in the book of Revelation has puzzled many interpreters, sometimes even leading readers to search for a secret code that unlocks the book's meaning. However, when we read the book alongside other works of Jewish apocalyptic literature, such as 1 Enoch, the style of the book becomes less obscure. The images and patterns of Revelation were not idiosyncratically pulled out of the air; rather, they share characteristics with other works of the same genre.[27] If we were to read a parable like we read a recipe or view a newscast, our expectations of the text would lead to a misconstrual of the text's sense. Behind-the-text research into a book like Revelation can keep it from being an esoteric book; instead, the reader can follow the text's genre cues in communicating urgent truths about Jesus Christ as the glorified Lamb of God who triumphs amidst the visible persecution of his bride, the church. Understanding the genre of a work is important in giving a close theological reading of the text.

While extrabiblical literature can help readers discern the genre of biblical books and the mode of their culturally embedded communication, this discernment is still not in the realm of secular reason. Even with the wealth of extrabiblical works to which we can compare and contrast biblical works, questions of genre are difficult ones: they require a marriage of historical and theological reasoning. What genre are the Gospels, and how does that relate to the history of Jesus? Are the opening chapters of Genesis "myth," and if so, how does this genre function? Theological interpreters of Scripture should not simply be

---

26. We return to this issue in chap. 3's discussion of biblical inspiration per se in light of a doctrine of revelation.

27. See Adela Yarbro Collins, "Revelation, Book of," *The Anchor Bible Dictionary* (New York: Doubleday, 1992), 5: 704.

apathetic about these questions, because they relate to the creational side of the origin of the scriptural texts. But neither should we approach history as if it were an immanent field sealed off from the Spirit's productive, sustaining, and sanctifying action.

Even apart from the important issues of genre, all readers of Scripture depend on the work of critical scholarship in some way, even if it is hidden. Do you read an English translation of the Bible? Translators depend on lexical information about how words and grammar are used both inside and outside of biblical writings. On points of dispute concerning translation, one can often see the ambiguity of this historical and contextual task. Even if we are not working with Hebrew and Greek ourselves and thus assessing the variants among the received texts (textual criticism), *someone* is making critical assessments for translations. We cannot read a translation of Scripture without being dependent on multiple levels of critical scholarship.

How can critical and theological reasoning be held together, particularly in dealing with behind-the-text issues? There is no single "global" answer to this question, for it depends on the particular biblical issue in question, as well as the critical and theological questions being posed to the text. In the same way, no single critical method always leads to a faithful interpretation of Scripture, and all methods must be "tamed in relation to the theological aims of Scripture and the ecclesial context within which the Bible is read as Scripture."[28] In other words, critical methods need to be *recontextualized* within a theological framework: that is, they need to be evaluated and used according to terms that refuse to treat the Bible as nothing more than an object of historical inquiry.

This recontextualization of biblical criticism within theology is necessary because some biblical scholars use historical-critical tools in a way that marginalizes theological thought altogether. In general, these approaches do not seek to expand their horizon by hearing the address of the text about the subject matter of God's work in the lives of Joshua, David, Jesus, or Paul. Rather, they fixate on behind-the-text issues such as the date of the text's origin and the circumstances that gave rise to it, as well as issues and problems related to manuscripts, redaction history, the original audience, and so forth. In the course of

---

28. Joel Green, *Seized by Truth: Reading the Bible as Scripture* (Nashville: Abingdon, 2007), p. 125.

these explorations, they lose the subject matter of the text itself.[29] Therefore, in interpreting the prologue of the Gospel of John, rather than allow themselves to enter into play with the possibility of Jesus being the "Word made flesh," these approaches move that question to the sidelines in their preoccupation with behind-the-text issues. When they use their explorations in this way, these purveyors of historical-critical methods do not lead to a receptive reading of the text; they simply use texts as steppingstones for reconstructing a history behind the text.

For the readers of Scripture, the history behind the text is important. But its reconstruction is not the final goal of interpretation. Scripture itself offers a revelatory history: that is, it portrays a history and a narrative about history fused together. While I will examine this further through an exposition of what is meant by the "historical sense" (chap. 5), for the purposes of this chapter I wish to say that Christian readers should not make behind-the-text issues the center of interpretation. When historical events such as the Exodus or the life of Jesus are narrated, our modernist tendency is to test the truth of these accounts by looking behind the text. But when we do, we end up with an account of the Exodus or Jesus' life that is narrated by our own historical reconstruction. At that point we risk exchanging the narrative of Scripture for our own historical narrative. Instead, we need to engage in historical reconstruction in a way that is oriented toward the illuminating text itself. This is not to assume that the biblical texts occupy an autonomous, textual reality that is divorced from history. Rather, it is to claim that it is impossible to access the reality mediated by the text apart from the text itself. The biblical text is not primarily a historical source for accessing a reality behind the text; rather, it is the Spirit's instrument for narrating the revelatory history, a history that is not simply a secular history but one in which God is active in the world.[30]

Another misuse of historical reconstruction is when it leaves readers with a sense that the ancient text does not address them, but only addresses the ancient community. On this issue, Christian interpreters

29. One should note that in a Christian interpretation of the Bible as canon, the subject matter of each individual text is shaped by the overall canonical claim that Scripture is God's instrument for shaping his people into Christ's image through the Spirit.

30. For more on this important difference, see Francis Watson, *Text, Church, and World: Biblical Interpretation in Theological Perspective* (Edinburgh: T&T Clark, 1994), pp. 2-3, 255-64.

need to be clear that we read as part of the one people of God; we are not reading "other people's mail." "The initiating error of standard modern exegesis is that it presumes a sectarian ecclesiology," Robert Jenson says. This approach fails to recognize that "the text we call the Bible was put together in the first place by the community that now needs to interpret it."[31] When Christians analyze the text, its history, and background, we should not assume that the historical gap between our contemporary horizon and the ancient one is a great canyon to be bridged by clever analogies or parallels. In a very real sense, this gap is bridged by the Spirit — the same Spirit who unites together God's people across culture and time. The books of the Bible are not just "addressed to" ancient Israel or the early church. Through Scripture, the Spirit addresses *all* of God's people, not just the original hearers.

Ultimately, the "critical" dimension of interpreting Scripture within a theological hermeneutic can be used for two positive ends: 1) By reengaging the features of the text, it opens readers to the otherness of the text in all of its historical and cultural particularity, reshaping preunderstandings that domesticate or poorly construe the text's sense. 2) The Christian's interpretation of Scripture is then put back into play: it becomes traditional in the fullest sense, not simply compliant to a previous reading but expanding a tradition by continuing to participate in the Spirit's work, which uses Scripture as an instrument of God's transforming word. While Christian readings of Scripture still occur within the rule of faith, the critical moment can be a human process that the Spirit uses to overcome sinful resistance to God's powerful, transforming word through Scripture. Indeed, refusing the gifts of critical scholarship on Scripture can, in fact, be a way of resisting the Spirit's work through Scripture.

Understanding and Explanation Together: Critical Naiveté in Scriptural Interpretation

The integration of the modes of understanding and explanation into a receptive mode of receiving Scripture is sometimes called reading with

31. Robert Jenson, "The Religious Power of Scripture," *Scottish Journal of Theology* 52, no. 1 (1999): 98.

a "second," or "critical," naiveté.[32] After Karl Barth makes some technical and explanatory comments on a biblical text, he says, "[W]hen the distinctions have been made they can be pushed again into the background and the whole can be read [with this tested or critical naiveté] as the totality it professes to be."[33] Though a part of the hermeneutical process does involve analyzing and assessing the features of the biblical text as an object, even this should be done in a distinctly Christian way. The reader needs to keep even critical analysis of the text within the realm of theological reasoning, receptive to the surprises and new insights that can be gleaned from this analysis. Ultimately, the text must remain in play so that the reader is vulnerably listening to the text as part of the canon of Scripture, reading Scripture as a way of entering into the Spirit's work of conforming the people of God to the way and image of Christ.

As I have indicated by way of the example of Augustine above, engaging in theological interpretation means integrating back together what the last few centuries of hermeneutics have tended to pull apart: a clear sense of the function of Scripture as that which leads to the love of God and neighbor, with a historical and anthropological sense of the ancient context and its customs, and a conviction that all scriptural interpretation is done on the path of Jesus Christ and leads to conformity to Christ by the Spirit, with a facility in textual criticism and ability to work with the linguistic features of the text. As a result, a theological approach to the interpretation of Scripture should not lead to an apathy about historical and critical questions, but should lead toward a more comprehensive hermeneutic that holds together understanding and explanation, theological and critical studies, in a way that seeks to "take every thought captive to obey Christ" (2 Cor. 10:5).

---

32. The notion of "second naiveté" is associated with Ricoeur, and "critical naiveté" is associated with Karl Barth. While I use these terms side by side, Ricoeur's account involves a second stage after critical distance from the text, whereas Barth's account does not involve a second, separate stage. See Richard E. Burnett, *Karl Barth's Theological Exegesis: The Hermeneutical Principles of the Römerbrief Period* (Tübingen: Mohr Siebeck, 2001), p. 116. For more on Ricoeur's notion of a second naiveté, see Mark I. Wallace, *The Second Naiveté: Barth, Ricoeur, and the New Yale Theology* (Macon, GA: Mercer University Press, 1990), chaps. 2 and 3.

33. Karl Barth, *Church Dogmatics,* trans. G. W. Bromiley, IV:2 (Edinburgh, T&T Clark, 1960-61), p. 479.

While there is no method to use on a biblical text to assure a faithful interpretation, there are different kinds of inquiry that we can identify that characterize a close and theological reading of a biblical text.[34] Some inquiries focus on the *text itself,* as when one pursues issues regarding the genre of the text, the text's internal argument, or textual criticism. Another kind of inquiry focuses on the text's larger *literary context,* which informs the passage in question and may share key words and motifs that are contained in the text itself. In the midst of this examination, issues of the *context* from which the biblical text emerges and into which it is received come into play. The text has a sociohistorical setting and addresses issues that interface with the reader's context. In addition, there are *intertextual* issues, where the biblical text may quote or echo other texts in the canon, where creeds and the church's worship may provide special insight into the biblical text that would otherwise be inaccessible.

These four types of inquiry are not separate steps for biblical interpretation, because dimensions of all four should be operative in the vulnerable play into which one enters with the text. All of these types of inquiry should occupy a broadly theological space, as they are all part of the dying and rising with Christ that takes place through our reading of Scripture — by the Spirit's power. An impressionistic reading of Scripture does not give the Spirit more room to work than does a close reading of Scripture, as described above. Rather, when we enter into these human processes of interpretation as a way of participating in the Spirit's work of judging and redeeming through Scripture, a close reading can be an act of faithfulness that is open to the rich food that God has to offer through the Bible.

As we think through the dynamics of participating in the Spirit's work through a close reading of Scripture, our example below shows how a revitalized notion of reading Scripture as part of a tradition can go hand in hand with receiving fresh insights from Scripture in a congregational context. Such a view requires us to rethink some common ways of thinking about tradition on a congregational level.

---

34. I adapt these four areas from Green, *Seized by Truth,* pp. 126-36.

Exegetical Example

When contemporary Western Christians hear about "church tradition," many of them may think of something like the following: 1) the way we've always done things, as opposed to "new" ways of doing things; 2) the old and outmoded ways of the past. But when we recognize that coming to Scripture from within a particular horizon of understanding is inevitable, and that traditions can help enable deeper understanding of Scripture rather than just block understanding, then the situation has changed. The traditions of the church can be seen as rich resources for deepening our encounter with Scripture. Rather than being "the way we've always done things" or the outmoded ways of the past, church traditions can be a newly appropriated, fresh mode of drawing on the Spirit's work in the past in the Christian community.

With our exegetical example, our use of a tradition will come through the congregational singing of a hymn by twelfth-century theologian Bernard of Clairvaux. The hymn could be sung a cappella, with the accompaniment of guitar and drums, or with an organ. There are many possible arrangements that help the congregation enter into Bernard's poetic and worshipful hymn. Furthermore, the hymn draws on a key image from the passage being preached in the worship service — Jesus Christ as the bread of life in John 6 — but it is not a direct commentary on the verse. It emerges from Bernard's rich, scripturally informed theology of communion with Christ that pulls together images from books such as John's Gospel, Song of Songs, and Paul's Epistles. As such, though it emerges from a theology that *develops* these scriptural themes, it provides a canonical canvas that displays the theme of communion with Christ in a new light. In the hymn, the congregation is not just taught about this communion, but it enters into the communion by performing the hymn in a community that is gathered to worship and commune with Christ and his body.

Here is a translation of Bernard's hymn:

Jesus, thou Joy of loving hearts!
Thou Fount of life! Thou Light of men!
From the best bliss that earth imparts
We turn unfilled to thee again.

Thy truth unchanged hath ever stood;
Thou savest those that on thee call;
To them that seek thee, thou art good,
To them that find thee, all in all.

We taste thee, O thou living Bread!
And long to feast upon thee still;
We drink of thee, the Fountain Head,
And thirst from thee our souls to fill!

Our restless spirits yearn for thee,
Where'er our changeful lot is cast;
Glad, when thy gracious smile we see,
Blest, when our faith can hold thee fast.

O Jesus, ever with us stay!
Make all our moments calm and bright!
Chase the dark night of sin away!
Shed o'er the world thy holy light!
Amen.

Now consider the Scripture passage to be read and proclaimed in the worship service:

So Jesus said to them, "Very truly, I tell you, unless you eat the flesh of the Son of Man and drink his blood, you have no life in you. Those who eat my flesh and drink my blood have eternal life, and I will raise them up on the last day; for my flesh is true food and my blood is true drink. Those who eat my flesh and drink my blood abide in me, and I in them. Just as the living Father sent me, and I live because of the Father, so whoever eats me will live because of me. This is the bread that came down from heaven, not like that which your ancestors ate, and they died. But the one who eats this bread will live forever." (John 6:53-58)

The literary context of this Scripture passage focuses on the identity of Jesus Christ. And Bernard's hymn provides an expansive context for understanding the subject matter of John 6:53-58: Jesus Christ as the bread of life. The congregation confesses that Jesus is the source for their life, the light of all people, the fountain of life, the source of nourishment that all of the "bliss" provided by the earth alone cannot provide. Thus the congregation turns to Christ with a distinct disposition, one evoked by the Johannine text: hunger. In this hunger for Jesus Christ, Christians adore his works — the work of mercifully saving "those who call on thee," of standing "unchanging" in his faithful, saving work. Yet this reality of being saved in Christ is not just an ethereal reality, but one of delight. We "taste" and "drink" Christ, the "living bread," but we are not satisfied; we long for Christ even more. Much like the concluding section of John 6, this eating and drinking of Christ directs our attention both to the eucharistic feast of the church and the eucharistic character of life in Christ — feeding on Jesus Christ.[35] Bernard's point in the theme of continual hunger is that, the more they feed on Jesus Christ, the congregation's appetite for him is not satiated but continues to grow deeper.

In the final verses of Bernard's hymn, the congregation members confess that they are "restless" and "changeful," plagued with "the dark night of sin." The congregation is not complaining about hardships that they may endure, but they are confessing their inclination to find nourishment in places other than Jesus Christ. Rather than focusing on Jesus — the unchanging lover — and feeding on him, the congregation confesses a tendency to find life elsewhere. But they call on Jesus to "ever with us stay" and to shine his "light o'er the world." Just when the congregation might be tempted to look to their own resources to overcome their inattention to Christ and the darkness of sin, they join together their voices to petition Christ, the light of the world, to bring them deeper into the feast of the bread of life.

As sung in a congregation, Bernard's hymn is a rich living tradition that can help the congregation encounter the same Jesus Christ who is held up in John 6:53-58. The hymn points clearly to Christ, the source of our life and nourishment, and confesses the ways in which we seek our nourishment in places other than Christ. Its performance can bring a congregation deeper into considering the subject matter of the text: the call to feed on Christ and abide in him.

In addition, there are other insights from the text that can come

---

35. See George R. Beasley-Murray, *John,* Word Biblical Commentary, 2nd ed. (Dallas: Word, 2002), pp. 94, 96-99.

from reengaging the text in the mode of critical, explanatory inquiry. The textual possibilities opened up by Bernard's hymn say relatively little about the connection of these themes with Israel and the Old Testament. Exposure to extracanonical Jewish sources through critical commentaries can help to disclose the richness of the "bread of life" image in Jewish thought and its connections with the rich themes of wisdom and law in the Hebrew Bible.[36] Critical inquiry can help keep our engagement with the text in play, a situation in which we remain open to surprises and new insights as readers. These new, yet ancient traditions could be highlighted in the proclamation of the word.

Conclusion

In the end, the renewal of theological interpretation means fusing together what modernity has torn apart: an attentiveness to creeds and hymns in interpreting Scripture, as well as behind-the-text issues; a receptivity to the challenging address of the Spirit through Scripture, and a facility in historical and linguistic analysis; the importance of tradition in reading Scripture, and the importance of critical inquiry. Both tradition and critical inquiry are important dimensions of a larger drama in which the Spirit is addressing God's people through Scripture, calling us to stop attempting to control Scripture, and to receptively respond to God's call through Scripture to enter into the Spirit's work of making all things new in Jesus Christ.

The implications of this account of reading Scripture closely within a tradition can be quite surprising. Imagine a congregational discussion of a possible change in the music in worship. In many congregations, the question comes around to something like this: Do we want something traditional or something contemporary? Some members of the congregation quote Bible verses about the importance of the past and tradition, and others quote verses about God's new work and singing a new song, and so on.

In this chapter I suggest that both sides of that debate need to reframe their position on the basis of their use of Scripture. In a sense,

---

36. For an account of the relevant rabbinic passages on this point, see Beasley-Murray, *John,* p. 99.

when it comes to worship, there is no such thing as "traditional worship" versus "contemporary worship." All worship is traditional in the sense that certain traditions are operative. The real question is: What traditions should be enacted in our worship? When it is approached theologically, Scripture gives a rich account of the traditions that should be operative in the church's worship: practices of prayer and praise, of word and sacrament, which call the church to her identity as Christ's bride, God's holy temple, the chosen ones of God. Through the use of Scripture in the celebration of word and sacrament, the Spirit unites believers to the people of God through the ages, and the church of the past. But in this worship the Spirit also calls forth for those who are in Christ to live into the "new creation" of the Spirit, the "new thing" that is not the result of catching up with cultural trends, but living into the Spirit's word through Scripture, which is not completely immanent, in our past or present.

In other words, the portrait of reading Scripture that emerges from this fusion of *understanding* and *explanation* is one that values reading Scripture in tradition but also values new insights from Scripture. In Protestant circles, some speak of the church "always being reformed by the word of God."[37] In light of the discussion of this chapter, I think that this slogan can be saved from some possible misconstruals. The continuing process of "always being reformed" is not about the church seeking to catch up with contemporary culture. Indeed, tradition itself is not something old and worn out, something from which God must reform the church into something new. Operative traditions are inescapable. Instead, God's word empowers the reshaping of the church because, on this side of the *eschaton,* the church is always in need of further transformation through Scripture. Tradition is not just about what we have done and been in the past. Tradition can be the bridge of the Spirit for today's church to live deeper into its identity in Christ. Moreover, scriptural exegesis that uses a variety of critical methods to reengage the text does not make exegesis "up to date"; nor does it necessarily displace the value of past traditions. Rather, when this process is brought into the Spirit's transformative work, "always being reformed" is a process of wrestling

---

37. On the context of the overall slogan "Reformed and always being reformed by the word of God," see Harold P. Nebelsick, "Ecclesia Reformata Semper Reformanda," *Reformed Liturgy and Music* 18, no.2 (Spring 1984): 59-63.

with Scripture to hear afresh how the Spirit addresses those who are in Christ. "Always being reformed" is a process of entering into the Spirit's work as we read Scripture closely, open to the surprising old and new work of being reshaped into the image and likeness of Jesus Christ.

For Further Reading

Markus Bockmuehl, *Seeing the Word: Refocusing New Testament Study* (Grand Rapids: Baker Academic, 2006).

Bockmuehl presents a powerful argument that the New Testament's "implied readers" are ecclesial readers, and that many approaches to New Testament studies assume a "sectarian" ecclesiology in interpreting Scripture from the standpoint of "the autonomous reasoning subject, isolated from the worshiping community."

Stephen Fowl, *Engaging Scripture: A Model for Theological Interpretation* (Malden, MA: Blackwell Publishers, 1998).

Fowl gives an account of a Christian reading of Scripture that both shapes and is shaped by Christian convictions and practices. He makes the case that Christians should be suspicious of buying into a broad general hermeneutical account of textual meaning that is then applied to Scripture, and he responds to the critique that this may leave the Bible open to misuse.

Joel B. Green, *Seized by Truth: Reading the Bible as Scripture* (Nashville: Abingdon, 2007).

Green gives a helpful account of the way in which critical methods can and should be incorporated into a theological hermeneutic of Scripture. Green is particularly helpful in his insistence on the ecclesiastical location of scriptural interpretation, and in his way of drawing on critical studies that enhances a theological hermeneutic for Scripture.

Anthony Thiselton, *New Horizons in Hermeneutics: The Theory and Practice of Transforming Biblical Reading* (Grand Rapids: Zondervan, 1992).

Thiselton gives a wide-ranging survey of contemporary biblical scholarship in light of key figures in philosophical hermeneutics. He has helpful discussions of Gadamer and Ricoeur, which interface with this chapter in particular.

D. H. Williams, series editor, *Evangelical Ressourcement: Ancient Sources for the Church's Future* (Grand Rapids: Baker Academic).

This series of books explores the ways in which Christians can draw on the an-

cient traditions of the church in a way that overcomes the Enlightenment prejudice against preunderstanding that I have explored in this chapter.

Jens Zimmerman, *Recovering Theological Hermeneutics: An Incarnational-
Trinitarian Theory of Interpretation* (Grand Rapids: Baker Academic, 2004).

*Zimmerman gives an appreciative yet critical account of Gadamer and other
recent hermeneutical philosophers in the midst of an exposition of the
hermeneutical relevance of Reformation and Puritan authors. Rooted in a theology of the incarnation and the Trinity, Zimmerman proposes a general hermeneutic that is based on specifically Christian theological claims, placing
communion with God and with others at the center.*

CHAPTER 3

Revelation and Scripture Interpretation

Theological Decisions We (Must) Make

"This is the word of the Lord."
"Thanks be to God."

IN THE CONTEXT of worship, the church declares that the Bible is "the word of the Lord." The words have a familiarity that may veil how extraordinary this claim is. The books of the Bible are written by human hands, emerging from the thought and linguistic world of ancient times. What does it mean to say that these words, written long ago and spoken today, are the word of God?

The church's affirmation of the Bible as the word of God is not a simple case of *transferring* authorship from a creature to the Creator. Christians do not claim that, though it appears that Paul wrote the letter to the Roman churches, it was actually God, *apart from* Paul, who wrote it. Paul wrote the letter. But the audacious Christian claim is that the primary author was, in fact, God: the God who chooses to use Paul's writing as an instrument for his own purposes. The primary author of Scripture is not just Paul and the other human writers, but a unique author: "the LORD, and there is no other; besides me there is no God" (Isa. 45:5).

Thus the question of what it means to receive Scripture as the word of God is inseparable from the question of who God is. Who is God? The question itself should signal to us that we cannot properly talk about receiving the Bible as Scripture without evoking the material content of

71

Christian theology itself: the triune nature of God, the attributes of God, the nature of salvation, and so forth. No amount of information about the ancient world and the biblical context can give us answers to these questions. Neither can we expect all of our theology to leap from a particular Scripture passage, because even the content of a particular passage cannot fill us in on this broader question: Who is this God from whom we receive this word?

Perhaps we should simply avoid the question. "Avoid speculation — just keep with what the Bible says" is common advice. But as I have suggested in earlier chapters, such an avoidance is simply impossible apart from an act of self-deception. Anytime that Christians act, a functional theology is at work. Whether this theology is recognized or not is beside the point. There is no way to free ourselves from presuppositions about God when we approach Scripture. For example, consider a key moment in the Genesis account of God's response to human wickedness immediately before the narrative of Noah and the ark:

> The LORD saw that the wickedness of humankind was great in the earth, and that every inclination of the thoughts of their hearts was only evil continually. And the LORD was sorry that he had made humankind on the earth, and it grieved him to his heart. So the LORD said, "I will blot out from the earth the human beings I have created — people together with animals and creeping things and birds of the air, for I am sorry that I have made them." But Noah found favor in the sight of the LORD. (Gen. 6:5-8)

How is this passage, particularly verse 6 ("the Lord was sorry that he had made humankind on the earth") to be received as the word of the Lord? There are numerous possibilities, and they all depend on certain presuppositions about who this Lord is. Some exegetes have focused on verse 6, saying that this verse is a God-given analogy to a human experience of grief, given by God to express his great love for human beings. Does that mean that God made a mistake, or that God changed his mind? No, these exegetes say, because God is not a finite being who can be overtaken by surprise. The sorrow and grief is affirmed, but as a divinely given analogy, rendered by a human author.

A second possibility with verse 6 is to say that this passage shows a God with some limits, a God who risks and who can make mistakes.

God is changeable and subject to emotions, just as human beings are. This is a more literal rendering of the passage. With this interpretation, the human language of Scripture provides nonanalogical access to the being of God.

A third possibility is to perceive the sorrow and grief of God as an analogy, but an analogy with a purely human origin. The ancient author seeks to express his or her experience of the transcendent through speaking about God in personal terms, even anthropomorphic terms. The point of verse 6 is not about God at all; it is a human construction of God that imagines the transcendent as favoring good over evil.

Of these three, which interpretation do you favor? Think carefully about your reasons why. There are certain pieces of information in the text itself that you could point to in favor of one interpretation or another. But chances are, your primary reason for favoring one interpretation over another goes far beyond inner textual issues. Who is God? That inescapable question faces us Christians every time we open our Scriptures.

Moreover, there is likely to be a relationship between your response to that question and how you pray, how you worship, and how you approach your Christian life. Is God mysterious yet made known to us in a relational way through divine revelation? Is God accessible and relevant to today's world, meeting us on our own terms? Is God-talk a human construction that needs to be rhetorically directed toward good ends? While there are many ways of living in the embedded contexts from which these questions arise, a little imagination can see how people who pose questions in these ways are likely to have a different set of practices and actions that shape the theological preunderstandings of their context. Topical sermons, contemplative prayer, involvement in the market economy, shifting gender relations — all these are part of the complex mix of inclinations, commitments, and understandings that help to make some interpretations of Scripture seem plausible and others not.

The influence of the contextual location of biblical interpreters is an important topic in its own right, and it is the focus of the next chapter. But rather than focusing on that global issue here, we are going to ask about the different possibilities of interpreting what it means to affirm the Bible as the word *of God*. If we are to avoid collapsing our differences of biblical interpretation into a boring, shoulder-shrugging act of saying, "I guess we come from different backgrounds," we need to think clearly about some key theological dynamics in the reading of Scripture itself. Specifically, we need to face the reality of two either/or's.

By posing two sets of either/or's, I am not advocating simplistic or dichotomous thinking. It is not a way to divide exegetes into simple categories of right or wrong, "orthodox" or "deviant." Although some may think that these are speculative issues, it is indeed impossible for Christians to be agnostic on them. The either/or's of this chapter are not merely methodological questions (i.e., concerning which method one should use in interpreting scriptural language about God); the either/or's are *ontological* questions, questions about the nature of God, human beings, and the world itself. Nor are these speculative issues — issues where there is a theologically neutral way for Christians to construe their response. In our practice of the reception of Scripture, our decisions on these either/or's are already forced. Either revelation is grounded in *inherent, universal human capacities* or in the *particularity of God's action* with Israel and in Jesus Christ. Either Scripture is received from within a *Deistic hermeneutic* or Scripture is received within a *Trinitarian hermeneutic.*

I will be advocating the second approach in each either/or scenario posed above: it is an extension of the approach I have outlined in the last two chapters, an approach that sees Christian knowledge of God as occurring on a Christ-formed path of "faith seeking understanding." However, in this chapter I will outline both approaches. The key question for readers is where they will find their *practice* to be with respect to these two trajectories, and where they may want to move more deeply into one approach or the other. Readers may be surprised where their own practice now falls, as these either/or's map quite differently from conventional dichotomies such as conservative or liberal, traditional or progressive.

These either/or's are unavoidable; yet each approach can have a wide range of theological and exegetical construals. Each side has a spaciousness to it. Nonetheless, on key issues of revelation, they can also be specific: they stand in a particular place with regard to the particularity of Jesus Christ, the work of the Spirit, and the triune nature of God. On these issues there is no halfway house, no midpoint. While there are many possible positions on both sides, our practice in the reception of Scripture will put us on one side of the dividing line or the other.

Either/or #1: Either Revelation is Grounded in Inherent, Universal Human Capacities or in the Particularity of God's Action with Israel and in Jesus Christ

One of the clearest ways to encounter this either/or is to draw on Danish philosopher Søren Kierkegaard's work entitled *Philosophical Fragments.* Kierkegaard was a mid-nineteenth-century Lutheran writer who sought to look beneath the surface of people's stated professions of belief to their real, functional beliefs. In *Philosophical Fragments,* Kierkegaard uses the analysis of Johannes Climacus, a pseudonym, to penetrate two different functional views of revelation and its reception: the Socratic way and the Christian way.[1] Even people who think they are followers of Jesus may, in fact, be following Socrates. Indeed, as we shall see, some Christians consciously adopt an account reminiscent of Climacus's religion of Socrates. For our purposes, the crucial insight will be to perceive what is at stake in the two approaches.

In the way of Socrates, the teacher is one who acts as a midwife: the teacher helps to give birth to knowledge, which is inherent in human beings themselves. For example, in a Socratic dialogue called the *Meno,* Socrates leads a slave boy to articulate some basic concepts in geometry. Socrates does this by posing question after question to the boy. The resulting knowledge of the slave boy is not just a subjective opinion but a knowledge of geometry that is universally valid. Socrates acts as a midwife because he assumes that the human mind already has a shadowy form of this knowledge; then, when the mind apprehends the truth, it will embrace it.[2]

This portrait of the religion of Socrates can be an illuminating parable for theologies of revelation in the Enlightenment. For example, in *The Education of the Human Race,* Gotthold Lessing argues that the Bible gives revelation to the human race, but it contains nothing that could not be discovered by human reason on its own. Because ancient peoples were so primitive, the Bible was a necessary source of "education" on the oneness of God and the importance of ethics. God only gave the

---

1. My account draws on various sections of chap. 1 in Søren Kierkegaard, *Philosophical Fragments, Johannes Climacus,* ed. Howard V. Hong and Edna H. Hong (Princeton, NJ: Princeton University Press, 1985).

2. See Kierkegaard, *Philosophical Fragments,* pp. 10-12.

75

Israelites what they were ready for at that moment, so in the Old Testament the references to rewards and punishments are necessary accommodations to teach the importance of morality. The New Testament is a more advanced primer for human reason because it teaches the immortality of the human soul. But revelation, by definition, cannot reveal anything that contradicts the universal claims of natural reason. Natural reason can tell us that certain parts of the Bible (such as the rewards and punishments) are connected to historical moments in time rather than universal truths. Truth does not emerge from a historical moment in time; rather, it emerges as the human mind elicits it from the "necessary truths of reason."[3]

Immanuel Kant, in *Religion within the Limits of Reason Alone,* gives us an example of what this looks like in his Enlightenment appropriation of Jesus. Kant thinks one needs to move beyond the "mystical veil" of seeing Jesus in metaphysical terms like "Son of God," or as the object of Christian worship. Rather, one needs to extract from the Gospel narratives the way Jesus could be an instantiation of "the moral law." As such, the Christian message can be given a "rational meaning" that is "valid and binding for the whole world and for all time." What is the meaning, then, of Scripture's narrative about Jesus' atoning death? "Its meaning is this: that there exists absolutely no salvation for man apart from the sincerest adoption of genuinely moral principles into his disposition." Why does Kant push Jesus into this exclusively moral frame of reference? Because Kant believes that the moral law has an a priori basis: it is not grounded in human observation or a moment in human history. Rather, like geometry in the Socratic dialogue, it is a universally accessible rule that humans from any time or culture can access if they have the right teacher. Therefore, Kant claims, reason itself provides the "archetype," or moral exemplar, that we need.[4] A person may draw on Buddha, Jesus, or another religious hero as an exemplar, but whoever this figure *is* needs to fit within a framework that draws on universally valid ethical truths. Kant's approach reflects the spirit of an age when many were dispensing with doctrinal creeds in favor of ethical

3. See Lessing, "The Education of the Human Race" (pp. 82-98) and "On the Proof of the Spirit and of Power" (pp. 51-56), in *Lessing's Theological Writings,* trans. Henry Chadwick (Stanford, CA: Stanford University Press, 1956); quotation from p. 53.

4. Immanuel Kant, *Religion within the Limits of Reason Alone,* trans. Theodore M. Greene and Hoyt H. Hudson (New York: Harper One, 1960), pp. 54-56, 78.

creeds; the church's doctrine was blamed for contributing to the wars of religion; it was argued that Europe needed to unite around ethical imperatives rather than doctrinal confessions. In this rendering, the Apostles' Creed no longer points to God, Jesus Christ, and the Holy Spirit; instead, it is a practical creed pointing to universal ethical truths.

While the eighteenth-century version of Socrates' religion in the hands of Lessing and Kant may sound distant from Christian reasoning, this kind of reasoning is widespread both outside and inside the church today. The core assumptions of many twentieth-century methodologies in "religious studies" assumed that only universally accessible and verifiable truth are worthy of inquiry. Truth claims that see truth as emerging from a particular moment in time — such as the history of Israel or the life of Jesus — need to be reconceptualized within a framework of thought with universal grounds in human rationality.

Some contemporary Christian theologians take this route as well. For example, Harvard theologian Gordon Kaufman explicitly denies the Christian approach of seeing theology as "faith seeking understanding": he seeks to construct Christian theology without presupposing faith commitments.[5] Kaufman describes theology as putting together a series of building blocks in which "any interested persons, whatever their faith-commitments," can participate. It is a "public activity" that is not grounded in "privileged presuppositions."[6] As Christians, our conceptions of God should not be guided by "biblical or traditional images" of God, but should be guided by a universally accessible ethic of "humanization." "The only God we should worship today — the only God we can afford to worship — is the God who will further our humanization, the God who will help to make possible the creation of a universal and humane community."[7] It is "provincial" and "chauvinistic," Kaufman believes, to rely on a conception of God that emerged within a particular tradition at a particular moment in history.[8] One should not follow the Apostles' Creed in basing a theology on one who "suffered under Pontius Pilate" at a historical moment in time. One should reori-

5. Gordon Kaufman, *In the Face of Mystery: A Constructive Theology* (Cambridge, MA: Harvard University Press, 1993), p. 85.

6. Kaufman, *Face of Mystery,* pp. 85-86.

7. Gordon Kaufman, *God, Mystery, Diversity: Christian Theology in a Pluralistic World* (Minneapolis: Fortress, 1996), p. 29.

8. Kaufman, *God, Mystery, Diversity,* pp. 113-14.

ent Christian theological language according to the universally accessible ethic of what is "humanizing." Kaufman's approach seeks to revise and modify truth claims that arise in moments of history according to (an ostensibly) more universal set of norms for knowing.

Through the voice of Climacus, Kierkegaard claims that such a trajectory embodies a radically different story of knowing than the Christian way. As a thought experiment, imagine that a moment in history was decisive rather than incidental for discovering the truth.[9] Imagine, as strange as it may sound, that the truth is something that could be right in front of your eyes, yet you could not recognize it as truth. Imagine that truth does not lie waiting within a human being to be brought out by a teacher as midwife. Imagine that a teacher could give all kinds of examples of the truth, yet it would still not be recognized as such. Imagine that natural reason, ethics, and even an ethic of humanization are not fertile soil for giving a context for the truth. Imagine that truth brings with it its own content, and that its content is from God and not from ourselves.

What would it mean if all of these radical claims were true, and the truth about God was not universally accessible? It would mean that our teacher would need to bring us the truth about God from outside of ourselves. It would mean that God himself would need to be our Teacher, since nothing within human beings gives them an inherent capacity to see or recognize the truth about God. This would mean that we would need eyes to see, ears to hear, and ways to apprehend this truth about God, and that God would need to provide the apparatus to receive the truth. Furthermore, rather than the truth about God being universally accessible, a moment in history would be decisive for discovering the truth. If this were the case, then God could be made known in the history of Israel and of Jesus Christ.

Climacus tells the story about these two different ways of approaching the knowledge of God so that familiar claims about Christian revelation could become strange again. Could it really be that we could have the truth in front of our eyes and not even see it apart from God? It is a radical moment when Jesus tells Nicodemus that "no one can see the kingdom of God without being born from above" (John 3:3). Could it really be that a moment in history is decisive in discovering the truth

---

9. Kierkegaard, *Philosophical Fragments,* pp. 18-19.

about God? The New Testament repeatedly gives a decisive "yes" to that question in verses such as 1 Timothy 2:5-6: "For there is one God; there is also one mediator between God and humankind, Christ Jesus, himself human, who gave himself a ransom for all — this was attested at the right time." The truth about God is inseparably connected to Jesus Christ, and that truth is eschatologically conditioned in its occurrence ("at the right time") and in our reception of it: "For now we see in a mirror, dimly, but then we will see face to face. Now I know only in part; then I will know fully, even as I have been fully known" (1 Cor. 13:12).

Not only is it true that humans don't have the inherent capacity for knowing the truth about God; Climacus points out that we are in fact bound to error and cannot free ourselves.[10] Climacus names this error as sin. Therefore, we need more than a teacher who is a midwife, more than a teacher with information that we do not have. We need a teacher who is a savior, deliverer, and reconciler if we are to know the truth about God.[11] Our theology of revelation, Climacus implies, must be inseparable from our theology of salvation. For the truth about God — which God alone enables us to receive — does not just enlighten us, but makes us into a new creation, leads us to repentance, and makes us disciples of the teacher. These developments in the Christian life are moments in coming to know the truth, a truth that is not accessible simply by the work of the mind, but whose knowing is a miracle itself, an act of God that changes human lives. As Jonathan Edwards elegantly argues, if you claim to know God but you are not drawn to worship and to delight in God's beauty, then you know that you have not encountered God.

One implication of this vision of the Christian way is that knowledge of God is given a heteronymous rather than autonomous character. Knowledge of God is not self-referential *(auto)*, but it is received as something irreducibly different *(hetero)* from one's own desires and conceptions. With this view, Christians do not believe that Jesus is the revela-

10. Climacus's account of the human capacity for knowledge of God may be supplemented with a theology of the image of God in human beings — and a seed of religion in fallen humanity. But this need not change Climacus's overall account. Unless one views the image of God as a distinctly human possession in autonomy from God, this image still relates to God's work in humans rather than something existing in human beings independent of God.

11. Kierkegaard, *Philosophical Fragments,* p. 17.

tion of God because it is an inherently compelling idea, or because it leads to the most benefits in life, or even because it makes the most sense of their experience. In receiving God's revelation, Christians enter into a world that they did not create. They receive a word from God that is external to themselves — an alien word that they are inclined to resist. What Rich Mullins sings about in his song "Creed" applies to this view of Christian revelation: "I did not make it, no, it is making me; it is the very truth of God and not the invention of any man."

Before continuing, let me anticipate three objections that the reader may raise to this account of revelation. First, doesn't this view of revelation grate against the principle articulated in chapter 2 that there is no interpretation without horizons or preunderstandings? Does this view of revelation seek to escape our culturally embedded location of interpretation? Second, does this view of revelation mean that the human is merely passive in the reception of revelation, while God does it all? Third, how does this theology of revelation relate to the notion that God not only speaks through Scripture, but that God speaks through nature as well?

The first objection might be valid if we proposed a strict identity between revelation and Scripture as a book. But as I will develop further below, my claim is that *revelation* is a dimension of the divine activity of *redemption.* The Bible is an instrument that God uses in the drama of redemption. Revelation is not identical with the Bible as a book; rather, it is an act of God. While we always interpret the Bible, in the act of revelation God "reads" us, reshaping us into Christ's image by the Spirit's power through Scripture. As Catholic philosopher Jean-Luc Marion puts it, we do not interpret revelation, in the sense of bringing questions, expectations, and presuppositions that then form the content of revelation. Rather, revelation is a phenomenon that is already full of meaning, "saturated" in itself. In revelation, God gazes upon us and changes us, rather than the other way around.[12]

Does this mean that, if we hold this view, we will be closed to anyone else's interpretation of the Bible because we have received certain revelation from God? Not at all. Revelation is the self-communicative

---

12. For a helpful exposition of Marion's concept of a saturated phenomena, see Robyn Horner, *Jean-Luc Marion: A Theological Introduction* (Burlington, VT: Ashgate, 2005), chap. 10.

fellowship of the triune God himself, and the Bible is God's instrument of revelation. Since we are still growing in our knowledge of the triune God, we are still growing in our understanding of Scripture. We have not arrived at a place of face-to-face knowledge with God. Yet God has not left us alone, but is renewing us through his word and Spirit; and this renewal relates both to our knowledge of God and our salvation in Jesus Christ. Revelation is inseparable from the divine act of our transformation into the image of Christ. It is not simply a set of propositions, even though it is also not a mere expression of human intuition.[13] Therefore, to claim that we receive revelation externally from God and not simply as the result of human construction is not to claim we have all the answers. It is to claim treasure from God in jars of clay, a taste of God's word by the Spirit that will not reach its culmination until we are face to face with God. Essentially, this view of revelation is a way of articulating what is at stake in the normative claims in chapters 1 and 2 above, that we read Scripture on the path of Christ by the Spirit, anticipating a vision of the triune God.

However, does this leave humans passive in the reception of revelation, while God does all of the work? In this account, revelation is a divine act that does not exclude human beings, but one that incorporates humans and empowers them by the Spirit. The images of humanity in this account of revelation involve a movement from blindness to sight, from sin's bondage to freedom in Christ, from boredom to delight in the beauty of God. Moreover, this process does not turn us into cookie-cutter Christians; instead, the rich diversity of global and historic expressions of Christianity are seen as the work of the Spirit along the path of Christ. This diversity exists not because there is a different Spirit in different places, nor because the Spirit testifies to different Christs. Instead, it is the indigenizing and transforming work of the Spirit in diverse cultural contexts.[14] Yet our transformation from sin to whole-

---

13. For more on the place of propositions, see chap. 1 of this book. Kevin Vanhoozer makes the helpful point that, although revelation is not a set of propositions, with revelation one must hold together the words and works of God. "There is . . . no reason to oppose persons and propositions: persons do things with words and propositions." Vanhoozer, "A Person of the Book?" in *Karl Barth and Evangelical Theology,* ed. Sung Wook Chung (Grand Rapids: Baker Academic, 2007), p. 56. God's word is a word that acts with power, as chap. 6 explores further.

14. I will explore this point in greater depth in chap. 4.

ness, from ignorance of God to knowledge of God by this revelation, is always partial. We are still sinners, and we are still on a journey. Right now we can only anticipate that the final end of the drama of revelation will be unity in confessing Jesus as Lord (Phil. 2:4-11). At that time, the widest possible variety of peoples and cultures will be confessing, for every tribe, people, language, and nation will be praising the triune God (Rev. 5:9; 7:9; 11:9; 14:6).

The third objection relates to the place of natural theology. If the knowledge of God derives from God rather than a source inherent within human beings, doesn't that deny that God not only speaks through Scripture but through nature as well? This question brings us back to the paradox we discussed in chapter 2. On the one hand, all truth is God's truth: hence, Christians should celebrate truth wherever it is found, whether through scientific inquiry, philosophical analysis, or other human disciplines. This gives us grounds for fruitfully drawing on history, philosophy, anthropology, and other disciplines in our inquiry. However, we should think carefully about what kind of knowledge we gain through these general disciplines of the liberal arts. Do they lead us to a knowledge of God in Christ? In one important sense, the answer is no. Examination of "the book of nature" — as distinct from "the book of Scripture" — may at best lead to a general knowledge of God. Knowledge of Israel and Jesus Christ, as part of the moments of history, is not something inherent within human beings, something that can be drawn out by a teacher as midwife. The study of the book of nature provides profound insight into many areas of human understanding, but it does not make possible an explicit knowledge of Jesus Christ. The book of Scripture, not simply the book of nature, is necessary for that knowledge.

But there is another sense in which the Spirit's work in creation may yield knowledge of "God's truth," one that fits the other side of the paradox: all truth is in Jesus Christ. Karl Barth speaks about this possibility in terms of "parables of the Kingdom," which come from voices outside the church. Since Jesus Christ himself is the truth, he acts as Lord over the church and creation. Believers in Jesus Christ do not "own" the truth as much as they are owned by the one who is the truth. The church is the bride of Christ, but it has not arrived in that identity: it is in the eschatological process of growing into the grace and truth that is in Christ. Thus, precisely because all truth is in Jesus Christ, and the Spirit is active in the world, at times those outside the church discover a dimension of an "in Christ" truth that the church needs to hear. But this requires a profound act of discernment on the part of the church, and Barth offers several crucial clarifications on this process of discernment. First, these are parables because they are indirect witnesses to Jesus Christ: they need to be reinterpreted in light of Jesus Christ as the hermeneutical key. Barth also calls them "lesser lights," because they do not have independent authority but only authority to the extent that they reflect the light of Jesus Christ.[15] Second, a Christian engagement with parables of the kingdom outside the church will not lead Christians away from Scripture but deeper into Scripture. "If it is a true word," Barth says, "it will be a good and authentic commentary sounding out the word of the Bible. It will not lead its hearers away from Scripture, but more deeply into it."[16] In other words, the "lesser lights" of creation do not provide a different truth from that of Scripture; nor do they present a revelation from a separate source from what is in Jesus Christ. But insights from these "lights," if authentic, can help awaken Christians to live deeper into the scriptural witness.[17]

In spite of this account of the lights of creation, Barth does not affirm the possibility of "natural theology" in the sense in which many Roman Catholics and Protestants have used the term. For Barth, Jesus Christ alone is the origin and source of revelation, even though that is reflected in various parts of revelation. But in terms of our third objection, what if, unlike Barth, we accept a theology of the "book of nature" as a source of revelation? While there are various ways to configure natural theology, it is important to recognize two things about the "religion of Socrates" and the "religion of Jesus." First, as noted above, even a very high natural theology cannot lead to an explicit knowledge of Jesus Christ through the study of nature. Scripture is necessary. But second, there are scriptural indications that if and when God is revealed through nature, God is the actor: "For what can be known about God is

---

15. "They are true words only as they refer back to their origin in the one Word, i.e., as the one true Word, Jesus Christ Himself, declares Himself in them." Karl Barth, *Church Dogmatics,* IV:3.1, p. 123.

16. Barth, *Church Dogmatics,* IV:3.1, p. 128.

17. For a helpful overview of Barth's "theology of lesser lights," see George Hunsinger, *How to Read Karl Barth: The Shape of His Theology* (New York: Oxford University Press, 1991), pp. 234-80.

plain to them, because God has shown it to them" (Rom. 1:19). In other words, even with "natural revelation," God is the agent of revelation and uses nature to reveal himself. Such revelation is not inherent in human beings in autonomy from God's work.

Thus natural revelation, if one grants the category," is still not "the religion of Socrates." It is God's use of nature as an instrument for the purpose of revelation. The profound limits of the natural revelation of God are apparent, however, from the biblical account that humans are not only naturally religious, but natural idolaters (Rom. 1:22-23). Enlightenment attempts to develop a natural religion show how a natural theology in the mode of the religion of Socrates is in fundamental conflict with a religion rooted in the particularity of Jesus Christ. The former is content with the "internal word" of natural reason. But when, as with Kant and Lessing, this internal word is given an independent authority over against the particularity of the Spirit's testimony to Jesus Christ through Scripture, then this internal word is little more than an attempt to replace the external word of God in Christ with the immanent word of human reason.

WHAT IMPLICATIONS might there be of this account of revelation? Climacus openly admits that, in this view, revelation itself is a miracle, an act of God. The teacher does not just bring out what is inherent within us; the teacher is the Creator, who gives us the eyes of faith to see, what Jonathan Edwards calls a "sixth sense" provided by the Spirit to apprehend the knowledge of God. The teacher must also be a Savior who delivers us from our sin, which binds and blinds us.

What Kierkegaard, in the nineteenth century, is pointing us toward is a distinctly nonmodern claim in classical Christianity, one that Barth forcefully restated in the twentieth century: only God can make God known. Strictly speaking, it is God who knows God. When we speak of human knowledge of God, we are speaking about how to get in on a God-thing. In this account of revelation, our knowledge of God cannot simply be our "best guesses" about an inaccessible God. Our knowledge of God is not an attempt to put God in a box, to tame and simplify the transcendent one of the universe. If there is to be any knowledge of God, we must, in fact, participate in something of God. We must access something *extra nos* — outside ourselves.

We encounter God's word as an external word because it is God who knows God; yet it is also because, as sinful humans, we are expert idolaters. As John Calvin points out, we are extremely adept at creating and projecting our own image onto God:

> They do not therefore apprehend God as he offers himself, but imagine him as they have fashioned him in their own presumption. When this gulf opens, in whatever direction they move their feet, they cannot but plunge headlong into ruin. Indeed, whatever they afterward attempt by way of worship or service of God, they cannot bring as tribute to him, for they are worshiping not God but a figment and a dream of their own heart.[18]

In some ways, Calvin's insight on this particular point is not far afield from the theories of Ludwig Feuerbach and Karl Marx, namely, that human beings project their own needs and desires on God by means of religious symbols.[19] A natural tendency of the human, Calvin says, is to "fashion for himself an idol or spectre in the place of God."[20] The ground of religion as it expresses itself apart from God is human desire and ambition, rather than one of receiving an external word from God. In a theology of revelation that is theocentric, the extent to which humans come to know God's word is the extent to which we encounter the judging and healing external word of God. The residue of sin as idolatry is inevitable until we see the one who is truth "face to face." Revelation from God is not fully and completely received until that final day. In the meantime, however, it is crucial to be clear about whether we think that knowledge of God comes from our own inherent human insight or from an external gift received from God.

If knowledge of God requires a teacher to bring us an external word, a savior to save us from our own sinful blindness, then coming to know God cannot simply be a textbook subject in a classroom. Nor can it sim-

---

18. John Calvin, *Institutes of the Christian Religion,* ed. J. T. McNeill, trans. F. L. Battles (Philadelphia: Westminster, 1960), 1:4:1. On this point, I am indebted to the illuminating analysis of Calvin in J. B. Webster, *Holy Scripture: A Dogmatic Sketch* (Cambridge, UK: Cambridge University Press, 2003), pp. 74-78.

19. For an enlightening account of how Marx, Nietzsche, and Freud can be useful for Christians in recognizing their own sinful practices of projection and self-deception, see Merold Westphal, *Suspicion and Faith: The Religious Uses of Modern Atheism* (Bronx, NY: Fordham University Press, 1998).

20. Calvin, *Institutes,* 1:5:12.

ply be a social act of observing religious practitioners or surveying the opinions of various religious experts. If this account of revelation is correct, then coming to know God takes place in a community that the Spirit has enlivened to receive the Word sent from the Father. While books — especially the Bible as God's chosen instrument of revelation — will be indispensable, we will ultimately need a community that loves and worships in its midst a God who has entered from outside. If God is the one who truly knows God, then humans need to get in on God's work in order to know God. But how could humans come to know God when it is God who truly knows God? In a word, the Trinity provides a clue to how this could be the case.

The first either/or leads us to the second. The Christian way of revelation I have described above is, implicitly, a Trinitarian way. This is why Karl Barth and some other theologians place the doctrine of the Trinity at the center of their account of revelation. If revelation is a "miracle," as Climacus says, in which God himself is the Creator of the human capacity for the knowledge of God, and God himself is the Savior and Redeemer, then we need the Spirit to open our eyes to Christ as the Word of God sent by the Father. Revelation leads us to a way of fellowship with God in and through Christ, empowered and illuminated by the Spirit, showing us a gracious Father.

Either/or #2: Either Scripture is Received from within a Deistic Hermeneutic or Scripture Is Received within a Trinitarian Hermeneutic

As I suggested in chapter 1, many American Christians are functionally Deistic, even if they would sign onto a Trinitarian creed as their official theology. What we confess in our theology is important, but our practice may tell a different story. How we act, how we pray, how we worship — all these say something about what we believe about God in our lived, operative theology. And for many Christians, their operative theology in reading Scripture is Deistic rather than Trinitarian.

For example, consider the question of what theologies are operative in a given worship service. Imagine entering a worship service in which the hymns are all about the church's own action: the action of obedience, of following God's way, of experiencing life together. Along comes the sermon, an exposition of Scripture. The punch line of the sermon does not relate to God but to a fresh understanding of how to respond to challenges at work, or to challenges in our relationships at home. God will take care of God. What we experience in this worship service is not speculation about God but more practical fare: words of insight and encouragement about how God wants us to succeed in all of our life endeavors.

Note the functional assumptions about God and Scripture in a service such as this: even if there are references to God, Jesus Christ, and the Holy Spirit, the basic assumption is that knowledge of God is an abstract affair that has little to do with our practical lives. Since direct talk about God is impractical (if not presumptuous), we read Scripture and write songs in a way that focuses on what is under our control — our own will, our own decisions. God has given us a revelation in Scripture, and that may include abstract things about God, the nature of who Christ is, and so on. But functionally speaking, God has given us messages about how to succeed, how to make good decisions, how to have a happy future, and so forth. The error of this approach is not that it sees the Christian faith as having practical outcomes; that is true of a living faith. The problem is that it sees Scripture's witness to God, Jesus Christ, and the Holy Spirit as incidental to these outcomes rather than central to how we are changed and who we are called to be. This pragmatic form of Christianity, which writes off Trinitarian language as "abstract," fails to recognize that all true Christian transformation takes place through the power of God, in Jesus Christ, enabled by the Holy Spirit.

In American Christianity, there are mainline and evangelical forms of this functional Deism. Who is the central object of focus in the Christian life? We are — our decisions, our actions, our will. God has already done his part. For evangelicals, this may mean that God has given Christ on the cross for the forgiveness of sins and eternal salvation, and once we accept Christ, our Christian life is about maintaining this faith commitment. In other words, God does an indispensable part, but now we are the main actors — in maintaining our commitment, in seeking to lead others to make a decision for Christ, and so on. On the mainline side, the focus may be on how God desires a kingdom of peace and justice, and it is now up to us to build the kingdom ourselves. Once again, for all the talk of Christ and the Spirit, both evangelical and mainline tendencies have a Deistic conception of the Christian life, in which our monarch, God, tells us what he wants, and we go about the implementation of it. When there is talk of the Spirit, it is often a way of speaking about our moments of progress in this salvation that is ultimately self-salvation.

In a Trinitarian theology of revelation, our lives and the knowledge of God are caught up in the triune activity of God. Worship and the Christian life are first and foremost about what God is up to, not what we desire in ourselves. For example, consider the following pattern of prayer in Romans 8:14-17:

> For all who are led by the Spirit of God are children of God. For you did not receive a spirit of slavery to fall back into fear, but you have received a spirit of adoption. When we cry, "Abba! Father!" it is that very Spirit bearing witness with our spirit that we are children of God, and if children, then heirs, heirs of God and joint heirs with Christ — if, in fact, we suffer with him so that we may also be glorified with him.

Paul speaks here about a Christian experience that is irreducibly triadic: those who are led by the Spirit move from slavery to adoption, where the Spirit speaks through them to call God "Abba, Father," in living into this adopted identity as heirs of Christ — united to Christ in his suffering and glorification. God uses this triadic process, Paul goes on to say, to conform the chosen ones "to the image of his Son" (Rom. 8:29). The Trinitarian Christian is not a basically good person who tries his or her best to follow God's rules. The Trinitarian Christian is one who was in bondage but now lives into an identity of being filled with the Spirit, united to Christ and his body, living in gratitude before the Father.

If one is a functional Trinitarian in this way, a worship service that understands and proclaims Scripture in a God-focused way is not abstract and speculative. It is about our life "hidden with Christ in God" (Col. 3:3). If we find our true lives in our union with Christ, in his death and resurrection, by the indwelling of the Holy Spirit, to live in thanksgiving to the pardoning Father, then God has broken into our autonomous human sphere. Our sermons can admonish, but no longer will they have the human will and ingenuity at their center. Rather, following the reasoning of Paul, the imperative will follow from the indicative: "Since, then, you have been raised with Christ, set your hearts on things above" and "put to death, therefore, whatever belongs to your earthly nature" (Col. 1:1, 5 [TNIV]). The gospel proclaimed is not that we should try harder to get involved with the things of God. Rather, the gospel proclaimed is that God himself has given us a new identity as ones united to Christ by the power of the Spirit; therefore, we are called to live deeper into this identity, our true identity as creatures in reuniting communion with God. For functional Trinitarians, God-centered services of worship are the most practical services of all, for through the gospel of the triune God our lives are cast on a canvas that is much larger than our own attempts at self-salvation.[21]

In this functionally Trinitarian account, our reading of the Bible comes to be something that takes place, in a profound sense, within the life of God. On the one hand, the word of God is received as a word from outside, a disruptive word that displaces our autonomous attempts to domesticate God. As veteran preacher Will Willimon puts it, the gospel is an "external word," so that "we don't discover the gospel, it discovers us." The good news is "not common knowledge, not what nine out of ten average Americans already know. Gospel doesn't come naturally. It comes as Jesus."[22] When we hear the Bible as God's word to us, it does not emerge from natural reason or an inherent human capacity. It emerges, scandalously, from God's revelation in the historical moments of Israel and Jesus Christ, and it continues in God's triune work in history and the present.

This functional Trinitarianism also means that the word of God is God made present with humanity, communing with humanity in Christ by the Spirit. The word of God is not an abstract word, but a word with us, a word for us. The word of the triune God is not the word of a generic God, but the word of a God who has shown himself gracious and forgiving in the person of Jesus Christ, and who desires and creates fellowship with those who are in Christ by the Holy Spirit. This Trinitarian economy of salvation makes normative claims about the expectations with which we should come to Scripture. We should not read Scripture

21. For more on the manifold effects of a Trinitarian hermeneutic on worship, see James Torrance, *Worship, Community and the Triune God of Grace* (Downers Grove, IL: InterVarsity, 1996).

22. William H. Willimon, *The Intrusive Word* (Grand Rapids: Eerdmans, 1994), pp. 42-43, 52.

in search of a God who desires our destruction, or one that makes all of our dreams of success come true. We should read Scripture as food and nourishment for our growth by the Spirit into our God-given identities in Christ.

Augustine makes this insight into a practical rule when he claims that all scriptural interpretation must serve the function of building up love of God and neighbor for the sake of God. Since all scriptural interpretation takes place on the path of Christ by the power of the Spirit, Augustine postulates that living into our identities in Christ involves fulfilling Christ's double command: love of God and love of neighbor. Augustine declares that if there is any interpretation that contradicts love of God or neighbor, it is by definition mistaken. It doesn't matter how much historical-grammatical evidence is marshaled, if a scriptural interpretation does not lead to double-love, in Augustine's view, it has failed to discern the divine intent. Indeed, for Augustine, it is better to misunderstand the grammatical and linguistic level of the biblical text yet direct it toward double-love than to promote an interpretation of Scripture that does not lead to double-love. That would be like someone who wanders off a path but eventually ends up at the right destination. It is best to stay on the path, Augustine says, and to follow the reasoning of the particular scriptural text in question all the way to the destination. But the destination — of double-love on the path of Christ — is the most important of all.[23]

Inspiration

In light of this discussion, how are we to understand the inspiration of Scripture? First, we should note that frequently the doctrine of inspiration is taken out of an explicitly Trinitarian context. Emerging from the fundamentalist-modernist controversy of the early twentieth century, many Christians sought to determine the nature of inspiration in advance of hearing the content of Scripture about the saving work of the triune God. In other words, the heirs of fundamentalism tended to isolate the doctrine of inspiration from the material teaching of the

---

23. See Augustine, *On Christian Teaching,* trans. R. P. H. Green (Oxford: Oxford University Press, 1997), pp. 26-27.

church in order to have indubitable grounds on which to build doctrine; the heirs of modernism often relied on the appeal to universal human capacities rather than the particularity of Israel and Jesus Christ. As a result, both left behind the Trinitarian and soteriological context for the doctrine of inspiration.

But leaving out the Trinitarian and soteriological context for inspiration, and turning it into a cornerstone of a building, puts weight on the doctrine of inspiration that it cannot bear. Whether inspiration became the expressionistic "inspiration" of biblical authors to write (as though from a Muse), or inspiration became a theory that proved, in advance, the validity of its contents, inspiration became detached from the biblical and theological doctrines that brought about this doctrine. The doctrine of inspiration is part of the church's teaching not because it is an indubitable cornerstone, but because it is a teaching emerging from Scripture itself.

"Inspiration" is actually a broad term used to speak about the variety of ways in which God is described as generating Scripture. For example, 2 Peter refers to the Christian testimony about Jesus as a "prophetic message," of divine origin and authority (2 Pet. 1:19): "First of all you must understand this, that no prophecy of Scripture is a matter of one's own interpretation, because no prophecy ever came by human will, but men and women moved by the Holy Spirit spoke from God" (vv. 20-21). Jesus himself recognizes the Hebrew Scriptures as authoritative (Matt. 5:17-18), and even attributes words to God that are spoken by a narrator in Genesis but are not in a "God said" passage (Matt. 19:3-6; cf. Gen. 2:24; see also Matt. 24:35; Luke 16:17; John 10:35). Perhaps the most powerful ways in which Jesus speaks about the divine origin of Scripture (particularly in his own words) is in the proto-Trinitarian passages in John, for example, "Do you not believe that I am in the Father and the Father is in me? The words I say to you I do not speak on my own; but the Father who dwells in me does his works" (John 14:10).

The key New Testament text from which the language of inspiration itself is derived is 2 Timothy 3:16-17: "All Scripture is inspired by God and is useful for teaching, for reproof, for correction, and for training in righteousness, so that everyone who belongs to God may be proficient, equipped for every good work." While it is often noted that "all Scripture" in this passage probably refers to the Hebrew Scriptures, it does give "inspiration" as a category for "Scripture" that other parts of the New Testament widen to include the apostolic writings.[24] The key Greek word in the 2 Timothy 3 passage is θεόπνευστος (God-breathed): the breath of God generated by the Spirit. Reference to the Spirit as the origin of the Scripture comes immediately after Paul refers to "how from childhood you have known the sacred writings that are able to instruct you for salvation through faith in Christ Jesus." Scripture is received from the Spirit of God, given to build up believers in Jesus Christ, so that "everyone who belongs to God may be proficient, equipped for every good work." The notion of inspiration in this key passage takes place within the larger Trinitarian economy of grace: believers receive Scripture as that which is generated by the Spirit to build them up in Christ, to the service of God himself.[25]

Thus, an affirmation of inspiration is an indispensable part of a bigger picture. All of these passages occur in the context of a community that hears God's word in an authoritative way through Scripture. But the divine generation and authority of Scripture is not an end in itself, but functions for the purpose of God's salvation: it is for the liberation of the oppressed (Luke 4:16-21), the equipping of the saints for good works and the coming of Christ's kingdom (2 Tim. 3:10–4:5), the knowledge of the Father through the Son by the Spirit (John 14), and many other ends within the economy of salvation.

To some readers, the elephant in the room at this point may be this: *How* did inspiration happen? Did the human authors lose control, so that they recorded only God's words and not human words? I have intentionally de-emphasized the place of particular theories of how inspiration happened in my discussion so far. Why? Because it is a temptation to develop a mechanistic theory of "how inspiration happened," and to use that to ground the overall teaching of inspiration. But if my contention is correct that the proper context for understanding inspiration is the Trinitarian economy of grace, then our account of inspiration needs to emerge from this biblical and theological vision, not vice

24. For example, 2 Pet. 3:15-16 refers positively to the writings of Paul as "other Scripture," and 1 Thess. 2:13 assures the recipients that they receive Paul's letter "not as a human word but as what it really is, God's word."

25. On the Trinitarian dynamics of 2 Tim. 3:16, see Thomas Hoffman, "Inspiration, Normativeness, Canonicity, and the Unique Sacred Character of the Bible," *Catholic Biblical Quarterly* 44 (1982): 447-69, esp. p. 457.

versa. Thus the question becomes: How are we to think through the human act of authorship in light of Scripture as a Spirit-generated word from God to build up believers in Christ?

If this is our starting point, then we need to think in an incarnational and Trinitarian way about this human act. Would it be necessary for human authors to "lose control" or "escape their personality" for their words to be the instrument of God? In the incarnation we see that human agency is not competitive with divine agency. When we set our eyes on Jesus Christ, we see the one who is truly and fully human, yet the one who is united to God and God's action. The Word became flesh and took on all that is human. In Christ, we see that God's word is not a distant and disembodied word, but one that becomes one with us in all of the cultural embeddedness of our humanity. Herman Bavinck says it elegantly in his description of this "organic" view of inspiration: "The Holy Spirit, in the inscripturation of the word of God, did not spurn anything human to serve as an organ of the divine. The revelation of God is not abstractly supernatural but has entered into the human fabric, into persons and states of beings, into forms and usages, into history and life. It does not fly high above us but descends into our situation."[26]

Trinitarian reasoning can illuminate the human side of inspiration as well. While the incarnation shows us that God does not despise what is earthly, material, and human to use as his instruments, the Trinitarian economy of grace illuminates how redemption involves the restoration rather than annihilation of our human bodies, personalities, and selves. In the biblical language of the Epistles, the Spirit comes upon believers to unite them to Jesus Christ in his death and resurrection, simultaneously uniting them to his body, the church. In this process the Spirit generates a "new creation," but this new creation does not destroy what is human; it restores it. Human beings were not created to be autonomous from God, but in communion with God. In a Trinitarian economy of grace, divine agency does not shortcut human agency; rather, human agency is at its most full and free when it is in obedient communion with God.

Consequently, in the production of Scripture, divine and human agency are both active, though divine agency takes the initiative and de-

---

26. Herman Bavinck, *Reformed Dogmatics,* vol. 1: Prolegomena, trans. John Vriend (Grand Rapids: Baker Academic, 2003), pp. 442-43.

serves credit as the primary author of these "God-breathed" words. We should conceive of God's working within the human authors such that God acts "in, with, and over the creature" in the process of producing texts.[27] This includes their choice of words and also their use of oral and other materials in the composing and editing of the biblical texts.

The human words are inspired, not because of a strange ecstatic process of mind-channeling, but because God has chosen to use these creaturely words as instruments of God's word. Just as God uses ordinary water in baptism, and bread and wine in the Lord's Supper, God sets aside ("makes holy") the words of Scripture. This divine choosing takes the creaturely into the triune work of God: through Scripture the Spirit works to bring the church into conformity with its head, Jesus Christ, who speaks as the Word of the Father. To put it differently, Scripture provides the script for the church's performance of the drama of the gospel, empowered by the Spirit to live into the identity of Christ in myriad ways. The Bible as "script" is something functional, something the triune God uses in transforming his people.[28]

Canon

Closely related to the subject of inspiration is that of canon: the canon is the "rule" — or the list of authoritative, inspired texts — for the Christian tradition. Once again, there are temptations to extract reflection on canon from the Trinitarian and soteriological context described above. In the Enlightenment, such a practice becomes virtually a requirement for many thinkers, because they set "thinking for oneself" in opposition to the idea that truth can be received from an authoritative text or tradition. Since a canon is a list of authoritative texts, an a priori bias against the possibility of acquiring truth through an authoritative text will necessarily make the notion of canonicity unintelligible.

Historically speaking, canonization was a long process — for both the books of the Old Testament and the New Testament. The Torah

---

27. Karl Barth, *Church Dogmatics,* III:3, p. 136; cf. pp. 139-45. Barth's thought in this section focuses on divine and human agency more generally, but it has particular value for us as we think through divine and human agency in inspiration.

28. For more on the Bible as script in the triune drama, see chap. 6 below.

was the first "book" that was considered authoritative in Judaism; to it were added the Prophets, and later the other Old Testament "writings." By the time of Jesus, the Hebrew canon was relatively complete in Judaism, though it was not formalized until the end of the second century CE. Still, there was ambiguity, particularly for early Christian authors, about whether Judith, Tobit, and other books now considered deuterocanonical (or apocryphal, by Protestants) were canonical.[29] For the New Testament, the four Gospels and the thirteen Epistles of Paul were generally accepted as authoritative alongside the Old Testament by the middle of the second century. But there were still disputes about the exclusion of certain texts and the inclusion of others (such as Hebrews and Revelation) well into the fourth century. Frequently, the church was developing canonical lists as it was seeking to ward off heresy. Early Christians recognized that there were limits and bounds to the gospel of Jesus Christ, and thus canonical lists became a way of differentiating a gospel in which God truly became human in Christ from Gnostic strategies that denied the materiality of the incarnation. The stakes in such disputes were high, and canonical disputes were in no way isolated from the social, political, and cultural pressures of the day.

The key question for the theological interpreter of Scripture on the question of canonicity is this: How are we to understand this history in a theological way? In modernity we have become well acquainted with a functionally Deistic rendering of canon. The canonical process was one in which certain people exercised power over others by deciding that certain texts were canonical and others were not. Deism assumes that such judgments are arbitrary, as if God had abandoned both the world and the church to human judgments after the event of Jesus Christ. This perspective assumes that politics and society poison everything. The fact that the canon is worked out through historical processes makes the process radically contingent. Rather than assume that God works in and through human historical faculties and processes (as with a Trinitarian-incarnational approach), the Deistic view assumes that

29. Protestant, Eastern Orthodox, and Roman Catholic communions still disagree on whether these deuterocanonical books should be included in canonical lists. While this is an important difference between these communions, it is relatively rare that this difference leads to significant doctrinal divergence. See Stephen Fowl, *Engaging Scripture: A Model for Theological Interpretation* (Malden, MA: Blackwell, 1998), pp. 3-4.

the history of the church is reducible to a set of human actors vying for power.

Another possible interpretation of canon flows quite naturally from our Trinitarian theology of revelation above. God does not abandon the work of inspiration after the text has been written. On the contrary, if the Bible is to be God's ongoing instrument, God is active in each stage of the historical process in speaking through Scripture to the community of faith. Therefore, the canonical process is one in which the church comes to recognize the ongoing voice of Jesus Christ through the Spirit in Scripture, not simply one in which a certain group of people exercise their own power. As John Webster says, the church should see the process of canonization as "assent" rather than "authorization."[30]

In John Calvin's account of canon, we find an example of this Trinitarian-soteriological approach. For Calvin, the life of the church itself flows from God's triune activity, which uses Scripture as a divine instrument: "The highest proof of Scripture derives in general from the fact that God in person speaks in it." Calvin does not search for a nontheological space to ground this theological claim that God is the author of Scripture. Rather, he looks to the material content of theology itself: "[W]e ought to seek our conviction in a higher place than human reasons, judgments, or conjectures, that is, in the secret testimony of the Spirit."[31] It is the Spirit of God who opens our eyes and ears to God's active word, heard in the Scripture. In describing this soteriological context, Calvin speaks of the need to keep together "word and Spirit" so that, through the Spirit [the Scripture] "is really branded upon hearts, if it shows forth Christ, it is the word of life."[32] The recognition of a list of writings as canonical has everything to do with how the Spirit speaks through Scripture to conform us to Jesus Christ, bringing a life-giving word.

Note that if one adopts this Trinitarian-soteriological account of revelation, there are still many open questions about canon. What purpose might historical criticism fulfill when it seeks to isolate the precanonical sources and origins of the biblical writings? Following the work of biblical scholar Brevard Childs, one school of scholarly thought

30. Webster, *Holy Scripture*, pp. 62-63.
31. Calvin, *Institutes*, 1:7:4.
32. Calvin, *Institutes*, 1:9:3.

has worked out the implications of a "canonical approach" to Scripture by giving priority to the final, received form of the text.[33] This approach seeks to make use of studies related to the historical origins of the biblical texts, while integrating these reflections with the theological judgment that the final form of the text is the authoritative biblical witness. Other practitioners of the theological interpretation of Scripture may be more or less optimistic about the usefulness of inquiry into the compositional history of the text. But the final goal of the approach I am proposing is not to end with an account of the human origin of the texts, but to put this in the context of how God's speaking through Scripture is tied to a Trinitarian-soteriological view of biblical revelation. Therefore, the question of canonicity is (as it was in the patristic era) inseparable from that of orthodoxy, that is: What kind of gospel is being presented? When Christians respond to the claim that the Gnostic gospel of Judas should be canonical, they should not simply point to the decisions of the church but to the theological shape of the gospel therein. Does the Spirit use this book to form believers in the image of the God-human Jesus Christ, as children of the Father? Such a notion would be unthinkable for a Gnostic gospel.

Whatever specific account one gives of canonicity, if one follows this third approach to the canonical status of Scripture, two sets of theological claims are unavoidable. First, contrary to a Deistic view of history, we should see God as acting within the messy affairs of human history in the composition, transmission, and reception of the canonical writings themselves; second, it is not a "generic religious God" who is active in this process, but the God of Jesus Christ, through the power of the Spirit. Therefore, an account of canonical reception should give an account of how this is not a merely human authorization of texts but a reception through the illuminating power of the Spirit for the sake of shaping the hearers into the image of Jesus Christ.

33. In his summary account of a "canonical approach" in *Dictionary for Theological Interpretation* (pp. 100-102), Christopher Seitz argues that there are theological reasons for privileging the final form of the biblical text, for "only the final forms bear the fullest witness to all that God has said and handed on within the historical community of faith" (p. 102).

Extended Exegetical Example: Sallie McFague and Marianne Meye Thompson on Interpreting the Biblical Language of "Father" for God

For our exegetical example, we will examine how different functional theologies of revelation lead to quite divergent responses to a question that arises in contemporary Christian ministry: How should we interpret and receive the biblical language of "Father" for God? I choose to compare Sallie McFague and Marianne Meye Thompson, not only because of how their two perspectives contrast, but also because of what they have in common. Both women are respected scholars in the academy and ordained clergy in their denominations. Both speak self-consciously as Christians and as persons concerned with the flourishing of women in ministry and society. And both speak with an awareness of the deeply patriarchal tendencies of the church past and present. They hold all of these assumptions in common; but there are different functional assumptions in their theologies of revelation, and those lead to significant differences in their appropriation of the language of "Father" in Scripture.

While she is in some ways a critic of the Enlightenment, McFague embraces Gordon Kaufman's Kantian view of the absolute mystery of God: God is not disclosed by an act of revelation, nor is the direct knowledge of God available.[34] It is in the face of this absence of God's self-disclosure that we can recognize that all talk of God is "indirect," and we can develop life-giving metaphors for God.[35] Systems of religious symbols are inevitable. Thus, rather than probing what is "given" by way of religious language, we should recognize the radical mystery of God, and we should use pragmatic criteria to evaluate religious language: Is this language helpful, fruitful, and life-giving to religious believers? Does this language open up relationships of mutuality and responsibility rather than hierarchy and abuse?

34. This brief account draws from Sallie McFague, *Metaphorical Theology: Models of God in Religious Language* (Philadelphia: Fortress, 1982), and McFague, *Models of God: Theology for an Ecological, Nuclear Age* (Philadelphia: Fortress, 1987). For a brief but illuminating overview of McFague's theological project and its connections with Kaufman's theological method, see Sarah Coakley's account in *Modern Christian Thought, Volume 2: The Twentieth Century* (Upper Saddle River, NJ: Prentice Hall, 2000) pp. 428-33.

35. McFague, *Models of God,* p. 34; cf. Coakley, *Modern Christian Thought,* p. 430.

While the texture of McFague's ethical critique of religious language has a postmodern rather than a modern cast, her criteria for receiving or rejecting the language and metaphors of Scripture emerges from an anthropological starting point common in the Enlightenment. God is absolute mystery; thus God does not tell us how to speak about God. God is not our teacher of knowledge about God; rather, it is precisely when we realize the fallible, human status of our metaphors that a space opens up for creative new metaphors for God that serve humanization rather than oppression. From the human side of the equation, God is an open canvas for liberating metaphors of God.

Given this theology of revelation, McFague draws on Scripture as a set of possible resources for guiding and norming human practice. In Scripture we see how certain metaphors guided practice in the ancient world: for example, the model of God as father was a good one in the ancient world. But now, according to McFague, it is "a good model gone astray."[36] In our contemporary society, the model of God as father, along with images such as "king, ruler, lord, master," function to reinforce human hierarchies in society and the hierarchy of humans over the natural world. We need to move beyond imagining God as exercising "domination and control" to seeing God as involved in "co-creation" with us.[37] When our metaphors for God are those of sharing, inclusion, and intimacy, these images will shape communities to become sharing, inclusive, and relational. In terms of the language of God as "father," while McFague thinks that this language should not be strictly prohibited, it should give way to humanizing images such as God as mother, lover, and friend. These are three key metaphors McFague uses for God in her book *Models of God.*

Therefore, for McFague, the key question for what "father" means is how it fits into the symbol system of contemporary human communities. Although Scripture rarely addresses God as "friend," McFague believes that this metaphor needs to become a preferred one because of its egalitarian and humanizing qualities.

Like McFague, Thompson has a high view of the mystery of God. God is so mysterious that we cannot depend on our own cultural constructs to give us reliable knowledge of God. But Thompson, in her

36. McFague, *Metaphorical Theology,* p. 145.
37. McFague, *Models of God,* pp. 16-17, 18-19.

book *The Promise of the Father,* evokes Barth to suggest the "stark" options we face with the doctrine of revelation: "Either our understanding of God begins with revelation, or it begins with human beings."[38] Thompson rejects the anthropological starting point, claiming instead that "father" should be seen as a Scripture-given analogy for God: the analogy of father is thus "an appropriate way" for Christians "to speak of God" (p. 171). An analogy is mysterious, according to Thompson, and the analogy of father is not a name for God. But the analogy is not simply a human projection. God's revelation is in and through human language, metaphors, and analogies, and these analogies are given by God in Scripture. Therefore, father is one among a number of normative scriptural analogies for God. It does not mean that God is male or a cosmic version of "Dad." Rather, God's revelation itself provides the meaning of God as father. God's revelation in Scripture provides the positive content of what Scripture means when it refers to God as "Father," not our own experience of our fathers or our own experience as fathers.

Thus, in order to discern the significance of calling God "Father" in Christian speech and worship, Thompson examines the witness of Scripture itself. Thompson is attentive to an "eschatological trajectory" rooted in the Old Testament that connects God as father with the covenant in which God will be "God of all the families of Israel" (Jer. 31:1); this is extended in the New Testament through the inclusion of gentiles as God's children through Jesus Christ, offering to them the covenant promises of Abraham (p. 164). After examining the intertextual biblical senses of calling God "Father," Thompson says that "the real theological issue is not whether God can be experienced in a fatherly way but whether God can be trusted to fulfill the promises and obligations that the Bible ascribes to him as Father" (p. 174). In its biblical use, calling God "Father" is not giving priority to stereotypically masculine traits. On the contrary, Scripture often fleshes out the father image with traits that are far from typical cultural portraits of males or fathers. The key function of the image is that it refers to a relationship of trust and the covenant promises of God to Israel and the church.

Like McFague, Thompson is concerned about the possible misuse of the term "God as Father" in the present context, such that it might

---

38. Marianne Meye Thompson, *The Promise of the Father: Jesus and God in the New Testament* (Louisville: Westminster John Knox, 2000), p. 170.

suggest that "male is God." But Thompson notes that there is a "scandal of particularity" here: Jesus Christ was a historical person who lived and died and rose again in a particular context at a particular time. Yet God is revealed in Scripture, which witnesses to the life, death, and resurrection of Jesus Christ. Jesus calls God "Father" and teaches his disciples to do so. Therefore, though there are many other scriptural analogies for God that we should use as well, if we want to participate in God's revelation in Jesus Christ, we need to see ourselves in relationship to the one Jesus called "Father" (pp. 183-85).

In spite of their many areas of commonality, their different theologies of revelation lead McFague and Thompson to very different places in their interpretation and appropriation of the language of God as father. For McFague, all religious language has an anthropological starting point, and thus it is subject to critique and revision based on what is humanizing and helpful in our current religious symbol system. For McFague, Scripture is not an instrument of an external divine revelation; it is a possible sourcebook for human metaphors about God. Therefore, the fact that Jesus instructs his disciples to pray to God as father does not mean that it is appropriate for Christians today to continue to pray to or speak of God as father. Rather, the key question is whether we assess (on the basis of our own human criteria) whether an image for God is fruitful for the flourishing of human beings.

By contrast, for Thompson, trusting Jesus Christ for salvation involves trusting that his commands and the biblical narrative of salvation will be one of health and salvation. We do not have a criterion — apart from God's own revelation — to judge what we should edit from the content of the scriptural narrative. For Thompson, this does not mean that we should uncritically accept the practices and traditions of the past regarding how Christians speak of God as father. But the grounds for revising our practices needs to come via a receptive reading of God's living word spoken through Scripture. Reading Scripture in light of Christ, we find ourselves drawn into a narrative that we did not create, with norms that we did not approve of in advance. The key is not to edit the particularity of revelation in Christ, but to receive this revelation in a way that names patriarchal idolatry as the disobedience it is, while praying and speaking of God in ways that recognize Scripture as the instrument of God's revelation in a way that surpasses our own bright ideas. Interpreting the language of "father" puts us in a place like that of the gospel itself: coming to know God in Jesus Christ, as we are given ears by the Spirit to hear an external word that we neither expected nor constructed, a word of healing and salvation.

Conclusion

This chapter has explored a subterranean level of what is operative whenever Christians interpret Scripture: functional theologies of revelation. Every time we interpret Scripture, our action carries implicit testimonies of our belief about how God relates to Scripture and to our reception of it. On the one hand, we may assume that God's revelation through Scripture is no more than an expression of human religious experience, or perhaps a portrayal of truths that are true to the extent that they are grounded in universal human capacities apart from God. This set of approaches is quite compatible with a Deistic way of appropriating Scripture, in which the readers use Scripture for the purposes of solving their own problems, or deciding what from Scripture is "relevant" or "humanizing" that we can put into practice today. There are many variations among these themes on this side of the either/or. Practitioners of these kinds of approaches span a broad spectrum of theological traditions between liberal to conservative. But there is a common thread that is operative in this wide range of ways to receive Scripture: they operate from an anthropological starting point for revelation and from within a Deistic theology of salvation.

By contrast, I have argued that a more faithful and fruitful approach to interpreting Scripture involves living into a different operative theology of revelation. Instead of starting with inherent human capacities and assuming that humans can apprehend the truth when they encounter it, we see God's decisive action with Israel and in Jesus Christ as the ground for revelation. We do not come to know God's decisive action with Israel and in Jesus Christ through a Socratic method of having universal truths drawn out of us by a teacher as midwife; instead, as we come to know God in Christ through Scripture, we encounter a word that is *external* to our own expectations and devices. Moreover, only God can make God known. As our teacher, God must give us the eyes to apprehend the truth. This problem is addressed by way of a Trinitarian hermeneutic, one in which the knowledge of God arises from the initiative of the Spirit, who opens our eyes through Scripture to Jesus Christ, the Word of the Father. In this vision, scriptural interpretation is part of a process of growing ever deeper into the knowledge of God as we receive the word and fellowship of the living Christ by the Spirit's power.

In light of this theology of revelation, which is rooted in God's action and a Trinitarian theology of salvation, we can also move beyond common misconstruals of the inspiration and canonicity of Scripture. The doctrine of inspiration is the affirmation that God acts "in, with, and over" the human authors in generating the texts of Scripture as creaturely products by the Spirit's power. Affirming Scripture's inspiration involves recognizing Scripture as the Spirit's instrument for shaping God's people into Christ's image, the Spirit's instrument for mediating the living Christ's lordship over the church. The doctrine of canon is one in which the church recognizes and confesses the lordship of Christ over the church by affirming the canon of Scripture as the Spirit's chosen instrument of revelation. Canonicity is not about the church arrogating its authority over Scripture; nor is canonicity reducible to a human power struggle in the church. Instead, we should view canonicity as the part of the process in which the Spirit works in and through the composition, redaction, and gradual stages of reception of these books as Scripture, precisely because the Spirit speaks an external word through these human words to reshape God's people into Christ's image.

Just as water is taken up into the divine work of baptism, and bread and wine are taken up in the divine work of the Lord's Supper, so also the creaturely words of Scripture are taken up into the triune God's work of salvation. Through these creaturely products, God speaks a powerful word that opens up the possibility of knowledge of God in Christ through the Spirit, a knowledge that is always tied to God's presence and fellowship. The Spirit uses Scripture in our journey of faith seeking understanding, mediating the self-presentation of the Word, Jesus Christ, through Scripture. This journey of reading Scripture is not just about texts, meaning, and interpretation. It is about receiving Scripture as the Spirit's word that unites God's people ever deeper to Jesus Christ and his ways, mortifying sin while vivifying the community for service in Christ. Scripture is not God; it is an instrument in the triune God's work. But we should receive it as God's chosen instrument, with a functional theology that is attentive to God's external word mediated by the Spirit. For it is by the Spirit that readers are empowered and called to an ever-deepening communion with God in Christ, and to a love of neighbor in service and witness.

For Further Reading

Karl Barth, *Church Dogmatics,* I:I; I:II (Edinburgh, T&T Clark, 1960-1961), chap. 3; Hans Urs von Balthasar, *Theo-Drama: Theological Dramatic Theory,* 5 vols. (San Francisco: Ignatius Press, 1988-98).

Barth and von Balthasar are two of the most significant thinkers on the doctrine of revelation in the last century, and they continue to be influential in the contemporary discourse on the theological interpretation of Scripture. Both are deeply Trinitarian thinkers who are acutely aware of the significance of operative theologies of revelation.

James B. Torrance, *Worship, Community and the Triune God of Grace* (Downers Grove, IL: InterVarsity, 1996).

In this very accessible account, Torrance gives a concrete analysis of operative theologies of worship, contrasting a Trinitarian approach to worship to a Unitarian one. Torrance's book is helpful for pastors or worship leaders who are seeking to discern the implications of moving toward a Trinitarian way of receiving Scripture in worship.

J. B. Webster, *Holy Scripture: A Dogmatic Sketch* (Cambridge, UK: Cambridge University Press, 2003).

Webster is a significant thinker in the contemporary discourse on the theological interpretation of Scripture. His book Holy Scripture *is particularly helpful in its view of how Trinitarian teaching should be central in a Christian reading of Scripture, and how these Trinitarian convictions can help one avoid misconstruals of the doctrines of inspiration and canon.*

Telford Work, *Living and Active: Scripture in the Economy of Salvation* (Grand Rapids: Eerdmans, 2002).

Work gives a constructive proposal that draws on both ancient and contemporary thinkers in considering the consequences of placing one's doctrine of Scripture within the overall economy of God's working in salvation.

CHAPTER 4

The Impact of the Reader's Context

Discerning the Spirit's Varied
Yet Bounded Work

H OW DOES God speak through Scripture to a Latin American Christian living under an oppressive political regime? How does God speak through Scripture to a first-generation Christian convert from Islam in east Africa? How does God speak through Scripture to a white Methodist parishioner in Nebraska? Questions such as these presuppose that God speaks through the instrument of Scripture, as I have already argued in this book. But that leaves open the question of how the interpreter's contextual location impacts the event of God's speaking through Scripture.

It is a truism that there is no context-free interpretation of Scripture. The historical critic who interprets the Bible from a library desk in Harvard Divinity School is just as shaped by the sociocultural context as the Masai Christian who takes a rest from herding cattle in Kenya to recollect a memorized passage of Scripture. "Contextual" manifestations of Christianity are not just for the global South or ethnic minorities in the West. All scriptural interpretation is shaped, to some extent, by the social and cultural location of the interpreter.

It would be tempting to move from this *descriptive* observation about the contextual location of interpretation to several different kinds of *normative* claims about how one should practice interpretation. Consider the following normative claims that one might make based on the observation that interpretation is contextual.

1) Since all interpretation of Scripture is culturally conditioned (descriptive), then all interpretation of Scripture must be equally valid (normative).

2) Since all interpretation of Scripture is culturally conditioned (descriptive), then one culture never has the right to criticize another culture's interpretation of Scripture (normative).

Although both of these claims may sound like they follow from the descriptive observation that "all interpretation of Scripture is culturally conditioned," neither conclusion necessarily follows from the premise that all interpretation of Scripture is culturally conditioned.

In fact, these normative claims bear traces of the Enlightenment prejudice against preunderstanding: they assume that only an objective, context-free interpretation of Scripture could properly evaluate other interpretations. However, as we have explored in chapter 2, there are reasons from the field of general hermeneutics to reject that claim. For example, among the many interpretations of Leo Tolstoy's *Anna Karenina,* some interpretations are better than others. In fact, this is exactly what readers of literary criticism about *Anna Karenina* must assume as they sort through the different views of it. Nevertheless, all views are culturally conditioned.

Moreover, since we are dealing with the interpretation of Scripture, there are also theological reasons to reject the norms in claims one and two above. Consider the contextual interpretation of Scripture in the German Christian movement in Nazi Germany. Influenced by various social and cultural forces tied to the rise of Nazism, these German Christians interpreted Jesus to be the first and greatest anti-Semite. They understood Jesus' cleansing of the Temple to be an example of his antipathy toward Jews. Thus, enlightened in their understanding of Scripture by the new Nazi movement, they followed the Nazi plan of exterminating the Jews, which they said was an act of following Jesus.[1]

Not many of us today can claim to inhabit the same social-historical-cultural world as did these Nazi Christians. But should that silence our protest against the use of Scripture in a way that cuts Jesus

---

1. For more on Nazi Christianity and its interpretation of Scripture, see Richard Steigmann-Gall, *The Holy Reich: Nazi Conceptions of Christianity, 1919-1945* (Cambridge, UK: Cambridge University Press, 2003).

off from Israel and justifies Aryan domination and violence against Jews? Does this interpretation of Scripture have just as much claim to be a valid reception of God's word as the Barmen Declaration's protest against Nazi Christians, which rejected the "false doctrine" that "events and powers, figures and truths" (such as the Nazi movement) besides God's word can be considered "God's revelation"?[2] If we really hold to normative claims one and two, we have no choice but to say that the Nazi interpretation and the Barmen interpretation are equally valid and beyond criticism. While this form of cultural relativism may sound tolerant or even progressive in the abstract, it actually silences genuine debate about the meaning of texts. Moreover, it leaves us with a mute God, for a God who tells Nazis to exterminate Jews and tells other Christians to resist the Nazi regime is an incoherent God, one who does not speak beyond the level of our own wishes.

I BELIEVE THAT the two normative claims above represent dead ends for those of us who affirm that the Bible is God's instrument for transforming his people into the image of Christ. But we are still left with an unavoidable question: How should we think about the implications of the observation that all scriptural interpretation takes place within culturally conditioned contexts?

This chapter addresses this question by proceeding in three sections. The first two sections present a dialectic of two sides of our thinking about the place of context in the interpretation of Scripture. First, the contextual reception of Scripture is not only an observable human phenomenon; it is something that reflects a key feature of how God makes himself known to human beings. Just as the Word became flesh and inhabited a human culture in Jesus Christ, God's word is properly received in a culture only when it comes to inhabit that culture by the Spirit's indwelling power. As such, the cultural differences manifested in various interpretations of Scripture are God's gift to the church, a product of the Spirit's work in animating God's word in various cultures of the world. This dynamic of the Spirit's work is one of "indigenizing" the Christian story for various cultures.[3]

---

2. *Book of Confessions: Study Edition,* Part 1 of the Constitution of the Presbyterian Church (U.S.A.) (Louisville: Geneva Press, 1996), 311.

3. For the language of "indigenizing" and "pilgrim" dynamics in the cultural recep-

However, since all human cultures bear the marks of human sin, the gospel's "inhabiting" of culture by the Spirit will also involve the Spirit's critique, challenging the culture through Scripture. All Christians are on a pilgrim road of living into God's reign, which is present but not yet fully consummated. As the living Christ speaks through Scripture by the Spirit, God's people are called to be set apart for God's way and service, often in conflict with cherished cultural values. For the Christian, reading Scripture is inseparable from the act of discipleship and carrying the cross in following Jesus. Therefore, reading Scripture is not simply an act of self-realization or the realization of a given culture's ideal. Instead, it is a path leading us into the mortification of our personal and culturally formed desires, as we come to live into the new reality of the Spirit. I frame the dialectic of the Spirit's work in culture through Scripture in this way:

> First, the Spirit works to indigenize God's word in Scripture in various contexts and cultures, bringing unity in the person of Jesus Christ; as such, scriptural interpretation from diverse contexts can be received as mutual enrichment, gifts of the Spirit for the whole church.

> Second, the Spirit uses Scripture not only to indigenize the gospel, but also to call people of all cultures to transformation; as such, the Spirit uses Scripture as a tool to confront the cultural idols that seek to make the Spirit's word through Scripture captive to its own cultural interests and priorities.

In light of this dialectic, how should we discern faithful acts of culturally informed reception of Scripture from unfaithful ones? How are we to discern whether our act of interpretation is participating in the Spirit's work or resisting the Spirit's work of transformation? The third part of the chapter describes this norm for the interpretation of Scripture:

> As a result of the dialectic above, Christians should engage in a task of *spiritual discernment* as a dimension of the faithful reception of

---

tion of the Christian message, I am drawing on the language of Andrew F. Walls but developing his terminology somewhat differently. For an excellent account of how these two dynamics have been at work in Christian history, see Walls, *The Missionary Movement in Christian History: Studies in Transmission of Faith* (Maryknoll, NY: Orbis, 1996).

Scripture, seeking to discern the particular shape of the Spirit's spacious yet bounded work in using Scripture to transform the church ever deeper into Christ's image.

I describe this act of spiritual discernment in three ways: first, by examining the insufficiency of direct appeals to "experience" as a criterion for discerning the Spirit's work in Scripture; second, exploring the guidance provided by the Spirit's work in community for discerning the Spirit's work in Scripture; third, discerning the constructive role of suspicion toward one's own cultural captivities in scriptural interpretation, even as this is combined with a trust in the Spirit's power to speak through Scripture. All of these ways suggest that spiritual discernment involves reading Scripture as the church, yet submitting as the church to the life-giving word of the Spirit through Scripture. I conclude this chapter with an extended exegetical example from a Christian ministry in Uganda.

Mutual Enrichment: The Spirit's Work of Indigenizing the Word

Cultural variety in scriptural reception:
Is it really the work of the Spirit?

When one looks at the great variety of scriptural interpretation around the world and through time, why attribute this variety to the Spirit's work? Although I advocate doing so, such a claim is far from self-evident. For many, the variety of scriptural interpretations in various cultures suggests that scriptural interpretation is nothing more than a projection of our own desires.

For example, consider the divergence among the portraits of Jesus in various cultures. Even when based on a common set of Scripture texts, such as the Last Supper, Jesus in Christian art typically reflects the complexion and cultural values of the receiving culture. For instance, in a form of iconography standardized since the Middle Ages, a traditional Ethiopian icon of Jesus and the holy family depicts the family of Jesus with relatively dark skin, typical of the Amhara tribe. Darker skin would have made Jesus the color of the non-Orthodox in the southern tribes of Ethiopia; lighter skin would have made Jesus closer to a European complexion. Thus Jesus and his family are identified with the Amhara tribe.

Joseph, Mary and Jesus leave Bethlehem, 1756. Joseph leads the donkey bearing the Virgin Mary and the Christ Child, as the family leave Bethlehem.
(© HIP / Art Resource, NY)

In contrast, consider Gaudenzio Ferrari's early sixteenth-century Italian painting of the Virgin Mary and Jesus. The complexion of Jesus and his mother is relatively light. The painting has perspective to show the relative distance of characters, and the finely tuned accounts of the human body. These traits — as well as other characteristics of the painting — reflect the artistic conventions of Italian Renaissance humanism in the sixteenth century. Just as the Bible's account of the birth and family of Jesus enters into an Amharic Orthodox context in an Ethiopian icon, it takes on a distinctively early-modern Italian cast in the painting of Ferrari.

Gaudenzio Ferrari, *Madonna and Child* *(© Scala / Art Resource, NY)*

Examples like these could be multiplied indefinitely. Whether or not the Bible's stories are portrayed in art, they tend to be received in a distinctively Italian way by Italians, in a distinctively Ethiopian way by Ethiopians, in a distinctively Japanese way by Japanese, and so on. What are we to conclude from observing this cultural variety in receiving the Bible's narrative about Christ and his family? On the one hand, some see a danger in creating Jesus in our own image: a blue-eyed, meek, and mild Caucasian Jesus for Caucasians, a warrior Jesus for those involved in political conflict, and so forth. Indeed, the danger of idolatry is a real one. Cultures can and do project their hopes and values onto Jesus, potentially compromising his revelatory identity.

This may lead some to conclude that the cultural reception of Scripture is nothing more than projection. Allegedly, the Bible is simply a tool to justify the ideals and agendas of particular cultures. In light of such great cultural variety in the reception of Christian Scripture, some claim that the Bible can "mean anything you want it to mean," testifying against the possibility of divine revelation being received through Scripture.[4]

But while there is a genuine danger of idolatry, this is not the only way to interpret the significance of this cultural plurality. In light of the scriptural witness, there is good reason to believe that the indigenization process of Christianity is inherent to the Christian message itself. If that is the case, then cultural variations in the visual accounts of Jesus' family, along with the other varied cultural appropriations of Scripture, can testify to the Spirit's work. Ethiopians perceive something true about the gospel when they see Jesus as not simply a foreigner but as the Savior who has become one with their own people — "like his brothers and sisters in every respect" except sin (Heb. 2:17; 4:15). Different cultural receptions of Jesus Christ in works of art can point to the Spirit's gifts, the Spirit's indigenizing work. The Spirit enables the reception of the Christian faith in a way that makes the gospel a living message in various cultural contexts. We will examine the biblical and theological rationale for these claims below.

The Scriptural Witness: The Spirit's Work in Indigenizing

The God of Scripture makes himself known in particular, culturally specific ways. Scripture does not begin with a list of necessary or transcendental truths about God; rather, it begins with a narrative about God and particular people. God makes himself known in the garden to Adam and Eve, later to Noah and his family, to Abram and Sarai, and to

---

4. See a discussion of this issue in Ann Monroe, *The Word: Imagining the Gospel in Modern America* (Louisville: Westminster John Knox, 2000), chap. 2.

Moses at Mount Sinai. There was a corporate dimension to this knowledge of God: it was connected to God's covenantal promises to the family of Noah, then to the descendents of Abram, then to the people of Israel. The God of Israel speaks in culturally particular ways to particular peoples, and not through universal theorems. Yet the cultural particularity of God's way of speaking had implications not only for Israel but for "all the families of the earth" who will be blessed through God's covenant with Abram (Gen. 12:3).

In the New Testament, God's love was manifested through the sending of his Son, Jesus Christ, the eternal Word who was in himself beyond the particularity of a specific culture. It was the Word through whom "all things came into being" (John 1:1, 3). The Word was "the true light, which enlightens everyone" (1:19). But since the Word came "into the world" in Jesus Christ, the Word took on all the particularity of a human culture: the "Word became flesh and dwelt among us" (1:14).

Jesus Christ, as the incarnate Word, was culturally Jewish through and through.[5] In the Gospel accounts, when Jesus prays, speaks, and even when he argues with other Jews (such as the Pharisees), Jesus does so in distinctively Jewish ways.[6] Moreover, Jesus' ministry was first and foremost directed to "the house of Israel" (see Matt. 10:5-7; 15:21-28), though the Gospel accounts of Jesus' ministry sometimes suggest an opening of God's covenant to peoples beyond Israel as well.[7] God does not switch from a culturally particular mode of revelation in the Old

---

5. While it is fruitful to consider the incarnation in terms of the cultural-particularity of the descent of the Word, one must keep in mind that the incarnation is a unique event. Only Jesus Christ is "truly God" and "truly human" in one person. Sometimes Christians speak of the Bible itself in directly incarnational terms, as "truly divine" and "truly human." But while the incarnation can be instructive for the way in which God's incarnate Word inhabits a particular culture, Scripture is best understood as an instrument of the *Spirit,* who bears witness to the eternal Word made flesh in Jesus Christ. In other words, the doctrine of Scripture should be seen as an extension of the doctrine of the Spirit, from within a Trinitarian theology of salvation.

6. There is a wide-ranging literature about the Jewish nature of Jesus' practice. A particularly rich account of the Jewish identity of Jesus can be found in the multivolume series by N. T. Wright, *Christian Origins and the Question of* God (Minneapolis: Fortress Press, 1992-2003).

7. The inclusion of gentiles in Jesus' mission is anticipated in passages such as Luke 15:11-32, but it is extended much more explicitly in the second part of the composition, the book of Acts.

113

Testament to a "universal" mode in the New Testament. Rather, the culturally particular covenant with Israel is extended, in Jesus Christ, to include non-Jews of various languages and cultures.

The culturally particular work of the triune God was extended as the earliest Christians bore witness to the gospel and it was received into other cultures. In the book of Acts, the cross-cultural transmission of the Christian message is framed explicitly in terms of the Spirit's work. At Pentecost, the Spirit enables the followers of Jesus to speak in the various languages of the gathered Jews, "from every nation under heaven living in Jerusalem" (Acts 2:5). Peter addresses his fellow Jews and proclaims a distinctively Jewish account of the gospel, quoting the prophet Joel and speaking of "our ancestor David," who foresaw "the resurrection of the Messiah" (Acts 2:29, 31). Peter proclaims: "Let the entire house of Israel know with certainty that God has made him both Lord and Messiah" (Acts 2:36). Many who heard were baptized and received the Holy Spirit (vv. 41-42).

As the message of the gospel spreads, the Spirit authorizes a shocking course of action: a Jewish message about the Jewish messiah is directed by God to extend to non-Jews. Peter and a gentile, Cornelius, both receive visions. The Spirit tells Peter to welcome gentile visitors, even though this violates the Jewish law. Cornelius is told in his vision to seek out Peter, for God has heard his prayer and has seen his generous giving of alms (Acts 10:1-33).

When Peter presents the message to Cornelius, it is still a message of Jewish origin that God "sent to the people of Israel" (10:36). But instead of speaking of Jesus as the Messiah — with all of the Jewish weight of the term — Peter speaks about Jesus as the "Lord of all," and he says that "everyone who believes in him receives forgiveness of sins in his name" (10:36, 43).

There is both a great gain and a great loss in translating the Christian message into those terms. Although both Jews and gentiles had the category of *kyrios,* ("Lord"), it differed in meaning for the two cultures. In a Jewish cultural context, "Lord" was a Greek translation of the divine name YHWH in the Septuagint, the Greek translation of the Hebrew Bible that was used by Second Temple Jews: its early application to Jesus Christ brings with it the weight of its Old Testament context.[8] In a

8. This is not to say that declaring "Jesus is Lord" was directly a divine title in a Jewish

gentile cultural context, "Lord" was a term more commonly used for gods, political rulers, or those exercising power with regard to servants.[9] There is a gain in this translation into Greek culture: it emphasizes the cosmic authority of Christ's lordship and reign. But there is also an irreducible loss from the Jewish context: its association with the divine name of the God of Israel and the religious thought of Second Temple Jews. This gain and loss is inevitable with any translation from one language into another.

What is striking about the book of Acts is that it attributes the translation to the work of the Spirit: it is the Spirit who enables the Pentecost speech to be understood by linguistically diverse (Jewish) hearers; the Spirit orchestrates Peter's meeting with Cornelius; and the Spirit "fell upon all who heard the word" that Peter spoke, bringing them to believe in Jesus Christ as Lord. At the Council of Jerusalem recorded in Acts 15, Peter says that it was God's decision that Peter would be "the one through whom the Gentiles would hear the good news and become believers." God spoke to them (through the words of Peter) "by giving them the Holy Spirit, just as he did to us" (Acts 15:7). The Spirit verifies for Peter — and the Jerusalem Council — that the gentiles have had a genuine encounter with the living Christ, that they know God through Christ. Yet gentile understandings of Christ inevitably had differences from Jewish understandings.

How are we to conceive of the legitimacy of gentile understandings of Christ as distinct from Jewish ones? The Jerusalem Council attributed the gentiles' incorporation into Christ to the work of the Spirit; thus the laws that were distinct to Jewish identity and culture should not be applied to gentile believers. It only maintains a bare minimum of dietary laws to follow, ones that would assure the possibility of Jewish-gentile table fellowship in Christ.[10] The Council of Jerusalem did not frame different cultural manifestations of Christianity as a threat to Christian identity, but as part of the work of the Spirit, who brings people of many histories and backgrounds to faith in Jesus Christ.

---

context, but it does relate the Jewish context to the exaltation of the risen Christ by the God of Israel. See Gerhard Kittel, *Theological Dictionary of the New Testament,* vol. 3 (Grand Rapids: Eerdmans, 1985), pp. 1058-59, 1088-92.

9. See Kittel, *Theological Dictionary of the NT,* 3: 1049-58.

10. See Joseph Fitzmyer, *The Acts of the Apostles* (New York: Doubleday, 1998), pp. 553-54.

The idea that Jesus Christ is made known by the Spirit to peoples of various cultures also fits with other New Testament teaching about the Spirit. The Spirit "will guide you into all truth" (John 16:13); the Spirit does this not by "speaking on his own," but the Spirit will "glorify" Jesus Christ, "because he will take what is mine and declare it to you" (16:15). In Pauline writings, it is impossible to be "in Christ" without also being "in the Spirit": the two are closely tied together.[11] Paul uses the image of the body of Christ as an image of bounded diversity and differentiation of function within the church. The Spirit unites a diversely gifted body of believers into Christ's body (1 Cor. 12), and as such the Spirit's work shows, for Paul, that salvation is received by faith, "not national custom and social affiliation."[12] It is for this reason that Paul was angry when Peter withdrew from the gentiles so as not to offend some Jewish Christians. "I opposed him to his face, because he stood self-condemned; for until certain people came from James, he used to eat with the Gentiles. But after they came, he drew back and kept himself separate for fear of the circumcision faction" (Gal. 2:12). Peter's temporary refusal to accept the gentiles and their sociocultural identity was a failure to honor the Spirit's own work in granting salvation through faith in Christ — not on the basis of the law.

Note that even though Jesus Christ would inevitably be understood differently in early Jewish and gentile Christian communities, these differences were not necessarily problematic in New Testament terms. Judaizers and Hellenistic proto-Gnostics presented culturally colored accounts of Jesus and his work that New Testament writers did consider problematic. But aside from certain examples in which cultural forces overwhelmed the distinctiveness of the gospel, Jews and Greeks were seen as "one in Christ Jesus," a work of the Spirit that overcomes the privileging of national and ethnic origin (Gal. 3:28). The Spirit testifies to the living Christ, who is active in communities of various cultures and histories, incorporating them into Christ and hence into being "Abraham's offspring, heirs according to the promise" (Gal. 3:29).

As chapter 3 explored concerning the doctrine of inspiration, the

11. See Lewis Smedes, *Union with Christ: A Biblical View of the New Life in Jesus Christ,* 2nd ed. (Grand Rapids: Eerdmans, 1983), pp. 43-45.
12. See Lamin Sanneh, *Disciples of All Nations: Pillars of World Christianity* (Oxford: Oxford University Press, 2008), p. 8.

Spirit breathes life into the words of Scripture as an instrument for bearing witness to Jesus Christ. In light of the passages from the book of Acts and the others above, there is a Spirit-enabled knowledge of Jesus Christ that takes place through Scripture. This does not require one voice in interpretation, for the Spirit is also the bond that holds together Jews and gentiles in the Christian community as one body (Eph. 2:11-17; 4:3-6). Lamin Sanneh says:

> The New Testament describes Christian Gentiles and others as bonding with Christianity not by tying themselves to the apron strings of Jesus' Jewish origins but by clothing themselves with the authentic vestments of their own culture. Jewish Christians themselves, chiefly Peter and Paul, were the first and the most adamant in urging upon the Gentile church such a radical move. It is, consequently, not a betrayal of faith for believers elsewhere to embrace Christianity and to fold it into their native traditions rather than to turn against their culture.[13]

Since the Spirit enables different receptions of Scripture to lead to the knowledge of Jesus Christ, we should be attentive to the Spirit's work by learning from culturally diverse receptions of Scripture. Culturally informed differences in Scripture interpretation (as in the artistic portrayals of Jesus and his family mentioned above) are not simply a problem to be overcome; they can be a sign of the Spirit's work in indigenizing the gospel, that is, something to be celebrated!

The Continuing Work of the Spirit: Reading with God's People in Diverse Cultural Contexts

Concretely speaking, how might we encounter the Spirit's work in different cultural receptions of Scripture in a way that illuminates our own reception of Scripture? Some examples may help to make this clear.

While teaching for a year at a theological school in Ethiopia, I grew in my understanding of how to interpret the Bible as I learned from the reception of Scripture among my students. Our students came from various regions and tribes of Ethiopia, and each tribe had

---

13. Sanneh, *Disciples of All Nations,* pp. 55-56.

its own code of food taboos. Remaining faithful to that code was part of a person's self-identification with his or her tribal identity. The Old Testament dietary laws made a great deal of sense to those students: they saw them as laws given to Israel by God as a way for Israel to remember that they were God's chosen people. I discovered that many Christians from my home culture in the United States did not know how to make sense of those dietary laws: they either ignored them, or they saw them as cryptic guides to healthy eating. As in many cultures in the ancient Near East, my Ethiopian students knew that food taboos were not about healthy diets. Those cultures used dietary laws to express cultural differentiation: other cultures may eat camels, and there may be nothing biologically wrong with eating camels, but that's not what *our* people do.

While my Christian students did not keep kosher (in light of the Council of Jerusalem's decision in Acts 15), they were able to have deep insight into the Old Testament narrative of God's people through their own cultural practice of dietary taboos. Even though all foods are now "clean" for those in Christ, my students had a strong sense of how the dietary laws are still operative for Christians: we are called to be a holy people, set apart from the world for God's purposes. We should live in a way that distinguishes us from those around us.

Why did my students have special insight into the biblical text? In this particular case, their cultural background was much more similar to the cultures in which the Bible itself was written. The particularity of their culture made a connection to the particularity of ancient Near East and Second Temple Jewish cultures. Philip Jenkins gives numerous examples like these in *The New Faces of Christianity: Believing the Bible in the Global South.* For example, Jenkins points out that many readers in the global South are much closer to the kinds of agrarian cultures that gave rise to scriptural images and cultural situations involving seed and planting, famine and exile. Many can relate to the circumstance of day laborers who have been asked to work in a vineyard (Matt. 20:1-15), and to work at pruning vines and branches (John 15).[14]

Yet the Spirit's enabling of an indigenized reception of Scripture is not just based on the relative cultural distance between the receiving

---

14. Philip Jenkins, *The New Faces of Christianity* (Oxford: Oxford University Press, 2006), pp. 69-73.

culture and the originating cultural context in Scripture.[15] The account in the book of Acts, and the consequent growth of Hellenistic-Roman Christianity, tells us as much: there is little doubt that the first Jewish converts' understanding of Jesus as the Jewish messiah and Lord is closer to the cultural context of the New Testament writings than that of early gentile converts — and the many gentile converts to follow. However, though there is great value for gentiles to come to terms with the Jewish context of the messiah, the council of Jerusalem does not allow for a basic priority of Jewish culture over Greek culture.[16] Appropriations of the Christian message in various cultures are seen as the work of the *same* Spirit in one Christ: "So he [Christ] came and proclaimed peace to you who were far off and peace to you who were near; for through him both of us have access in one Spirit to the Father. So then you are no longer strangers and aliens, but you are citizens with the saints and also members of the household of God" (Eph. 2:17-19). A culturally diverse group of believers is united as one in the Spirit in Christ, as members of "the household of God."

The oneness of the Spirit that holds together the cultural plurality of the church's reception of Scripture manifests itself in the phenomenon of translation, which is central to the Christian faith. The New Testament was not written in the language Jesus spoke (Aramaic) or even in the highly cultured Greek of Philo. It was written in the Greek vernacular. Was there a gain and loss in receiving the Aramaic teachings and traditions of Jesus in Greek? Yes. Was there a gain and loss in putting the apostolic witness to Christ into the commonplace language of the

---

15. Reflecting in broad terms on the relationship of the gospel to culture, Darrell Guder says: "No particular cultural rendering of the gospel may claim greater validity than any other, and all cultural formulations of the faith are subject to continuing conversion as the gospel challenges them." Darrell Guder, *The Continuing Conversion of the Church* (Grand Rapids: Eerdmans, 2000), p. 92. Guder's point is not to say that all renderings of the gospel (or scriptural interpretation) are equally valid, but that there are not privileged cultures that are so "pure" that they do not need the Spirit's transformation, or cultures so "corrupt" that the Spirit cannot work through them.

16. Indeed, rediscovering the distinctly Jewish context of the New Testament has led to many significant insights in the last several decades of New Testament scholarship. For an excellent overview of the diverse yet fruitful renewal of interest in Second Temple Judaism in scholarship on the New Testament and Christian origins, see Markus Bockmuehl, *Seeing the Word: Refocusing New Testament Study* (Grand Rapids: Baker Academic, 2006), pp. 185-205.

people? Yes. "The New Testament Gospels are a translated version of the message of Jesus," says Lamin Sanneh, "and that means Christianity is a translated religion without a revealed language."[17] Just as the cultural gain and loss in the many tongues of Pentecost is attributed to the Spirit, so the *koine* (common) Greek of the New Testament is taken up into the Spirit's work.

This feature of the New Testament corresponds to a notable feature in Christian history: the audacious willingness of Christians to translate Scripture into thousands of vernacular languages around the world. Often Christians have shown vigilant loyalty to one particular translation, whether the Latin Vulgate or the King James Version. But to a surprising extent, Christians have been willing to follow the trajectory of Pentecost by making Bible translation one of the first acts of missionary work. The contrast with a religion such as Islam is striking. For Islam, the Arabic words themselves are the words of God, and no translation of the Koran can truly be called the Koran. Translations may be used for study, but not in public worship, and certainly not as a substitute for the Arabic.[18] By contrast, the Christian tradition has generally worked with an assumption that holds unity and plurality together in biblical interpretation: the Spirit will use Scripture in various languages to bring people to the knowledge of God in Jesus Christ — and the unity therein. But just as the differences between translations are irreducible, so will the differences between the reception of Scripture in various cultures also be irreducible.

In *Christianity Rediscovered,* Roman Catholic priest Vincent Donovan gives an account of his attempt to share the gospel message among the nomadic Masai tribe in Kenya. One of his most important lessons was that if he were to simply present his own account of the Christian message, Jesus would be received as a Western cultural commodity, a steppingstone on the path of Westernizing the culture. On his own, Donovan did not have the resources to describe how the gospel could be received by the Masai. Immersing himself in the culture, Donovan was able to see the ways in which the Masai had been seeking after God. Gradually, Donovan shared the message of Jesus and Scripture with re-

17. Lamin Sanneh, *Whose Religion Is Christianity?* (Grand Rapids: Eerdmans, 2003), p. 97.

18. Sanneh, *Whose Religion?,* pp. 99-100.

gard to these indigenous practices, beliefs, and narratives. The Christianity embraced by the Masai was not just a translation of Donovan's Western Christianity, but a translation of the New Testament account of the good news into their own culture. Here is a Masai creed:

> We believe in the one High God, who out of love created the beautiful world and everything good in it. He created man and wanted man to be happy in the world. God loves the world and every nation and tribe on the earth. We have known this High God in darkness, and now we know him in the light. God promised in the book of his word, the bible, that he would save the world and all the nations and tribes.
>
> We believe that God made good his promise by sending his son, Jesus Christ, a man in the flesh, a Jew by tribe, born poor in a little village, who left his home and was always on safari doing good, curing people by the power of God, teaching about God and man, showing the meaning of religion is love. He was rejected by his people, tortured and nailed hands and feet to a cross, and died. He lay buried in the grave, but the hyenas did not touch him, and on the third day, he rose from the grave. He ascended to the skies. He is the Lord.
>
> We believe that all our sins are forgiven through him. All who have faith in him must be sorry for their sins, be baptized in the Holy Spirit of God, live the rules of love and share the bread together in love, to announce the good news to others until Jesus comes again. We are waiting for him. He is alive. He lives. This we believe. Amen.[19]

This creed displays how the translation of the Christian message need not remove Jesus from his Jewish identity ("a Jew by tribe"). Moreover, the creed is explicit about some issues that many other creeds are not explicit about (e.g., the roles of the Bible, God's love for the whole world, the healing ministry of Christ), while it does not include reflection on issues that are common in many other creeds (e.g., Jesus' return for the final judgment, the precise nature of Jesus' deity and humanity). The last two sentences of the first paragraph address issues present for a culture that has heard a new message, from a new source (the Bible): Is this a "different God" from the one our ancestors worshiped? Why should we pay attention to the God discovered through this book, the Bible? These are different questions from those posed at the Councils

---

19. Vincent Donovan, *Christianity Rediscovered* (Maryknoll, NY: Orbis, 2003), p. 158.

of Nicea or Constantinople. But they are crucial questions for the Masai in receiving the Christian message. The culturally conditioned interpretation of Scripture represented by a creed like this one is not simply the projection of long-standing cultural preunderstandings: it is the product of a wrestling with Scripture by the Masai people. In this wrestling and indigenization of the gospel, there are echoes of the Spirit's work at Pentecost of making God's word understandable to people of many tongues and cultures.

In summary, the indigenizing of the Christian message — tied to contextual readings of Scripture — is a work of the Spirit that we should celebrate. In terms of our norm stated at the outset ("scriptural interpretation from diverse contexts can be received as mutual enrichment, gifts of the Spirit") that indigenizing can be used by God to open new doors for the understanding of Scripture. Unlike the Enlightenment tendency embedded in some historical-critical approaches to see the cultural particularity of the reader as an obstacle to be overcome, cultural difference in scriptural interpretation can be a sign of the Spirit of Pentecost making the word of God penetrate the idiom, narratives, and practices of various cultures. The very act of translating the Bible into many languages implies the striking claim that Christianity is a religion of revelation "without a revealed language." There is no such thing as a noncontextual reading of Scripture, just as there is no such thing as an untranslated manifestation of Christianity. "The church anywhere and everywhere is situated . . . in a translated environment."[20]

Receiving Scripture as a Work of the Spirit's Critique of Culture and Ongoing Conversion of the Church

The Bounded Character of the Spirit's Work

All interpretation of Scripture is shaped by the context of the receiving culture. The Spirit indigenizes the Bible's message to be at home in all cultures and nationalities. Yet there is no culture that is beyond the need for the Spirit's converting work through Scripture. As a second-century author noted about the way Christians relate to culture, for

---

20. Sanneh, *Whose Religion?*, pp. 110-11.

Christians "every foreign land is to them as their native country, and every land of their birth as a land of strangers."[21] Christians are at home in all cultures — and in no culture. For Christians have an identity shaped by the Spirit's work in speaking God's word: "The word of God is living and active, sharper than any two-edged sword, piercing until it divides soul from spirit, joints from marrow" (Heb. 4:12). The Christian inhabitation of culture is always in need of surgery by the word of God. God's word does not simply inhabit cultures; it transforms them.

This transformation is not simply a human work, something that a particular exegetical method can produce through disciplined human effort. It is the work of the Spirit, even as God incorporates and includes human activities in the Spirit's work. Lesslie Newbigin says that if a culture encounters the gospel as God's revelation, "it will involve contradiction [of the culture], and call for conversion." This conversion, "which is the proper end toward which the communication of the gospel looks, can only be a work of God, a kind of miracle."[22] This should not surprise us: as I showed in chapter 1, our reading of Scripture is part of our continual transformation into the image of Christ. Yet this transformation involves both a death to our old self — a mortification of some of our cherished cultural wishes and conceptions — as well as a rising again in Christ. The Spirit animates both aspects of our reading of Scripture in union with Christ: mortification and vivification. The Spirit uses Scripture as an instrument in this process of dying, rising, healing, and restoration in Christ.

In terms of the church and Scripture, this means that the church does not "own" the Bible. The Bible is the Spirit's tool to constantly disrupt sinful cultural patterns, a process of both critique and healing that does not end. There is a subtle but powerful danger in considering Christian Scripture to be one religious sourcebook among others. Viewed anthropologically, one can explain religious phenomena by how texts such as the Vinaya Pitaka lead to certain practices among Buddhists, the Koran to practices among Muslims, the Old and New Testaments to practices among Christians. But if the story is left there,

---

21. *Epistle to Diognetus,* in *Ante-Nicene Fathers: The Writings of the Fathers Down to* A.D. *325,* ed. and trans. Alexander Roberts and James Donaldson (New York: Christian Literature, 1884), 1:26.

22. Lesslie Newbigin, *Foolishness to the Greeks: The Gospel and Western Culture* (Grand Rapids: Eerdmans, 1986), p. 6.

then we are left with a Deistic account of religion that is bereft of God's continuing action in history. For Christians, the Bible is not "our own book" in the sense that it simply legitimates and endorses our practices. It is a book used by the God who owns us, reshaping us into Christ's image.

Stated in terms of a biblical theology of the Spirit, the Spirit does not simply produce undifferentiated celebration of "difference" in biblical interpretation. Some hermeneutical difference is due to human idolatry and sin, a cultural resistance to Scripture's transforming work. In our day, it is especially tempting to equate the Spirit's work in indigenizing with a postmodern fascination with "the other." But in Scripture itself, the realm of the Spirit is a realm of discernment. As Paul wrote to the Corinthians, "We have received not the spirit of the world, but the Spirit that is from God," not "taught by human wisdom" but by the Spirit so that we can "interpret spiritual things." And this Spirit is not an ahistorical, free-floating sensibility, but one that reflects "the mind of Christ" (1 Cor. 2:14-16).

Indeed, various New Testament books go out of their way to delineate for us the very specific shape of life in the Spirit, showing that not all culturally embedded differences are from the Spirit. Paul gives great specificity to the "works of the flesh" in contrast to life in the Spirit. The works of the flesh and the Spirit are mutually opposed: the works of the flesh include "fornication, impurity, licentiousness, idolatry, sorcery, enmities, strife, jealousy, anger, quarrels, dissensions, factions, envy, drunkenness, carousing, and things like these"; in contrast, "the fruit of the Spirit is love, joy, peace, patience, kindness, generosity, faithfulness, gentleness, and self-control" (Gal. 5:16-26). Here Paul is extending a theme already present in the Old Testament, wherein life in the Spirit is connected with obedience to God's commands (e.g., in Ezek. 37:27, the Lord declares, "I will put my spirit within you, and make you follow my statutes and be careful to observe my ordinances"). It would be difficult to think of something more culturally shaped than a set of ethical admonitions and prohibitions. Yet that is precisely what the Pauline writings connect with the work of the Spirit. While Paul, the apostle to the gentiles, champions the idea that the Spirit has been given to peoples of all nations and customs, he retains quite specific ideas about which behaviors emerge from life in the Spirit and which ones do not.

The Synoptic Gospels present a similar portrait of ethical demands with regard to Jesus himself. Jesus offers a great deal of ethical teaching in these Gospels, teaching that is unafraid to get specific even on sticky matters related to God's law — such as wealth, divorce, and loving enemies. Repeatedly, Jesus warns those around him to put his teaching into practice (Matt. 7:15-27; Luke 6:43-49), and he warns that the kingdom will not be inherited by those with certain patterns of behavior (Matt. 25:31-46; 13:36-43). However one interprets passages like these in the Synoptic Gospels, it is clear that Jesus does not simply "celebrate difference" when it comes to different patterns of ethical behavior.

In addition to these culturally loaded ethical criteria, God's work in diverse peoples leads to a bounded diversity of theological confession in the New Testament. As I have noted above, within the book of Acts itself there is already a diversity of culturally informed perspectives on Jesus between Greek and Jewish circles, and this difference is attributed to the Spirit's work. But there are limits as well. Immediately before laying out the variety of gifts from the Spirit in 1 Corinthians 12, Paul flatly declares some broad boundaries: "No one speaking by the Spirit of God ever says, 'Let Jesus be cursed!' and no one can say 'Jesus is Lord' except by the Holy Spirit" (1 Cor. 12:3). In other words, the Spirit alone enables one to confess "Jesus is Lord" — a weighty confession in the New Testament context.[23] In 1 John, the "liar" is the one who "denies that Jesus is the Christ," the Messiah (1 John 2:22). This is a theological confession, but also one still tied to ethical practice, for "whoever says, 'I have come to know him [Jesus Christ],' but does not obey his commandments, is a liar, and in such a person the truth does not exist" (1 John 2:4).

From the earliest to the latest New Testament Epistles, there are warnings to early Christian congregations about false teaching, doctrine and practice that leads astray. Indeed, from a historical-sociological standpoint, "the letters of Paul owe their existence to the threat of heresy in his churches," and the composition of the Deutero-Pauline letters and the Synoptic Gospels continued to be shaped by early Christian debates about orthodox teaching and practice.[24] As Christians, we trust that God's Spirit was active in and through these de-

---

23. See Kittel, *Theological Dictionary of the NT,* 3: 1088-1094.

24. See Hans Dieter Betz, "Heresy and Orthodoxy in the New Testament," *The Anchor Bible Dictionary,* vol. 3 (New York: Doubleday, 1992), p. 145.

bates and in these documents. But in some ways, at the origin of the New Testament documents themselves is a conviction that some ways of understanding God's work in Jesus Christ are superior to others. A diversity of views of God and Jesus Christ exist in the New Testament, but it is a bounded diversity. Establishing those boundaries was a central impetus to the writing of the books that were received into the New Testament canon.

In a similar way, the Spirit's work in shaping the church through Scripture has a bounded and specified character. The Spirit does not shape churches to conform to one cultural form or ideal. Rather, the Spirit generates a bounded diversity as it conforms many peoples to the image of Jesus Christ. The "boundaries" of this diversity are ultimately constituted by Jesus Christ himself.[25] The living Christ has made himself one with all cultures and peoples, yet no culture can — or ever will — be a full reflection of Jesus Christ. Therefore, we must maintain a great paradox: the incarnate Word speaks through Scripture so that our faith can become our own, amidst all of our cultural particularity; yet the incarnate Word calls his disciples to a continuing conversion, wherein the Spirit uses Scripture to reshape God's people into Christ's image.

Discerning the Spirit, Part I: The Insufficiency of Direct Appeals to "Experience" as a Criterion for Discerning the Spirit's Work in Scripture

While nearly 80 percent of Americans profess to be Christians, fewer than 40 percent of them attend worship services weekly.[26] In the face of

25. To say that the positive content and the boundaries of the diversity of the Spirit's work is constituted by Jesus Christ is not to move away from the Trinitarian vision of revelation I examined in chap. 3. Rather, Jesus Christ is the one through whom humans enter into knowledge and communion with the triune God, by the power of the Spirit, the Son sent by the Father. This approach is christocentric and also Trinitarian. For an exposition of a similar approach in Thomas Aquinas's theology of revelation, see Matthew Levering, *Participatory Biblical Exegesis: A Theology of Biblical Interpretation* (Notre Dame, IN: University of Notre Dame Press, 2008), pp. 28-35.

26. According to a Pew study, 78.4 percent of Americans affiliate as Christians, while 39 percent of Americans attend religious services at least once a week. See Pew Forum on Religion and Public Life, *U.S. Religious Landscape Survey* (Washington, DC: Pew Research Center, 2008), pp. 5, 154.

so much nominal Christianity, American pastors, church leaders, and other religious professionals can frequently become obsessed with framing the gospel in a way that reflects and confirms the experience of the hearers. Like advertisers, church and parachurch groups begin to "repackage" the gospel in a way that makes it attractive to potential consumers. In this context, the goal of Scripture interpretation is to make it "relevant": that is, to take away the rough edges that may conflict with shared American experience and to make it appear useful for people who want a "value-added" life. God's word through Scripture functions to support preestablished goals: to be successful, comfortable, and healthy. The real criterion, then, for discerning a proper interpretation from an aberrant one is whether it functions to help religious consumers become successful, comfortable, and healthy. It doesn't take much time browsing the aisles of a Christian bookstore to discover that this is a mainstream approach to the use of Scripture in many American circles, not a small sideshow.[27]

Some advocates of an approach to biblical interpretation that places *relevance* as the central criterion claim that they are simply seeking to *contextualize* the message of the gospel. Broadly speaking, "contextualization" is a term used to speak about the process by which the gospel is communicated, received, and lived in the particularity of a specific cultural context.[28] As such, the indigenizing work of the Spirit may lead to a contextualization of the gospel and scriptural interpretation in a particular cultural context, as I have explored above. But does a concern to contextualize the gospel mean that any effort to make the gospel relevant to a culture's shared experience is a participation in the Spirit's work?

Ultimately, I think that the answer is "no." There are at least two reasons for this. First of all, if we see our scriptural interpretation as part of the work of the Spirit, then we must recognize the way the Spirit's specified work rooted in Christ involves a contradiction of the values present in all cultures, even broadly shared American values

27. For further analysis and theological reflection on this phenomenon, see Philip D. Kenneson and James L. Street, *Selling Out the Church: The Dangers of Church Marketing* (Nashville: Abingdon, 1997).

28. For a helpful overview of different approaches to the issues involved in contextualization, see R. Musasiwa, "Contextualization," in *Dictionary of Mission Theology* (Downers Grove, IL: InterVarsity, 2007), pp. 66-71.

such as being successful, comfortable, and healthy. While we may be eager to use the Bible in a way that relieves us of stress and helps lead us to financial security, the Spirit uses Scripture to bear witness to the cross-formed path of following Jesus Christ. In Matthew's Gospel, Jesus not only says, "Come to me, all you that are weary and are carrying heavy burdens"; he also says, "Take up your cross and follow me," losing your life for Christ's sake (Matt. 11:28, 16:24-25). The Spirit does speak words of comfort through Scripture; but it is not "comfort" as defined by upper- or middle-class American values. The Spirit offers comfort in testifying that we belong to Christ and are members of his body as we follow Christ's cross-formed path. But this kind of comfort, delivered by the Spirit, often subverts the "comfort" sought after by Americans. When our efforts to make Scripture relevant or contextual simply lead to reinforcing cherished cultural values, we are using it for purposes that conflict with the purpose of the Spirit.

The second reason that one does not necessarily participate in the Spirit's indigenizing work when attempting to make Scripture culturally relevant is this: proper contextualization does not involve simply conforming scriptural interpretation to shared cultural patterns of experience. In fact, experience itself is a rather muddy concept. I draw on the category of experience because it is often used as a category to justify a particular hermeneutic of Scripture. Supposedly, since we are Americans, we should apply Scripture to "American experience." We live in a culture that thinks it needs success, comfort, and health, so we should make the Scripture applicable to this experience.[29]

This claim is striking because it assumes that experience is something primal and fixed, so that Scripture must be adapted and conformed to the shape of the concerns and questions contained within "American experience." But we should challenge that assumption. On the one hand, there is something unavoidable about experience: we cannot put our experience on the shelf when we interpret Scripture, for experience is part of our cultural way of being in the world. An interpretation of Scripture unaffected by experience is just as much an impossibility as an interpretation unaffected by the reader's cultural context.

However, experiences — and religious experiences in particular —

---

29. See the critique of the "Centrality of Felt Needs" among church-growth experts such as George Barna, in Kenneson and Street, *Selling Out the Church*, pp. 71-79.

are not fixed or self-evident in their meaning. Experiences must always be interpreted, and they are frequently *re*-interpreted in light of our encounter with Scripture and Christian teaching. For example, consider the experiences discussed by Jesus in Matthew 7:21-23:

> "Not everyone who says to me, 'Lord, Lord,' will enter the kingdom of heaven, but only the one who does the will of my Father in heaven. On that day many will say to me, 'Lord, Lord, did we not prophesy in your name, and cast out demons in your name, and do many deeds of power in your name?' Then I will declare to them, 'I never knew you; go away from me, you evildoers.'"

There are few experiences in the Christian life that appear to have a more self-evident meaning than dramatic experiences of spiritual power — of prophecy, exorcism, and "deeds of power." But Jesus says something remarkable in this passage: even these vivid outward displays of service done in the name of Jesus are not necessarily true acts of discipleship. How could that be? The true disciple is "the one who does the will of my Father in heaven," and even vivid deeds of power may not be what they appear to be. They need to be interpreted in light of the words of Jesus and his criterion of obedience to the Father's will.

In this passage we can see that experience needs to be interpreted by a norm outside of itself. This theme is extended by Jonathan Edwards, who drew on Scripture for resources to interpret Christian experience in the first Great Awakening. Since experience itself does not have a self-evident meaning, one needs to look to the "fruit of the Spirit," particularly in acts of obedience, to discern where the Spirit has been active.[30] Whether or not we accept Edwards's own criterion for the Spirit's work, it is a helpful model in two ways: first, it takes seriously the experiential dimensions of the Christian life, that the gospel accessed through Scripture should engage our mind and heart, bearing fruit in our practical lives; second, Edwards affirms a criterion for discerning the Spirit's work that is external to our own experience, namely, a scriptural account of the Spirit and the fruits of the Spirit.

The example of Edwards shows that using Scripture as a criterion for the Spirit's work need not involve ignoring our experience, but we

---

30. Edwards, "A Treatise Concerning Religious Affections," Part 3.

129

must understand that our experience needs to be transformed under the lordship of Christ. On a conceptual level, one of the reasons we tend to use experience as a fixed criterion for interpreting Scripture is because we fail to see how culturally contingent our own experiences are. We must apply Scripture to the typical experiences, or "values," of the readers. However, as theologian George Lindbeck has argued in *The Nature of Doctrine,* our experiences themselves are not primal and fixed. "The relation of religion and experience . . . is not unilateral, but dialectical."[31] Religion is not about finding external forms that express the "inner experience" of persons, such as religious expressions or "relevant" sermons. Rather, religious experience itself is shaped and interpreted in light of the sermons we hear, the Scripture we read, the community in which we are involved. We should not search Scripture to find what is compatible to a fixed internal need of experience. We should recognize that "religion is above all an external word" that "molds and shapes the self and its world." Thus, according to Lindbeck, the Christian message accessed through Scripture should not be seen as an expression of our experience but a reorientation of our experience, such that we learn "the story of Jesus and Israel well enough to interpret and experience [ourselves] and [our] world in its terms" (p. 34). We should not let experience dictate how we receive Scripture so much as allow Scripture to reshape how we experience the world.

In light of Lindbeck's account, we can see how our experience need not be a straitjacket for Scripture, but Scripture can be the Spirit's tool to transform even our interpretation of our experiences. Scriptural interpretation *should* be relevant in a certain sense: it should address the hearers, holding forth the word of the living Christ that calls hearers to continual conversion. But this kind of relevance does not seek to conform the message to a fixed set of experiences; rather, it requires the Spirit to reshape our experiences and how we interpret them.

The question of whether to assume a "fixed" theory of experience penetrates many decisions related to biblical interpretation in Christian ministry. When the church youth group is choosing curriculum, they have many options that target what is supposedly the "experience of American youth": sex, dating, drugs, and peer pressure. While these

31. George Lindbeck, *The Nature of Doctrine: Religion and Theology in a Postliberal Age* (Philadelphia: Westminster Press, 1984), p. 33.

are important issues to address openly, if our youth Bible studies give the impression that the Bible has little to offer besides advice on sex, dating, and peer pressure, then we have failed to trust in the Spirit's power to use Scripture to reframe youthful experiences in light of Christ. When a Memorial Day worship service makes allegiance to Jesus Christ subordinate to allegiance to the United States and its flag, we have failed to enter into the Spirit's transforming work through Scripture that forms us, first and foremost, into citizens of Christ's kingdom. There is nothing fixed about the experience of Christians in whatever cultural context they find themselves; so we need to participate in the Spirit's work of transforming our experience through Scripture.

In the approach I am advocating, a willingness to destabilize a fixed notion of experience in spiritual discernment requires a trust in the Spirit's work to bring a redemptive, healing word through Scripture. This is not compatible with some critical approaches, which involve using a set of experiences as the final standard in discerning liberating biblical texts from "toxic" ones.[32] Indeed, for some critics, the very idea that Scripture can be the instrument of revelation is simply a covert ideological maneuver by one person to gain power over another. "The insistence on the Bible as the Word of God," says Itumeleng Mosala, "must be seen for what it is: an ideological maneuver whereby ruling-class interests evident in the Bible are converted into a faith that transcends social, political, racial, sexual, and economic divisions," thus veiling its true ideological nature of imposing control over others.[33]

The Bible has been and continues to be misused for oppressive ends. But unless we are to exchange one form of cultural captivity for

32. For example, in a move that contrasts with a more nuanced account of experience among many other feminist theologians, some scholars make a particular rendering of women's liberating experience a fixed standard for grounding the need for an "exorcism" of "oppressive" texts in the Bible. Rosemary Radford Ruether recommends a "liturgy" for groups to cast the "demons" out of the biblical texts that Ruether deems oppressive. After casting out the "demons" from numerous biblical texts, a participant in the rite says, "These texts and all oppressive texts have lost their power over our lives. We no longer need to apologize for them or try to interpret them as words of truth, but we cast out their oppressive messages as expressions of evil and justifications of evil." Rosemary Radford Ruether, *Women — Church: Theology and Practice of Feminist Liturgical Communities* (San Francisco: Harper & Row, 1985), pp. 136-37.

33. Itumeleng Mosala, as quoted in the Bible and Culture Collective, *The Postmodern Bible* (New Haven: Yale University Press, 1995), p. 283.

another, we are called to a place of vulnerability in trusting the Spirit's transforming work through Scripture, even as we are vigilant in exposing the cultural idols that distort the Spirit's witness through Scripture. We are called to read with a hermeneutics of receptive trust, even as we use suspicion toward sinful interpreters (see the third section on "spiritual discernment" below).[34] A transformative encounter with Scripture allows experience itself to be reshaped through the Spirit's work in the reading of Scripture, even as our particular context continues to inform this transformation each step of the way.[35]

Discerning the Spirit, Part II: The Guidance Provided by the Spirit's Work in Community for Discerning the Spirit's Bounded Work in Scriptural Interpretation

If we are to be guided by the Spirit in discerning faithful interpretations of Scripture from unfaithful ones, how are we to discern the Spirit's work? When we look to Scripture itself to learn of the Spirit's work, we see several things that relate to the issue of discernment in scriptural interpretation: 1) The Spirit works to bind together believers into a community held together in oneness rooted in Jesus Christ, and through Christ given "access in one Spirit to the Father" (Eph. 2:17). 2) The Spirit brings fruit manifested in community and witness. "Love, joy, peace, patience, kindness, generosity, faithfulness, gentleness, and self-control" are all characteristic of life by the Spirit (Gal. 5:22-23). 3) As a covenant community, the church is in the sphere of the Spirit's spe-

---

34. For an excellent account of the importance of combining a hermeneutics of trust (that calls into question our experience) with a hermeneutics of suspicion, see Richard Hays, "A Hermeneutics of Trust," in *The Company of Preachers,* ed. Richard Lischer (Grand Rapids: Eerdmans, 2002), pp. 265-74. As Hays points out, "many practitioners of the hermeneutics of suspicion . . . are remarkably credulous about the claims of experience. As a result, they endlessly critique the biblical texts but rarely get around to hearing Scripture's critique of us or hearing its message of grace" (p. 267).

35. For a fascinating study of the transformative use of Scripture in African-American communities, see Vincent L. Wimbush, ed., *African Americans and the Bible: Sacred Texts and Social Textures* (New York: Continuum, 2000). For a review essay that highlights the role of experience and transformation in this book, see Wesley A. Kort, "African Americans Reading Scripture: Freeing/Revealing/Creating," *Christianity and Literature* 51, no. 2 (Winter 2002): 263-73.

cial influence, having moved from being "aliens" and "strangers to the covenants of promise" to being a people joined together into "a holy temple in the Lord," "built together in the Spirit into a dwelling place for God" (Eph. 2:12, 21-22).[36] 4) The Spirit bears witness to Jesus Christ: the teachings, commands, and confession of Jesus Christ (John 14:23-26; 16:12-15; 1 Cor. 12:3).

Through all of these works of the Spirit, we see how God uses the Christian community of the church as a part of the discernment process of hearing what the Spirit speaks through Scripture. Yet the Spirit is not the possession of the church; rather, it is the transcendent God who bears witness to God's Word made manifest in Jesus Christ. The Spirit's work through time and in various cultures provides guidance for scriptural interpretation; nevertheless, the church itself is not the final standard for the interpretation of Scripture. The Spirit retains the freedom to speak afresh through Scripture as the final standard for Christian conduct and belief.

On this point, we are required to hold together two sides of a paradox: on the one hand, the Spirit's work is connected to the life and history of the church catholic, and the church must be part of the discernment process; on the other hand, as a community of sinners still awaiting the final consummation of redemption, the church should not be the final standard for scriptural interpretation in a way that arrogates itself above Scripture.

Since modernity, Protestants in particular have been weak on the point of discerning the Spirit's work in and through the church throughout its history and across cultures. In the sixteenth and seventeenth centuries, Protestants such as the Lutherans and Reformed saw themselves self-consciously as "catholic." This was not just an ecclesiastical statement but a statement about the Spirit: they saw themselves in continuity with the early ecumenical councils and creeds of the church, assuming that the Spirit was active in leading the church "into all truth" through these decisions. Even though the Nicene Creed was written well over a thousand years before the Reformation, these Protestants still saw it as a legitimate, catholic standard for them. Why? Because it contained a deposit of the Spirit's work, a standard by which

---

36. I have opted for the alternate translation of the NRSV of "in the Spirit" over "spiritually" for an English rendering of Eph. 2:22.

the universal church could discern a faithful interpretation of Scripture from an aberrant one. For both Roman Catholics and most Protestants in the sixteenth and seventeenth centuries, the creeds and teachings of the ancient church were standards of discerning the Spirit even though they emerged from cultural and historical circumstances that were vastly different from their own. Instead of assuming that these cultural differences made attention to the ancient church irrelevant, a trust in the Spirit's work in the Christian community through time made them draw upon ancient creeds, councils, and teachings as a check and balance for their own time.

This point is an extension of the case I made in chapter 2 for connecting the work of the Spirit with the church's tradition. But associating the Spirit with the tradition of the church may strike some readers as counterintuitive, if not wholly implausible. Isn't the Spirit always doing a "new work"? Shouldn't we see the Spirit at work in spontaneity and new ideas rather than in tradition?

This is a legitimate point. The Spirit always calls the church beyond itself, to its identity as God's new creation. But it is false to assume that this fresh calling of the Spirit is contrary to affirming the Spirit's work in the Christian community of the past. If we are to believe God's promise through Scripture to send the Spirit to the church to lead her into all truth, to bind together the church as Christ's body, to give her gifts and bear fruit through the Spirit's power — then we should expect to see the Spirit's work in past Christian communities. In Enlightenment-influenced Christianity, interpretation of Scripture is frequently seen as the task of the individual; thus is the Spirit like an ethereal little voice in the head speaking to the individual. But that is not how Scripture portrays the Spirit's work. The Spirit forms believers into a community that has its own checks and balances, both in a given local church and across time and cultures. The community of the Spirit is the church both living and dead, the church of cultural multiplicity held together in oneness in Jesus Christ.

For example, consider the possibility that an adult education teacher in your church claims that Jesus, as the firstborn of all creation (Col. 1:15), is our model for how to submit to God the Father, who alone is the supreme authority. This teacher encourages members of the congregation to set their eyes on the Father, who possesses God's glory and power, for becoming Christlike is simply a means for knowing how to submit our will to the Father.[37] The teacher says that the Spirit has instructed him that this teaching is true, and he points to various New Testament passages to support his position.

There are several ways in which a more communal (and biblical) view of the Spirit can help in the spiritual discernment of this situation. First, the teacher can be confronted by other members of the congregation as a check and balance on the Spirit's communal work. As the congregation goes to Scripture together, other members can point to the scriptural insufficiency of this view. This very process of communal discernment of the Spirit's word through Scripture counteracts the individualistic approach of the teacher. In addition, members of the congregation can point out the ways in which the Spirit's work in the church's past has implications for this discernment: the teacher's position clearly conflicts with the Nicene Creed's affirmation that the Son is of "one essence with the Father," to be "worshiped and glorified" together with the Father and the Spirit. This creed is, again, the result of a debate over Scripture interpretation. But it also provides guidance about the Spirit's work in the past among interpreters of Scripture.

Since the Spirit speaks freely through Scripture, however, and is not strictly constrained by the church's past interpretation, the marshaling of evidence from the tradition does not necessarily close the issue on discerning what the Spirit is saying through Scripture. Yet, if our theology of the Spirit is to be biblical, the teacher above needs to show how his interpretation reflects biblical teaching and points to the teaching, commands, and confession of Jesus as Lord. The discussion of the Spirit's work in history and in other cultures can be a way to deepen and enrich the exploration of what Scripture itself teaches. The church can provide guidance and checks and balances for spiritual discernment in scriptural interpretation, even if it cannot arrogate to itself the role of being the final standard for scriptural interpretation.

---

37. Lest this kind of reasoning seem unlikely, it expresses the basic position of best-selling Christian diet author Gwen Shambling. Traditional Trinitarian doctrine is construed as insufficient in leading Christians to the self-denial necessary for the Christian life (and weight loss). See Jody Veenker, "The Weight is Narrow," *Christianity Today* (Sept. 1, 2000): http://www.ctlibrary.com/ct/2000/septemberweb-only/53.0a.html.

Discerning the Spirit, Part III: The Constructive Role of Suspicion Toward One's Own Cultural Captivities Combined with Trust in the Spirit's Transforming Power through Scripture

As Christians interpreting Scripture, we should exegete not only Scripture but our own culture, the culture that provides the lens through which we receive Scripture. This is not a secular or nontheological task; rather, it is a part of the theological process of discerning the Spirit's work. No culture is without the need for spiritual discernment for how it receives God's word through Scripture. For within all cultures are not only "secular parables" that may unwittingly testify to the truth that is in Jesus Christ, but also cultural idols that distort and domesticate the gospel of Jesus Christ.[38]

Is it really necessary to "read," or exegete, one's own culture?[39] Many Christians who approach the Bible pride themselves in focusing exclusively on exegeting the biblical text itself. In some sense, this emphasis is exactly right: it puts the focus on the text, which confronts our false and insufficient preconceptions about Scripture. But this idea has its problems, too. Many issues related to biblical interpretation arise from what exegetical possibilities are apparent to the receiving culture, yet these exegetical possibilities are formed and received in culturally specific ways. Without analysis of our cultural tendencies in receiving Scripture, we can be blinded to the ways in which we hold the Bible culturally captive to our own interests.

For example, imagine that you were attending a church service of a white church in the American South shortly before the Civil War. If the subject of abolition were to come up, the pastor might quote certain Scripture verses suggesting that slavery is an institution that God supports — and therefore one that we should support as well. Yet, if you were in a church in the American North, Scripture verses might be quoted suggesting that God abhors slavery, that it is a sinful human institution that needs to be abolished. In one church service the impera-

38. For more on the notion of "secular parables," see chapter 3 above.

39. In an essay that makes the case for the Christian obligation to exegete the culture and one that also gives some helpful guidelines, Kevin Vanhoozer argues that to be Christians who make a "mark on culture rather than simply submit to culture programming," one needs to be able to "read culture." Vanhoozer, *Everyday Theology: How to Read Cultural Texts and Interpret Trends* (Grand Rapids: Baker Academic, 2007), p. 55.

tive drawn from Scripture would involve the support of slavery, in the other the abolition of slavery. What would it mean to be a believer trying to be obedient to God in these two congregations?

Examples like this one display how obedience to God through Scripture is much deeper than having a good intention to obey Scripture. On the level of intention, both those Christians who obeyed the imperative of the Northern pastor *and* those following the interpretation of the Southern pastor could be considered obedient in that they both intended to obey Scripture. However, now that we have some cultural and historical distance from that moment, many (including me) would claim that even a sincere act of obedience to a proslavery interpretation of Scripture would be distorted, serving a cultural idol rather than God. Sincerely obeying Scripture in a way that endorses slavery is not made right by good intentions. The Bible became culturally captive to the idols of Americans who sought to maintain race-based slavery and segregation.[40]

Since all cultures have idols resistant to God's transforming work through Scripture, how are we to discern them? Cultural exegesis is notoriously difficult. Culture is like the water that fish swim in: it's just "the way things are," the lens through which we see the world. Because of this, one of the most effective ways of coming to know one's own culture is to encounter another culture. We don't realize that we have been swimming in a stream until we encounter a pond or an ocean! This cross-cultural encounter provides both illumination and criticism of how one receives the Bible in one's own culture.

As I came to know various Christians in Uganda and Ethiopia, I noticed how they received the Bible differently than did my home culture. For example, the narratives of Christ's healings and exorcisms were very significant to those Christians: they appropriated the stories as a daily help in an area with few doctors, frequent struggles to provide for the body's basic needs, and numerous encounters with people struggling with spiritual powers. As I compared their response to these Gospel narratives to the reception they received in my home church in America, I realized that these narratives are often ignored or translated into a disembodied realm of souls, in which "healing" becomes a metaphor for

---

40. For a thoughtful historical exploration of the debates about biblical interpretation and slavery in the nineteenth century, see Mark Noll, *The Civil War as a Theological Crisis* (Chapel Hill, NC: University of North Carolina Press, 2006).

new psychological resolve or the deliverance of the soul to heaven. Passages about healing were being truncated as they were read in my Western context, which assumes a great separation between spiritual and material realities. This encounter with East African Christianity exposed some assumptions about my own scriptural exegesis that I did not know I had. Even more, it became possible to "see" the cultural idols that were resisting God's transforming work through these Scripture passages. I did not just have a transformation of the will; I had a transformation of sight, and I could sense how the Spirit could use passages in the Gospels to critique and reform deep-seated cultural priorities.

While there is particular value for Western Christians in encountering the exegesis of non-Western Christians (and vice versa), the differences in culture within Western Christianity itself can be powerful in exposing the cultural captivity of the gospel. In a class discussion in America on the troubling narrative of Hagar in Genesis, one middle-class white student said that she could not imagine her church discussing this disturbing narrative of suffering and isolation, which does not seem to receive full resolution in the Genesis text. In contrast, an African-American student said that biblical stories like this one were frequently discussed in her urban black church: that is, troubling, ambiguous suffering was a central theme in many church services in her congregation. To some extent, this difference may be one of contextualization: the differences in how the gospel is received amid differences in culture, ethnicity, race and class, urban vs. suburban, and so on. But I also sensed that this Hagar text had exposed a cultural idol in the first student's white, middle-class, suburban congregation. Church services are supposed to be encouraging, sanitized from the struggle with ambiguous suffering and injustice that is a dynamic in the biblical narrative itself. This sanitizing represents a blind spot that functions as a sinful resistance to the Spirit's transforming power through Scripture.

What all of these approaches have in common is that we hear Scripture as part of the "communion of the saints," a Spirit-formed community that spans the globe and spans time.[41] The Spirit transforms God's

41. In addition to encountering the cultural difference in interpretations of Scripture based on geography, class, ethnicity, and gender, one of the most powerful forms of culture critique comes through encountering different receptions of Scripture through time. Encountering the history of interpretation while interpreting Scripture brings up its own set of issues, and I will explore these issues in some depth in the next chapter.

people through Scripture, and some of how this gets done is through the illumination and criticism that comes through cross-cultural encounters with other readers of Scripture. In addition, various historical and sociological tools of analysis can help to "read the culture" for interpreters of Scripture as well. In order to understand the issues and challenges in the reception of Scripture in Ethiopia, I not only developed relationships with people in that culture, but also pursued the academic study of Ethiopian history and culture. Sometimes we think we can skip those steps with our home culture. But that simply reinforces the cultural myth that one's own reception of Scripture is ahistorical and beyond the particularity of cultural blinders.

One recent study provides an example of the value of sociological analysis in exposing the cultural idols that shape the reception of Scripture. As I noted briefly in chapter 1, in their book *Soul Searching,* Christian Smith and Melinda Lundquist Denton studied the religious beliefs of American teenagers from a wide variety of religious traditions, geographical and social locations, and ethnicities. Smith and Denton report the explicit theologies expressed through the in-depth interviews, but they also sought to describe the implicit or operative theologies. In terms of operative theologies, Smith and Denton speak of "Moralistic Therapeutic Deism" (MTD) as a widespread belief system underlying the faith of a wide variety of religious teens. They summarize these beliefs in this way:

1. A God exists who created and orders the world and watches over human life on earth.
2. God wants people to be good, nice, and fair to each other, as taught in the Bible and by most world religions.
3. The central goal of life is to be happy and to feel good about oneself.
4. God does not need to be particularly involved in one's life except when God is needed to resolve a problem.
5. Good people go to heaven when they die.[42]

Notice that there is no mention of sin, the need for a mediator with God, Jesus Christ, or the Holy Spirit. Apparently, as long as we are gen-

---

42. Christian Smith and Melinda Lundquist Denton, *Soul Searching: The Religious Lives of American Teenagers* (New York: Oxford University Press, 2005), pp. 162-63.

erally "good, nice, and fair to each other," we will be okay with God, and reconciliation through Jesus Christ is unnecessary. Moreover, we do not need the Spirit's power to be good; we just go to God when we have a particular problem that needs resolution. At the center is the conviction that we should be happy and feel good about ourselves — and the assumption that God consents to this center.

It is crucial to recognize that this MTD creed is not on the level of consciously recognized theology. These teens would not say, "I am a moralistic therapeutic Deist." Yet when they were asked to talk about their faith and its meaning in their lives, these are the common themes that arose. They rarely mentioned Jesus Christ, the Holy Spirit, or the Bible. At times, a church-going teen would be asked, "What do you believe about Jesus?" Silence. The same teen who could talk eloquently about sexually transmitted diseases was stunned into silence when asked about Jesus Christ.

As Smith and Denton point out, MTD is not limited to American teen culture, for American teens have, to a large extent, absorbed the operative theologies of the adults around them. As a cultural phenomenon, it becomes the lens through which religion is perceived, and as such it brings certain things into focus and shakes others out of focus. This is particularly important in the interpretation of Scripture. The functional creed of MTD distorts how Scripture is heard. Being aware of how it is heard is crucial for someone seeking to communicate biblical teaching. Here is a list of examples of biblical exposition in a church youth group context, and "how it is heard" with an MTD-operative theology.

Biblical Exposition:	*What People Hear:*
In baptism, people are united to the death and resurrection of Christ so that they are "dead to sin and alive to God in Christ Jesus" (Rom. 6:1-11).	People should be baptized and try hard to be good people, like Jesus was a good person.
God is our rock, our sole deliverer and strength, so we should live lives of dependence on and gratitude to God (Ps. 18:1-6).	God is our rock, so that we can go to God in those [rare] difficult times when we have trouble getting by on our own.

Jesus Christ is the way, the truth, and the life — the way to the Father (John 14:6).	God wants us to be happy, so he sent Jesus to forgive our sins and provide entrance to heaven.
While we were still sinners, Christ died for us, showing God's love (Rom. 5:6-11).	Jesus died on the cross so that we can get forgiveness from God after we do things that are wrong.

In my own work in youth ministry, I have seen the benefits of asking youths to lead worship and interpret Scripture. It is usually a faith-building experience for the youths, and it can be a reality check for the leaders as they themselves learn how their interpretation of Scripture is being heard. If we listen closely, we can often hear the Bible's message being squeezed into conformity with the cultural idols of self-reliance and self-gratification contained in the MTD creed. Sociological analysis of the kind that exposes the operative theology of MTD can help us understand how to engage Scripture in a way that challenges these latent idolatries.

In summary, we encounter the cultural limits of our own horizon most clearly when we interact with interpreters from diverse social, cultural, and historical locations, as well as when we engage in historical and sociological analysis of our own culture. Receiving the Bible as Scripture involves exegesis of the text as well as exegesis of one's own culture of reception.

Spiritual Discernment in Summary:
The Call to Read Scripture as the Church —
Under and Yet Empowered by the Spirit's Word via Scripture

We have explored a number of dimensions of the process of discerning the Spirit as we read Scripture as Christians. Faithful readers are open to being reshaped by the Spirit through Scripture, refusing to set their own experience as a fixed standard by which to judge Scripture. We should approach Scripture with attentiveness to the other voices in the Christian community, both past and present. In this we are attentive to the Spirit's work in and through the traditions of the church. Faithful readers also apply a hermeneutic of suspicion toward their own culture's reception of Scripture, combined with a trust in the transforming power of the Spirit through Scripture. A common thread through all of these dimensions of spiritual discernment is a double-sided reality: first, the proper location for interpreting Scripture is the church, in the richest communal and historical sense of the term "church"; second, even though the proper interpretive location is the church, ecclesiastical readers are still sinners, and thus we must be attentive to our own tendency to use our own experience or cultural idols to attempt to block the Spirit's external, healing word through Scripture. Scripture should be interpreted from a self-consciously ecclesiastical place, yet the church finds its life by living *under* the Spirit's word through Scripture, not alongside or over it.

I use the image of living under the Spirit's word through Scripture to be clear about the relative authority of the church and tradition with respect to the Spirit's word via Scripture. Scripture should function as the final theological authority in relationship to the church and tradition, because Scripture is the Spirit's chosen instrument for speaking God's transforming word in Christ to the church. Jesus Christ is the Lord of the church, and Scripture is the Spirit's instrument to exercise that lordship. That does not mean that the Spirit is absent from the mutual accountability of the fellowship of the church, its creedal traditions, human experience, or culture. Indeed, we should not seek to interpret Scripture in a way that abstracts ourselves from tradition, creeds, experience, or culture. That would be a dangerous illusion, and it would also be an attempt to shut ourselves off from the Spirit's work in all these realms.

However, the sum total of what the Spirit speaks via Scripture is not simply a compilation of tradition, creeds, experience, and culture. If that were the case, then God's word would have become completely immanent: the Spirit would be mute apart from what we as readers bring to Scripture. Instead, we should remember that Scripture is the Spirit's instrument to communicate an external word that mediates the fellowship and saving work of the triune God. The church finds its life *within* this triune fellowship, but it does not find its life over or above it.[43]

43. It is in this context that the notion of Scripture as "self-interpreting" is properly understood. Though this notion that Scripture is "self-interpreting" and "clear" is often criticized as naïve, it is better thought of as a way to understand the priority of God's word

Thus, while it is correct to say that the church lives *under* the Spirit's word via Scripture, it is also valid to say that the church finds her life *within* the Spirit's work via Scripture — in the triune economy of salvation. The Spirit speaks an external word via Scripture, but it is not one that is over us in a coercive way; instead, it is a life-giving word that breathes life into what was dead. The church should approach Scripture expecting to submit to the Spirit's word, but also to be empowered and transformed by this word.

Extended Exegetical Example

As this chapter has explored, all receptions of the Bible as Scripture are culturally conditioned receptions. On the one hand, the Spirit works to indigenize scriptural reception in diverse contexts, giving gifts to the church in and through culturally shaped differences in biblical interpretation. On the other hand, Scripture is never fully "received" by any culture. Scripture interpretation participates in the Spirit's eschatologically conditioned work of uniting God's people to the death and resurrection of Christ. Readers of Scripture participate in the Spirit's work, but they are still sinners whose sin needs to be overcome through union with the death of Christ. Indeed, readers of Scripture are masters of sinful self-deception; for, as the prophet Jeremiah says, "The heart is devious above all else; it is perverse — who can understand it?" (Jer. 17:9) As a result, reading Scripture involves a balance of trust in the Spirit and the Spirit's work via Scripture, with a suspicion about how Christians have used Scripture in self-serving and oppressive ways. This suspicion of sinful interpreters (like ourselves) is part of the

---

by way of Scripture standing over the reader and all that the reader brings to the text. As John Webster says, "Scripture is self-interpreting and perspicuous by virtue of its relation to God; its clarity is inherent, not made, whether by magisterial authorities, the scholar-prince or the pious reader." Webster, *Holy Scripture*, p. 93. This self-interpreting clarity is not a formal property of the biblical text; rather, "Scripture is clear because through the Spirit the text serves God's self-presentation. Properly speaking, it is not Scripture which is self-interpreting, but *God* who as Word interprets himself through the Spirit's work." Webster, *Holy Scripture*, p. 94. In the triune economy of salvation, readers of Scripture enter into the Spirit's work — which is God's own "self-interpreting" of God's incarnate Word. The Spirit does not need our advice or input to speak God's Word.

process of putting to death the sinful old self and rising with Christ by the Spirit's power.

Let's consider an example from Christian ministry that displays some of the sinful distortions that can come into the interpretation of Scripture, yet shows how readers can nonetheless seek to enter into the Spirit's transforming work through Scripture. While living in a rural part of Uganda, I was the only Westerner in a Christian Ugandan community development group, located in an area that was 20 percent Christian and 80 percent Muslim. My Ugandan co-workers shared a common story about how the gospel had been shared with their people about one hundred years earlier. They were grateful for Western missionaries who had come to share the Christian message, and they appreciated having the Bible in their own language. But one of the significant things that the missionaries had emphasized to them was the teaching of Jesus from Luke's Gospel: "Blessed are you who are poor, for yours is the kingdom of God" (Luke 6:20). The indigenous people who heard this proclamation were living in subsistence-level poverty: the infant mortality rate was at about 50 percent, and they experienced many other debilitating effects of poverty.

My Ugandan colleagues in ministry considered this use of the Bible to be a culturally captive misuse of Scripture of the highest order. Regardless of the original motive, this use of Scripture put the poor on a spiritual pedestal. My Ugandan colleagues told me that this use of Scripture led to the following response: Ugandan Christians became apathetic about opportunities in agricultural and economic development. Since poverty was thought to be blessed by God, local Christians tried to be poorer than the next person in order to show their holiness. Passivity became a spiritual virtue, even as family members died of preventable diseases and people neglected opportunities for education. As the story goes, while the Muslims in the community rightly responded to opportunities to escape poverty, the Christian missionary had given the Christians spiritual incentives for staying in the bondage of extreme poverty. My Ugandan colleagues had good reason to have suspicions about this use of Scripture. They felt that, ultimately, this act of interpretation reinforced the difference in power between the missionary and his hearers, and that it led to deleterious results. But they combined a suspicion about the misuse of Scripture with a trust in the Spirit's power to speak a life-giving word via Scripture.

My Ugandan colleagues argued that the blessing of the poor in Luke 6:20, interpreted in its canonical context, was not glorifying abject poverty. They supplemented this passage with the Matthew 5:3 blessing of the "poor in spirit," not setting the verses off against each other but seeing both as complementary words spoken by God's Spirit. They had no doubt that God hears the cries of the poor, and that God loves the poor; but they were convinced that discipleship was not about becoming economically poorer and poorer, but growing in wholeness in Jesus Christ. They read Matthew 5:3 alongside the many petitions for life rather than death and destruction in the Psalms. They were careful to avoid simply reversing the missionary's imperative, which would say that riches are a measure of one's holiness. Instead, they revisited the notion of discipleship to clarify what it meant to be a disciple of Jesus Christ. The way of Jesus is not about poverty and suffering for its own sake, but about carrying the cross in following Jesus.

While my Ugandan colleagues had suspicions about the misuse of Scripture, their trust that the Spirit speaks via Scripture enabled them to overcome an interpretation with debilitating effects. It is precisely because Luke 6:20 is the word of God that it could not mean a glorification of dehumanizing poverty. Canonically speaking, God is a God who brings life, forgiveness, and healing, not the bondage of poverty. My Ugandan friends did suspect that there was something self-serving about the way the missionaries had taught Luke 6:20. But in their view, the problem was not with the text itself, or the fact that the missionaries said the Bible was the word of God. The problem was that the missionaries' interests took Luke 6:20 culturally captive and simultaneously tore it from the life-giving canonical context of Scripture. Affirming the Christian canon for my Ugandan colleagues was not simply a matter of intellectual assent; it was a deep trust in a spiritual reality that God speaks through Scripture as his special instrument, and that trust was nurtured in their own lives of worship, prayer, and proclamation.

As they interpreted Luke 6:20 canonically, they contextualized the passage in a way that showed the indigenizing work of the Spirit; but they also raised questions about spiritual discernment. God gives a special blessing to the poor, but God does not sanction poverty. Therefore, my co-workers looked for indigenous ways to escape poverty, while they also called into question some cherished cultural values. They sought to have positive relationships with their Muslim neighbors for the com-

145

mon good. They worked to bring a rice-huller to the community to provide higher income for local farmers; they also introduced rabbit farms to add protein to the local diet. Furthermore, they strongly advocated education for both boys and girls, believing that education could help give them more economic opportunities, as well as help to raise up articulate leaders to advocate for this impoverished area — both in Uganda's government and on the international stage. In some sense, all of these actions mobilized indigenous resources to move the community from passivity to activity. In some ways these actions were a Spirit-empowered performance of Scripture, a performance holding together God's care for the poor with God's salvation as one of life. But even these actions were not simply "indigenous"; they also challenged the cultural norms. They were in the realm of spiritual discernment.

On a number of occasions, the community-development group came into tension with the values and experiences of their fellow Ugandans. My colleagues asked hard questions when a family would decide to stop sending their daughter or son to school so that they could build a large memorial for another child, who had died. They called into question certain cultural norms that said it was "useless" to send girls to school. They became advocates of establishing new businesses in the area, even if it meant changing the traditional crops for farmers. They did all of this with a rationale from their scriptural interpretation of God's caring for the poor — but also wanting to free people from poverty.

In this situation, as in an American environment, one cannot simply interpret Scripture "once for all" and move ahead with one's plans. One must return to Scripture again and again. My Ugandan colleagues experienced the Spirit's work in coming to interpret Scripture in a way that was indigenous to their cultural situation. Yet this indigenous interpretation is not unrevisable: when it slips into a glorification of wealth, or it simply justifies the Westernizing of the economy, then this indigenous vision needs to be reshaped through the Spirit's voice via Scripture. In a similar way, while the Christian faith of many Americans has become indigenized in a way that connects to their social and economic life, the process of the Spirit's transformation through Scripture is not finished. When Scripture is used to flatly justify the systems of capitalism and the presence of great economic inequality in America, we need to return to Scripture to hear the Spirit's transforming word once again.

Conclusion

Just as it is impossible to interpret the Bible without theological assumptions being operative, a context-free interpretation of Scripture is an illusion. As we have explored, all scriptural interpretation is shaped by the context of the receiving culture. Yet this need not lead to relativistic conclusions that silence dialogue between various biblical interpreters. On the contrary, I have argued that Scripture itself claims that a bounded diversity in scriptural interpretation is the work of the Spirit, with the Spirit leading culturally diverse believers into the expansive yet bounded truth that is in Christ. Engagement with diverse contexts of scriptural interpretation not only gives us access to the indigenizing work of the Spirit; it can also be a tool of the Spirit to lead us to further transformation. We can receive gifts from a wide variety of cultural locations as we expose ourselves to the Spirit's indigenizing and transforming work in cultures that have both differences and commonalities with our own.

Given the diverse work of the Spirit in indigenizing the interpretation of Scripture, and in calling all cultures to transformation through Scripture, we face a situation of spiritual discernment. In scriptural interpretation, how does one discern the indigenizing or transforming work of the Spirit from cultural idolatry? While there is no easy answer to this question, this chapter has explored some dynamics of discernment. In the interpretation of Scripture, experience should not be hardened into something that acts as a judge over Scripture; but it should be open to being reshaped by the Spirit in our encounter with Scripture. In terms of positive resources, we can look to the work of the Spirit in the traditions of the church for guidance, and we can enter into a theological exegesis of our own cultural location, seeking to expose cultural blind spots and norms that seek to domesticate God's word. In the end, however, the final authority in the discernment of the Spirit is found in Scripture itself. Since Jesus Christ is the Lord of the church and Scripture is God's chosen means for holding forth Christ by the Spirit, no authority should supersede Scripture in the task of discerning the word of God that bears witness to Christ.

As Christians, we should not approach the subject of the contextual interpretation of Scripture with fear or despair, but with joy and wonder at the amazing work the Spirit has done through the ages and still does today. The Spirit has been bringing an indigenizing yet transforming word to extraordinarily diverse cultural contexts through Scripture. The Spirit continues to call all Christians to a life that is found in Jesus Christ, and continues to call for deeper transformation through the power of God's life-giving word.

For Further Reading

Lamin Sanneh, *Disciples of All Nations: Pillars of World Christianity* (Oxford: Oxford University Press, 2008); Lamin Sanneh, *Whose Religion Is Christianity? The Gospel Beyond the West* (Grand Rapids: Eerdmans, 2003).

> *These works by the Gambian-born professor of history and world Christianity at Yale Divinity School probe the biblical, historical, and theological implications of the gospel's spread through a great multiplicity of cultures around the world.*

Christian Smith and Melinda Lundquist Denton, *Soul Searching: The Religious Lives of American Teenagers* (New York: Oxford University Press, 2005).

> *This penetrating analysis of the religious lives of American teens has value in diagnosing the broadly held cultural idols that squeeze Scripture into a moralistic, therapeutic, Deistic mold.*

Lesslie Newbigin, *Foolishness to the Greeks: The Gospel and Western Culture* (Grand Rapids: Eerdmans, 1986).

> *Newbigin was one of the most significant theologians of culture in twentieth-century Christianity, and this book probes the ways in which the Christian gospel encounters Western culture in particular.*

Andrew F. Walls, *The Missionary Movement in Christian History: Studies in Transmission of Faith* (Maryknoll, NY: Orbis, 1996).

> *This book by a leading historian of Christian mission presents a constructive proposal for thinking through the relationship of Christianity to culture along with incisive historical analysis of how these dynamics have been at work in Christian history.*

Philip Jenkins, *The New Faces of Christianity* (Oxford: Oxford University Press, 2006).

> *Jenkins gives a topically oriented overview of how the Bible is read in the global South. It is particularly helpful in giving concrete examples of the ways in which the cultural context of Christians in the Two-Thirds World leads to understandings of Scripture that differ, in many ways, from those of Christians in the West.*

CHAPTER 5

Treasures in Jars of Clay

The Value of Premodern
Biblical Interpretation

I N THIS CHAPTER I explore the value of premodern (ancient, medieval, and Reformational) approaches to Scripture with two goals in mind. First, I seek to show how contemporary Christians need to rediscover and embrace some key premodern insights about how to approach the Bible as Scripture. As Wesley Kort writes, "At one time people knew what it meant to read a text as Scripture, but we no longer do, because this way of reading has . . . been dislocated and obscured."[1] While some aspects of modernity are to be valued, modernity must be critiqued for the ways in which its own cultural idols seek to squeeze God's word into its mold. Amid the great variety in premodern interpretations, there are nonetheless several key shared convictions about how Scripture functions within God's economy of salvation.

Second, I advocate a very particular practice for contemporary interpreters of Scripture: to supplement their reading of modern commentaries by reading patristic, medieval, and Reformational commentaries, sermons, and treatises that interpret Scripture. This practice draws on the great variety of premodern exegesis as a rich and varied feast, a renewal of the imagination to show the many ways in which God's word can function as a word that conforms believers to Christ's image by the Spirit's power. Premodern interpretation is not free-

---

1. Wesley Kort, *Take, Read: Scripture, Textuality, and Cultural Practice* (University Park, PA: Pennsylvania State University Press, 1996), p. 1.

wheeling or relativistic. It has distinct limits because proper interpretation must nurture growth in Christian discipleship, and premodern interpreters seek to be painstakingly faithful to the word of God in the whole counsel of Scripture. But Scripture is also filled with stories, law, and poetry that may not seem edifying at first glance. How could a Psalm that curses one's enemies be the word of the same God who speaks through Christ to love one's enemies? How can the Bible's narratives of rape and conquest help one grow as a disciple of Christ? In the particularity of its varied answers, the history of premodern biblical interpretation is a treasure for Christians, though it is one we must receive with discernment. Premodern interpreters of Scripture are, like us, simply "clay jars" holding forth the "treasure" of the gospel. "For we do not proclaim ourselves; we proclaim Jesus Christ as Lord" (2 Cor. 4:5-7). The value — and the limits — of premodern interpretation depend on the extent to which Jesus Christ shines in and through these frail vessels.

SINCE ENGAGING premodern interpreters may seem like a strange idea to some readers, and a new prospect for many others, I begin this chapter by addressing a common objection to reading premodern interpreters, and then I will move through a series of reflections to explore how and why premodern interpreters approach Scripture as they do. Each section begins with a series of objections and questions. First, the objection: Isn't premodern interpretation "esoteric and irrelevant" to the contemporary situation? Second, we move on to explore some basic theological features undergirding much premodern exegesis, specifically: What view of history and salvation do premodern exegetes share? Third, we explore the rationale for one of their exegetical practices: Why do premodern exegetes give spiritual readings of the Old Testament? Next, developing greater specificity in our consideration of giving spiritual readings to the Old Testament, we consider this question: How do premodern exegetes understand the different "senses" of Scripture? Finally, having surveyed key features of the theological rationale and exegetical practice of premodern interpreters, we return to a basic question: Why does premodern exegesis matter for the contemporary interpretation of Scripture? In each section, I hope to show the need to rediscover premodern interpretation, both in recovering its basic instincts toward the Bible as Scripture (the first goal mentioned above) and in appropriating its insights into particular biblical texts in a discerning manner (the second goal).

Esoteric and Irrelevant? Difference and Commonality in the Retrieval of Premodern Interpretation

If the idea of reading very old commentaries on Scripture is new to you, it may seem counterintuitive. Aren't we supposed to interpret the Bible as God's word for *today?* Don't congregations crave to see the ways in which the Bible is up to date and still relevant for their lives? If so, why would one read old commentators? They were part of a different culture, a different time in history, and they did not have the advantage of recent archaeological and textual discoveries. Haven't old commentators become obsolete? When Christians are aching for the word of God made relevant for today, isn't it an irresponsible, esoteric act to devote our attention to patristic, medieval, and Reformational interpretations of Scripture?

Several levels of response can be given to these questions. On the one hand, this objection betrays a tendency toward what C. S. Lewis calls "chronological snobbery," namely, "the uncritical acceptance of the intellectual climate common to our own age and the assumption that whatever has gone out of date is on that account discredited."[2] Unfortunately, the assumption that older is inferior can actually be a way to protect our own cultural idols. While we can read interpretations of Scripture from around the world and from different cultural groups today, we frequently still hold in common with these other interpreters certain assumptions from our shared experience of phenomena such as globalization, urbanization, and many other aspects of modernity. There is a distinct value in reading Christian authors who were *not* shaped by these modern forces: they show us new insights while they expose our own modern biases and idolatries as well.

Yet there is also something right about the "esoteric and irrelevant" objection: it points to a genuine theological concern for reading the Bible as God's word for us today. Ironically, that is precisely why

---

2. C. S. Lewis, *Surprised by Joy: The Shape of My Early Life* (Orlando, FL: Harcourt Brace, 1955), p. 201.

premodern biblical interpretation is relevant in our contemporary context. Let me explain.

Modern critical biblical commentaries tend to be primarily concerned with questions related to what John Webster calls the "natural history" of the biblical text: its authorship, textual history of redaction, and other aspects necessary for reconstructing the author's meaning in its original context. But these critical methods, in themselves, do not address the question of how this text is the word of God for today. While critical methods are truly necessary and can yield valuable results (see chapter 2), a Christian interpretation of Scripture cannot be content with simply rehearsing the natural history of the text. Christians must consider how this text, as Scripture, is an instrument of God's powerful word.[3] This question of how the whole of the Bible — even its difficult passages — can be God's word for the church was central for premodern commentators. Indeed, if one's goal is to teach or preach Scripture as God's word, modern critical commentaries may be more likely to be esoteric than premodern commentators are.

Consider the following example to clarify how this can be true. Imagine that you are in a small-group Bible study on the book of Genesis, and you are considering Genesis 12:1 as part of the calling of Abram: "Now the Lord said to Abram, 'Go from your country and your kindred and your father's house to the land that I will show you.'" Reflecting on the radical nature of this call, the study guide directs the group to discuss ways in which God has called them as Christians to leave behind their country and family in following Jesus. In the process, it quotes the words of Jesus in Luke's Gospel: "Whoever comes to me and does not hate father and mother, wife and children, brothers and sisters, yes, and even life itself, cannot be my disciple" (Luke 14:26). The group discusses what it means to follow Jesus above all other allegiances. Several comment that God is not directly calling them to leave their family, but that the faith and loyalty that God calls for is to rank above even allegiance to country and family. The discussion is both about the call of Abram and about the call to follow Jesus.

3. As John B. Webster argues, "The problem . . . is not the affirmation that the biblical texts have a 'natural history,' but the denial that texts with a 'natural history' may function within the communicative divine economy, and that such a function is ontologically definitive of the text." Webster, *Holy Scripture: A Dogmatic Sketch* (Cambridge, UK: Cambridge University Press, 2003), p. 19.

Whether or not you are satisfied with this interpretation of Genesis 12:1, consider a basic question: Is it plausible to see a small-group Bible study reading this way in today's world? I believe that it is, that Bible studies, sermons, and Sunday school lessons give such readings of Genesis very frequently — and in a great variety of cultural settings. Such a reading is not esoteric; rather, it is relevant: it applies to one's life in Christ and how one follows the radical call of Christ on a daily basis. But this approach has a great deal in common with premodern interpretations of passages such as this one. In fact, the general reading of Genesis 12:1 that I used in the above example was adapted from the interpretation of Didymus the Blind, a fourth-century teacher and monk.[4]

Both Didymus and the contemporary small group of my example are giving a "spiritual" reading of Scripture — reading an Old Testament text in light of Jesus Christ — one that is, by definition, rejected by the conventions of historical-critical scholarship, which limit a text's meaning to what was possible in its original context. In this practice, Didymus and the small group are in broad agreement with most of the history of the church's reception of Scripture. As Robert Louis Wilken says, "For most of the Church's history (the early Church, the Church during medieval times, and the Reformation era) the Old Testament was a book about Christ and the Church."[5] On this point, the intuitions of many Christian laypeople coincide with those of the historic church.

Ironically, the seminary training of pastors and teachers has been a major force in dislodging this approach of reading all of Scripture in light of Jesus Christ within the context of the Christian life. I recall the reaction of one of my fellow seminarians after seeing the implications of his newly adopted theory — that the Old Testament can mean only what the author intended in its original context. "Laypeople in my church interpret the Bible all wrong," he said. "They give meaning to the text that was never there!"

On this point, I sense that my fellow seminarian would benefit by becoming a student of Didymus the Blind and other premodern exegetes, as well as of the laypeople in his congregation. He is right to see

4. Mark Sheridan, ed., *Genesis 12–50,* Ancient Christian Commentary (Downers Grove, IL: InterVarsity, 2002), p. 2.

5. Robert Wilken, "Interpreting the Old Testament," series preface to Richard A. Norris, ed., *The Song of Songs,* The Church's Bible (Grand Rapids: Eerdmans, 2003), p. x.

that new insights about Scripture can come from historical-critical studies of the Old Testament. But "new" should not be equated with "better," for there is also deep theological wisdom in the premodern and lay intuitions of readers who read the Old Testament as a book that is ultimately about Jesus Christ. Many pastors and teachers learn this lesson the hard way: preaching and teaching based exclusively on reading the Old Testament in "its original context" strikes most lay Christians as esoteric rather than relevant, since it does not relate directly to their present lives in Christ. In many ways, modern approaches to the Bible are frequently more obscure than are premodern approaches.

So far I have emphasized how premodern interpretations of Scripture have commonalities with the use of the Bible among many Christians today. However, there are also significant differences, and I will explore many of those differences in the sections below. Even the commonality between premodern commentators and lay readers of the Bible today needs to be qualified. Although my Genesis 12:1 example shows crucial assumptions shared by early and present-day Christian readers about the entire Bible being God's word about Christ and the church, there are also strong counterforces in contemporary lay readings of Scripture. As I noted in chapter 1, it is common for contemporary Christians to see the Bible not as a book about Jesus Christ, but a "divine answer book" on what to eat to lose weight, how to be a successful leader, or how to be financially secure. Not all lay readings of Scripture exemplify the best intuitions of premodern interpretation; indeed, many do not. Contemporary Christians are likely to find premodern exegesis "at once strange, and yet strangely familiar."[6]

Probably the single greatest difference between premodern exegetes and most Christian exegetes today is one of habit: most premodern interpreters of Scripture saw the reading of their predecessors as a key part of the task of biblical interpretation. Even in the early centuries of Christianity, church leaders began to appeal to "the fathers" in their interpretation of Scripture. In the medieval period, Bibles were given an apparatus similar to today's study Bible, but with the interpretations of Christians of earlier centuries in the margins. In the Reformation and post-Reformation eras — indeed, up to the eighteenth century

---

6. Richard A. Muller and John L. Thompson, eds., *Biblical Interpretation in the Era of the Reformation* (Grand Rapids: Eerdmans, 1996), p. 344.

— both Protestants and Roman Catholics commonly gave concerted attention to the scriptural interpretation of the church fathers and certain medieval theologians.

Today, however, the vast majority of commentaries available to pastors give little or no attention to the church's exegesis of Scripture before the eighteenth century. English-translation projects such as The Church's Bible (Eerdmans) and the Ancient Christian Commentary on Scripture (InterVarsity) are seeking to remedy this situation. But it is worth noting that the library — and reading habits — of the modern pastor and teacher are very different from those of many premodern teachers of Scripture. Most premodern interpreters, whether Protestant, Roman Catholic, or Orthodox, shared a conviction that one should read Scripture in light of the Holy Spirit's work in the community of faith through history — in light of earlier interpreters of Scripture. They expected to disagree at times with these earlier interpretations; indeed, the early interpretations often disagree with each other. But the core conviction remains that one should read the Bible together with the saints that have come before.

What View of History and Salvation
Do Premodern Exegetes Share?

Before digging into the nuts and bolts of premodern approaches to Scripture, I should address some basic questions that inform all of their scriptural exegesis. First, in reading Scripture, should human history be understood *autonomously,* on its own terms apart from occasional divine interruptions, or does human history participate in the work of *God's provident action* within history itself? Second, are readers of Scripture ultimately seeking the *meaning(s)* of a text, or are they seeking to participate in God the Teacher by being *united to Jesus Christ* by the power of the Spirit?[7] The first question probes the nature of a Christian understanding of history and providence; the second question addresses the goal of scriptural interpretation itself in light of the realities Christians encounter in salvation.

---

7. See Matthew Levering, *Participatory Biblical Exegesis: A Theology of Biblical Interpretation* (Notre Dame, IN: University of Notre Dame Press, 2008), pp. 67, 79-80.

The question of history and providence is deceptively simple. The best of both premodern and modern exegetes seek to have a historical exegesis of Scripture; however, what they mean by "history" often differs. For many contemporary interpreters, historical exegesis of Scripture means correlating Scripture with the scholarly reconstruction of history outside of the text. For instance, modern scholarship on Joshua has sought to determine whether and in what way the historical people of Israel entered the land of Canaan. This task involves drawing on archaeological and other data about the ancient Near East to seek to explain the origin of the Joshua texts that speak about the conquest. Some conservative scholars have tended to defend the historical accuracy of the book of Joshua's account, while more liberal scholars have suggested that the conquest never happened, or that it happened in a way that differs greatly from the biblical Joshua's account. Yet both sets of scholars agree that the text, x, has an accessible, external history as its referent, y.[8]

But what if both sides of the modern scholarly debate were misguided? What if the ultimate referent of the biblical text (y) were not fully accessible through historical reconstruction? There are at least two ways that this alternative possibility could be understood. One is that the referent of biblical texts is a distinct realm of "theological ideas." Accordingly, the narrative of conquest has nothing to do with history, but it is simply the expression of religious and theological ideas. The conquest of Canaan could then be understood as a text that teaches the sovereignty of God and his faithfulness to the covenant, completely apart from the history of Israel. The act of faith in reading Scripture, then, would be to assent to this *theological* idea within the text.

But there is another possibility that retains an important place for the linear flow of history through time, yet still does not see Scripture's referent as one confined to a history "behind the texts," that is, accessible only through historical methods. Both modern scholarly approaches to Joshua introduced above seek to verify or question the truth of Scripture through historical reconstruction. The second option withdraws scriptural interpretation from history to the realm of ideas.

---

8. In this analysis and the following section I am indebted to John O'Keefe and R. R. Reno, *Sanctified Vision: An Introduction to Early Christian Interpretation of the Bible* (Baltimore: Johns Hopkins University Press, 2005), pp. 9-13.

But as Roman Catholic theologian Henri de Lubac has argued in his magisterial work on medieval exegesis, premodern exegesis, like that of medieval Christians, takes history much more seriously than that.[9]

In de Lubac's portrait of history, the incarnation is the supreme historical event that gives meaning to history. The incarnation of the Word in Jesus Christ is not merely an idea toward which Scripture points; the incarnation is supremely a historical reality, the key to the meaning of history itself. Thus, when premodern interpreters read Scripture in light of Christ, it actually is a *historical* reading because the incarnation is the definitive moment in history, the "prodigious new fact of Christ."[10] The history of God's historical action narrated in the Old Testament takes on meaning that would have been inaccessible to the human writers. What was thought to be history apart from Christ is shown to be what it really is, a "shadow" waiting fulfillment in Christ.[11] However, since Scripture points to Jesus Christ as its proper and final end, it is pointing to a mystery that will not be exhausted this side of the *eschaton.* Therefore, a historical reading of Scripture is necessarily an eschatological one as well, for the church reads Scripture in light of its own union with Christ, which has not yet reached its fulfillment.[12]

De Lubac's response to the question of historical interpretation may strike us as puzzling; we may think that he is perhaps speaking in a mistaken category. The question is about the role of history, but he has framed his answer about history largely in terms of Christian doctrine. To the modern mind, these are separate realities, ones that should stay apart even if they are correlated in terms of providing historical evidence to validate Scripture — or a particular theological position. But history and doctrine are interpenetrating realities for de Lubac. To assume that the linear flow of history, accessible only through ordinary historical methods, is the proper view of history is to functionally deny the (historical) reality of the incarnation: God and humanity have been united in the person of Jesus Christ, who shows the true origin and end of human history.

9. Henri de Lubac, *Medieval Exegesis,* 2 vols., trans. E. M. Macierowski (Grand Rapids: Eerdmans, 1998).

10. De Lubac, *Medieval Exegesis,* 1: xii.

11. Cf. Heb. 8:1-7; de Lubac, *Medieval Exegesis,* 2: 82.

12. See Susan Wood, *Spiritual Exegesis and the Church in the Theology of Henri de Lubac* (Grand Rapids: Eerdmans, 1998), pp. 44-45.

As I have noted above, most premodern interpreters understood the Old Testament to be a book about Christ and the church. Does this mean that the history of Israel in the Old Testament is necessarily eclipsed? No. Ultimately, to claim that the Old Testament is about Christ and the church means that the story of God's history of Israel does not stand on its own, but that it is illuminated by Jesus Christ, the key to history, and the church's (eschatologically conditioned) union with this same Christ. In the best instances of this union's practice, Abram, Joshua, and Esther do not disappear, to be replaced with Christ in premodern interpretation. Instead, they are understood in light of history's culmination in the Alpha and Omega, the true human being — Jesus Christ. When the risen Jesus "opened the minds" of his companions on the Emmaus road "to understand the Scriptures," he did not suggest that the "law of Moses, the prophets, and the Psalms" have been displaced; rather, they have been "fulfilled" in himself (Luke 24:44-45).

Matthew Levering, in the tradition of de Lubac, speaks about this christologically informed account of history, in his book *Participatory Biblical Exegesis,* as the "participatory" dimension of history. He argues that the linear flow of history "participates" in God's own providential work; thus is it more than it appears to be on its own. God himself has entered the internal life of history in Jesus Christ. History does not exist in an "immanent" realm, sealed off from God except for the occasional external intrusion. In the incarnation we do not see the divine and human agency in competition; rather, it is the way God works within history that finds its ultimate fulfillment in Jesus Christ. Creatures "cannot be fully understood by attending solely to their linear historicity," and there is no such thing as an "original context" of a biblical narrative that is strictly linear, functioning outside the way it participates in God's acts (Levering, p. 12). If the incarnation is a historical reality as Christians believe, then history itself — including the history "behind" the biblical texts — is caught up in a drama fulfilled in Jesus Christ.

Levering does not champion the participatory dimensions of history in order to exclude or denigrate historical approaches that focus on the messy human flow of linear history. Rather, the two are held together in Christ, such that "the participatory indwells the linear" (p. 14). Therefore, the history of Israel from which the Old Testament writings emerge should be an object of study. But ultimately, when it comes to scriptural interpretation, historical methods cannot serve as an autonomous means of verifying or denying the reality of the scriptural text. Instead, history and doctrine are held together as complementary, interpenetrating ways of accessing the realities held forth in Scripture (p. 15). For example, when we consider reading the conquest narrative in the book of Joshua, we should not simply understand the text in the light of a reconstruction of a sequence of historical events behind the text. The history of Israel also participates in the providential acts of God; thus do the doctrinal categories of providence, covenant, law, and ultimately the fulfillment of God's promises in Jesus Christ all supplement our understanding of the Israelite conquest narrated in Joshua.

The first question about history above leads quite naturally to the second question about God's saving purposes in the use of Scripture. Just as human history is illuminated by God's action within history that culminated in the incarnation, so also the restoration and fulfillment of creation's purpose leads us to this same Christ. Are readers of Scripture ultimately seeking the meaning(s) of a text, or are they seeking to participate in God the teacher by being united to Jesus Christ by the power of the Spirit? Premodern readers paid meticulous attention to what the texts of Scripture do and do not say. But they paid attention in this way because they saw the reading of Scripture as part of a larger process of transformation: being remade into Christ's image by the power of the Spirit.

I spelled out the general features of this christological-pneumatological function of Scripture in the opening chapters, where I was already drawing on the shared wisdom of premodern interpreters of Scripture. But there are two additional dimensions that premodern voices add to this theme, and they can help us understand their approach to biblical exegesis: first, the centrality of a Trinitarian soteriology (theological teaching on salvation) of participation, and second, the sense in which scriptural interpretation participates in God's own teaching by participating in the teacher, Jesus Christ. Because we do not read Scripture as a blank slate, but in trust that God is healing, restoring, and saving us in the process of reading Scripture, it is important for us to consider what *kind* of salvation we envision is being enacted. If salvation is simply "getting into heaven," then we will read Scripture with an eye toward what does and does not relate to getting into heaven. If salvation is simply a process of learning how to become more ethical and just, then we will read Scripture in a way that seeks out what is ethical and just. But many premodern interpreters had an operative theology of salvation that was much richer and more complex than either of these, namely, a Trinitarian soteriology of participation.

Trinitarian soteriologies of participation developed in their fullness during the fourth century, amid the Trinitarian disputes. Augustine and the Cappadocian Fathers both have theologies in which human beings are redeemed by participating in God through belonging to Jesus Christ, by the Spirit's power. Often these are called theologies of "deification" (or *theosis,* in Athanasius's famous formulation): the divine Word "became human, so that we may become divine."[13] When pressed, patristic authors would quickly clarify that the second part of the statement is somewhat hyperbolic: that is, humans do not become "God" in the sense of becoming assimilated to the divine. Rather, as Athanasius clarifies his position, he believes that there is only one Son of God by nature; others receive the name of sons and daughters of God by grace.[14] Creator and creature remain distinct. Nevertheless, there is a striking symmetry between God's descent to humanity and humanity's ascent to God, united to Christ, by the Spirit.

Although these soteriologies of participation were developed in the fourth century — and continue to be developed in the Eastern and Western theological traditions — they draw deeply on the language of the New Testament and the early church. One of the central images of salvation in the New Testament is union with Christ by the Spirit. Union with and participation *(koinonia)* in Christ is connected to baptism, the Lord's Supper, the forgiveness of sins, the giving of the Holy Spirit, and the new life in Christ that will continue via participation in Christ's resurrection, which was the "first fruits" of the age to come. Central to this image is the fundamentally Trinitarian one of adoption: as those who are united to Christ, we are able to cry out to God as "Abba, Father," by the power of the Spirit, who inhabits the prayers of Christians and bears fruit for those in Christ (Rom. 8:14-17, 26-27). The image of adoption is closely related to that of grafting branches into the vine, a covenantal

13. Athanasius, *Contra Gentes and De Incarnatione,* trans. Robert W. Thompson (Oxford: Clarendon Press, 1971), p. 268.

14. On this point, see Norman Russell, *The Doctrine of Deification in the Greek Patristic Period* (Oxford: Oxford University Press, 2004), pp. 169-71. Russell's book gives an excellent overview of theologies of deification among Greek patristic authors.

image for the incorporation of the gentiles into the covenant promises given to Israel (Rom. 11:13-24).

Union and adoption also relate to the key image of discipleship in the Gospels, as believers are not simply united to Christ in a mystical way by the Spirit, but are also called to do what Jesus commands of his followers. Salvation, in this theology of participation, entails participation in Christ by the Spirit, being incorporated into Christ's body, the church, and living out an adopted identity as God's children, who grow in love of God and neighbor through participation in God through Christ.[15]

Because of their rich biblical roots and wide-ranging theological implications, Trinitarian theologies of participation were significant soteriologies in all the main premodern strains — Orthodox, Catholic, and Protestant.[16] These soteriologies declined in modernity, and scholars have different accounts of why this decline took place.[17] At the very least, the decline is characterized by the following: a tendency to view the origin and destiny of humanity in autonomy from christological concerns, a suspicion of the doctrine of the Trinity and the inherent metaphysics in such a doctrine, and an increasing separation between biblical studies and Christian doctrine.

How does all of this relate to how we as the church read the Bible? If one interprets Scripture with an operative soteriology of participation, the location of scriptural interpretation is distinct: we interpret Scripture as the mystical body of Christ — the church — a people who find true life by participating more and more in Jesus Christ through the Spirit. Thus scriptural interpretation and doctrinal theology cannot be

15. For an overview of the wide-ranging New Testament language on union with Christ, see Lewis B. Smedes, *Union with Christ: A Biblical View of the New Life in Jesus Christ*, 2nd ed. (Grand Rapids: Eerdmans, 1983).

16. For an account of the Trinitarian soteriology of participation in the work of John Calvin, see Todd Billings, *Calvin, Participation, and the Gift: The Activity of Believers in Union with Christ* (New York: Oxford University Press, 2007). On Thomas Aquinas and Gregory Palamas, see A. N. Williams, *The Ground of Union: Deification in Aquinas and Palamas* (New York: Oxford University Press, 1999). For a broad overview of theologies of deification in the Christian tradition, see Michael J. Christensen and Jeffery A. Wittung, eds., *Partakers of the Divine Nature* (Madison, NJ: Fairleigh Dickinson University Press, 2007).

17. One common account blames the development of fourteenth-century nominalism for this decline, but genealogies on this point remain contentious. For an examination of further literature on this point, see Levering, *Participatory Biblical Exegesis*, pp. 3-4, 151-52.

set off against one another. The Spirit, as the primary author of Scripture, speaks through Scripture to conform us deeper into our identity as Christ's body, conforming us to the head, Jesus Christ. This transformation involves a movement from passivity and sin to active love of God and neighbor, by the Spirit's power. Therefore, the teaching of Scripture is not a set of abstract principles to be applied in our theology. The teaching of Scripture is God's teaching, teaching that we are missing if we are not moving ever deeper into participating in Christ by the Spirit.

As Levering says, in summarizing and extending Augustine's thought, "God teaches us in Christ, who brings to a radical fulfillment God's teaching in Israel. Christ is the true Teacher. Yet, Christ, as well as the Trinity and all realities of our salvation, must be taught to us in human words; and this is the task of Scripture" (p. 67). Thus, to look to the Old Testament and try to forget our knowledge of the New Testament's fulfillment in Christ is to move away from the teacher within Scripture itself. To be content with the "author's intended meaning" as the end to our reading of Scripture is to fail to perceive the church's own identity (as Christ's bride, growing in union with Christ), and the purpose of reading Scripture (participation in Christ by the Spirit). To read Scripture with an eye only for a cognitive meaning is to miss the end toward which we read Scripture at all: "To read Scripture properly means to encounter God's teaching and to have one's love reordered" (p. 69). The Bible is not a book of systematic theology or a collection of propositions about God. Nevertheless, when viewed with the eyes of those united to the living Christ, there is a sense in which all of Scripture becomes teaching (or "doctrine"), that is, dynamic, transformative instruction that moves those in Christ deeper into the reality of their adoptive identities as children of the Father, filled with the Spirit. As long as our study of the Bible and our theology are sharply separated, our Bible study can become an end in itself, not leading us to encounter the realities of which Scripture speaks: life in Christ, in the Spirit, as adopted children of God.

Why Do Premodern Exegetes Give Spiritual Readings of the Old Testament?

Why do premodern exegetes, in giving their spiritual readings of the Old Testament, understand the Old Testament not simply as the narrative of God's history with Israel but a book about Christ and those united to Christ (the church)? In general, there is both a biblical reason and a theological reason (which is also rooted in the Bible) for this widespread trend that finds its key exemplars in the patristic period. First, early Christians followed the pattern of "spiritually" interpreting the Old Testament that they found in the New Testament itself. Second, for early Christians, the practice of spiritual reading is not based on a peculiar hermeneutical theory about texts and interpretation, but on a particular set of theological convictions — articulated in the New Testament — about the identity of Jesus Christ.

What is a *spiritual* reading of the Old Testament? In the most basic sense, a spiritual reading is one that goes beyond the literal sense of the text. As a general phenomenon, it took place in a variety of religious contexts. For example, Philo (20 BCE-50 CE) gives an allegorical reading of the Hebrew Bible. However, seeing Christian spiritual readings as no more than a subset of a larger religious phenomena can be misleading. Christian spiritual readings of the Old Testament are distinctive in that they are directed toward Jesus Christ, and they assume the particular theological context of reading the Old Testament as those who are united to the living Christ.

We can see the distinctively Christian pattern of reading the Old Testament spiritually from the earliest New Testament documents. In 1 Corinthians, for example, Paul writes that "our ancestors" the Israelites were led "through the sea" into the desert. Why? In order to eat manna and drink water from a rock, as the Old Testament says? No, not simply that, says Paul, for "all ate the same spiritual food and all drank the same spiritual drink. For they drank from the spiritual rock that followed them, and the rock was Christ" (1 Cor. 10:3-4). Paul does not claim that the writer of Exodus secretly knew that Christ was the rock. But, in light of the living Christ, Paul is claiming, we see that it was Christ himself providing spiritual nourishment for the old covenant and new covenant alike. These things happened as "examples" (*typikōs,* or "types") and were "written down to instruct us" (10:11). As Paul articulates in 2 Corinthians, knowledge of the old covenant is "veiled" until "in Christ" the veil is set aside (3:14). Christ provides illumination of the old covenant because Christ himself is the fulfillment of all of God's covenant promises. "For in him every one of God's promises is a 'Yes'" (2 Cor. 1:20).

163

Many other New Testament passages use the Old Testament in a similar way. God's deliverance of Noah's family from the flood is said to "prefigure" God's salvation via union with Christ and his resurrection in baptism (1 Pet. 3:21-22). Typological reasoning is key in the Epistle to the Hebrews, which makes extensive use of the Old Testament, articulating the continuities and discontinuities of the old and new covenants in light of Christ's fulfillment of the old.[18] Hebrews begins with seven citations of Old Testament texts from divergent contexts (from the Psalms, Deuteronomy, and 2 Samuel), applying them all to Christ. How could this be coherent? Not because of quirky hermeneutics, but because of who Jesus Christ himself is in God's economy of salvation. "Long ago God spoke to our ancestors in many and various ways by the prophets, but in these last days he has spoken to us by a Son, whom he appointed heir of all things, through whom he also created the worlds. He is the reflection of God's glory and the exact imprint of God's very being" (Heb. 1:1-2). The Son was the fulfillment of such divergent Old Testament passages because, even though "our ancestors" did not realize it in their day, the Son is the Creator who is also the "heir of all things" and has been made known in history in Jesus Christ.

The New Testament also introduces a second word in describing a spiritual reading of the Old Testament: allegory. In speaking about Hagar and Sarah, Paul writes: "Now this is an allegory: these women are two covenants" (Gal. 4:24). In Paul's use of the Old Testament, there is an allegorical meaning — made possible through Christ — that was inaccessible before. Robert Wilken summarizes Paul's logic in Galatians 4:21-31: "Sarah and Hagar are not simply the names of the wives of Abraham; they also signify two covenants, one associated with Sinai and the other with the Jerusalem above."[19] We will return to this allegory in Galatians and nuance the notion of allegory later in this chapter; but we should note at this point that Paul explicitly names a certain sense of allegory in his use of the Old Testament.

Why do the New Testament writers use the Old Testament in ways that extend far beyond any "intended meaning" of the Old Testament's human authors? Were ancient readers naïve about the meaning and

---

18. On typological reasoning in Hebrews, see William L. Lane, *Hebrews 1–8,* Word Biblical Commentary, 47A (Dallas: Word, Incorporated, 2002), pp. cxxiii-cxxiv.

19. Wilken, "Interpreting the Old Testament," xii.

function of texts? Ultimately, the answers to these questions are not strictly hermeneutical, but christological. We will explore how this is the case by looking at the function of prophecy in the New Testament and then looking at some key biblical and patristic convictions about the identity of Jesus Christ.

How does the Old Testament point to Jesus Christ? Think of your own experience of Old Testament passages being used to testify to Christ in worship services. Quite likely, these passages have references to a Messiah, or a "suffering servant" interpreted in Messianic terms. These are crucial passages for Christians to connect with Jesus Christ, but sometimes we may be left with the impression that only particular Old Testament passages apply to Christ — such as those referring to a messiah — while others do not. This is what I call a connect-the-dots approach to prophecy and fulfillment. Particular points (or dots) in the Old Testament witness have a messianic scope, and those are then connected to the dot in Jesus' life. The suffering of the suffering servant (Isa. 53:3-12) is connected with the cross of Christ. The birth prophesied in Isaiah 7:14 is connected to Christ's birth from Mary (Luke 1:26-35).

These prophetic connections are important and legitimate ones to make. But here is the problem: the New Testament does not restrict itself to a connect-the-dots logic when applying the Old Testament to Christ. Instead, there is a sense in which the whole Old Testament — including its varied genres of law, poetry, and historical narrative — becomes a book of prophecy about Christ. Rather than connecting the dots, the entirety of the Old Testament comes to be applied to the person of Christ.

For example, when Hebrews 1:5-13 applies verses from the Psalms, Deuteronomy, and 2 Samuel directly to Jesus Christ, none of these references fits with a connect-the-dots approach. None of these works is in the genre of prophecy. None of them speaks about a messiah or a particular foreshadowed event in Christ's life. But these varied passages, in their distinct ways, speak about the Son of the Father, one who is worshiped by the angels, and exalted at God's right hand; thus, according to Hebrews, all of these verses speak about the identity of Jesus Christ.

As I noted in chapter 1, Irenaeus, in the second century, develops a term that is helpful for understanding this New Testament reasoning about Christ: recapitulation. In Jesus Christ there is a recapitulation (or replay) of the history of salvation. In the New Testament, Jesus Christ embodies Israel — and through Israel, the rest of humanity. But as the second Adam and the perfect covenant partner, he does not make the same mistakes as sinful humanity. Jesus Christ is the true covenant partner. "Do not think that I have come to abolish the law or the prophets; I have come not to abolish but to fulfill" (Matt. 5:17). Jesus Christ is the true priest, as Hebrews testifies, the true mediator between God and humanity. Jesus Christ is the second Adam, who reenacts or recapitulates the work of the first Adam to bring life rather than death. "For since death came through a human being, the resurrection of the dead has also come through a human being; for as all die in Adam, so all will be made alive in Christ" (1 Cor. 15:21-22).

Since Jesus Christ is framed as embodying the true Israel and the true second Adam, all of God's promises to Israel and righteous humanity apply first and foremost to Jesus Christ himself. Therefore, when the risen Christ explains his identity to his companions on the road to Emmaus, the Gospel narrative does not suggest a connect-the-dots relationship to his identity, but Jesus can claim that "all the Scriptures" point to himself. "Then beginning with Moses and all the prophets, he interpreted to them the things about himself in all the Scriptures" (Luke 24:27). Hugh of St. Victor typifies many premodern exegetes when he puts the approach this way: "All of Divine Scripture is one book, and that one book is Christ, because all of Divine Scripture speaks of Christ, and all of Divine Scripture is fulfilled in Christ."[20] Because of who Jesus Christ is as the consummation of God's promises, all Scripture bears witness to him, even the Old Testament, which temporally precedes the descent of the Word in the flesh in Christ.

The fact that these christological claims have implications for how to read Scripture has been unsettling to some Scripture scholars. In a fascinating essay, veteran New Testament scholar Morna Hooker begins an analysis of the hymn about Christ in Colossians 1:15-20 by asking the questions she has been trained to ask "in the methods of tradition-historical scholarship," namely, who, when, why, what?[21] None of these is a directly theological question; they are questions about the origin of the text. As she explores these questions, she notes

---

20. As quoted in Wilken, "Interpreting the Old Testament," xii.

21. Morna Hooker, "Where Is Wisdom to Be Found? Colossians 1:15-20 (I)," in *Reading Texts, Seeking Wisdom: Scripture and Theology*, ed. David Ford and Graham Stanton (Grand Rapids: Eerdmans, 2004), p. 116.

the ways in which the hymn is drawing on the language and thought of Old Testament and other Jewish literature. With the language of creation, word, and various wisdom themes, the passage speaks to the supremacy of Christ over all things.

> He is the image of the invisible God, the firstborn of all creation; for in him all things in heaven and on earth were created, things visible and invisible, whether thrones or dominions or rulers or powers — all things have been created through him and for him. He himself is before all things, and in him all things hold together. He is the head of the body, the church; he is the beginning, the firstborn from the dead, so that he might come to have first place in everything. For in him all the fullness of God was pleased to dwell, and through him God was pleased to reconcile to himself all things, whether on earth or in heaven, by making peace through the blood of his cross. (Col. 1:15-20)

By drawing from various Old Testament motifs, Hooker points out that Jesus is not just a "new" word or law, but that he is the fulfillment of God's word to Israel: "Christ, not the Torah, is now understood to be the supreme revelation of God's will or purposes, the fullest expression of his word or wisdom" (p. 123). Christ is "the agent of all creation," and in the larger context of Colossians, the one who "reveals God's purpose for humanity" as humans are restored in him (p. 125).

After giving this exegesis, Hooker poses this question: "What, then, can we learn from the way in which the author of this passage handles the Scripture?" Her response is telling. The exegesis of the Old Testament is "paradoxical," for though the author regards the Old Testament as authoritative, he "*subverts* the text" by pointing to his "fundamental *principle* of exegesis. The word spoken by God at creation and revealed on Sinai was not, after all, encapsulated in the written Torah, but it dwells in Christ. In Johannine terminology, this means that the incarnate Word reveals God in a way that Moses could not do." Hooker notes the striking hermeneutical implications of this. Paul "has no interest in the question which I was trained to ask: 'What did this mean for the original author?'" (p. 126) Why was Paul uninterested in this question? Because of who Jesus Christ is, the one in whom "all things hold together," the fulfillment of the law, of God's word — Jesus Christ himself is the reorienting factor for all Christian biblical exegesis.

For Paul, Hooker argues, the hermeneutical principle emerging from this christology is to "interpret Scripture in light of Christ," something quite different from the methods of her training as a biblical scholar (p. 127).[22] (However, we should bear in mind that Hooker's analysis itself uses a variety of critical methods, showing how critical methods can enhance a theological hermeneutic, as I suggested in chapter 2.) Nevertheless, Hooker's analysis does show the theological problems inherent in critical approaches that refuse christological readings of the Old Testament. Historical theologian David Steinmetz puts the issue quite forcefully: "The church which is restricted in its preaching to the original intention of the author is a church which must reject the Old Testament as an exclusively Jewish book."[23] Christians do not receive the Old Testament as a generic "word of God" to be received apart from Christ; it is because of Christ that Christians read the Old Testament as Scripture at all. That is why biblical scholars such as Christopher Seitz argue that Christians should prefer the term "Old Testament" over "Hebrew Bible." Christians receive Israel's Scripture as their own because of "the new covenant made by God in Christ," into which they are grafted by God's covenant with Abraham.[24] Paul and the apostles considered it "self-evident" that "the use of Israel's Scriptures [is] to preach Christ."[25] Israel's Scripture is not "someone else's mail" for gentile believers, but it is the Old Testament inextricably connected to the New Testament because it bears witness to Jesus Christ.[26]

22. For further analysis of the New Testament use of the Old Testament, and a variety of assessments about how this relates to modern exegetical practice, see G. K. Beale, ed., *Right Doctrine from the Wrong Text? Essays on the Use of the Old Testament in the New* (Grand Rapids: Baker, 1994).

23. David Steinmetz, "Theology and Exegesis: Ten Theses," in *Histoire de l'exégèse au XVIe siècle* (Geneva: Librairie Droz, 1978), p. 382.

24. Christopher R. Seitz, *Word Without End: The Old Testament as Abiding Theological Witness* (Grand Rapids: Eerdmans, 1998), p. 71.

25. Seitz, *Word Without End,* p. 74.

26. Seitz, *Word Without End,* pp. 71-74. As Brian Daley notes, "it is only the Church's faith in the risen Jesus as the Christ that has permitted it to receive and recognize this (apparently) hodge-podge of texts as 'Bible' at all." Daley, "Is Patristic Exegesis Still Usable? Reflections on Early Christian Interpretation of the Psalms," *Communio* 29 (Spring 2002): 185-216; quotation from p. 214.

How Do Premodern Exegetes Understand
the Different "Senses" of Scripture?

If one embraces the notion that Jesus Christ is the one to whom all Scripture points, even when that goes beyond the human authors' intentions in the Old Testament writings, how should we exegete Scripture? This is a significant question for premodern authors and for interpreters of the Bible in the church today. Making a commitment to the christology endorsed in the previous section — and the consequent practice of reading the Old Testament in light of Christ — is a crucial step. But there are many remaining possibilities and questions about how this can be done.

For premodern exegetes, this hermeneutic developed into different ways of construing the senses of Scripture. In patristic accounts, the most fundamental distinction was usually between the literal or historical sense of the text and the spiritual or figurative sense. The spiritual sense of the text would then be differentiated into several parts. Some gave a threefold exegesis that was variously named the literal, moral, and mystical senses.[27] Even more common was the fourfold sense, which highlights three aspects of the spiritual sense beyond the literal: allegorical, moral, and anagogical. This fourfold reading was systematized in medieval Christianity and frequently summarized in the following way:

> The literal sense teaches what took place,
> The allegorical sense what you ought to believe,
> The moral sense what you ought to do,
> The anagogical sense what you must strive for.[28]

An example from Rabanus Maurus (780-856) can illuminate its use. He first speaks about how interpretation is "divided into two parts, that is, into historical interpretation and spiritual understanding." But Maurus articulates this by speaking about the image being interpreted — Jerusalem — in a fourfold way. After mentioning a move from "history" to "allegory" to "anagogy" (the eschatological sense) and "tropology" (the moral sense), Rabanus gives this summary: "One and

---

27. See de Lubac, *Medieval Exegesis*, vol. 1, pp. 90ff.
28. See Wood, *Spiritual Exegesis*, pp. 27-28.

the same Jerusalem can be understood in a fourfold way, historically as the city of the Jews, allegorically as the Church of Christ, anagogically as that celestial city of God which is the mother of us all, and tropologically as the soul of man."[29] To extrapolate what undergirds an approach like this, note that all three spiritual senses relate to Christ and to believers as ones united to Christ: Jerusalem, as the special dwelling place of the God of Israel, refers to those who belong to the Word made flesh in Jesus Christ, the church (allegorical), which culminates in an eschatological "city of God" (anagogical), and entails God's dwelling in the human soul (tropological). Jerusalem does not simply denote a city in the Middle East, but connotes the way in which God in Christ dwells among and within his people that will be eschatologically consummated in the future.

In the Reformation, at first glance there may appear to be a break with the patristic and medieval traditions of three- or fourfold exegesis. Luther, Calvin, and other Reformers have a sharp polemic against the "allegories" and the spiritual interpretation of some church fathers, such as Origen, and they do not organize their exegesis around the medieval fourfold sense. But the situation is considerably more complex than this rhetoric may indicate. In terms of the broad christological issue in the previous section, the Reformers were clearly on the side of patristic and medieval interpreters: the Old Testament, and all of Scripture, was interpreted in light of Jesus Christ. Moreover, in some ways, Reformers such as Calvin renamed the senses of Scripture yet retained the content of the medieval fourfold account. Calvin championed the "literal sense" of the Old Testament. But as Richard Muller points out, the "literal" meaning of the Old Testament, for Calvin, was "not at all like the modern, higher-critical paradigm for interpretation." It was not seeking to view the Old Testament apart from Christ. For Calvin, the literal sense "held a message concerning what Christians ought to believe, what Christians ought to do, and what Christians ought to hope for."[30] In other words, Calvin folds the three spiritual senses back into an expansive understanding of the literal sense. In many ways, Calvin's approach is actually quite close to earlier authors, as interpreters as diverse as Origen and Aquinas all seek to

---

29. Quoted in de Lubac, *Medieval Exegesis,* vol. 1, p. 108.
30. Muller and Thompson, *Biblical Interpretation,* p. 11.

firmly ground the spiritual senses in the literal or historical sense of Scripture.[31]

While premodern interpreters frequently speak about the "literal" sense of Scripture, what they mean by this sense can be confusing to newcomers to premodern exegesis. Indeed, various authors do not use the terminology consistently. But there are still some basic features that we can discern about a premodern rendering of the literal sense of Scripture.

First and foremost, the literal or historical sense was not what we ordinarily denote as "literal" or "historical" in contemporary English usage. To take the text literally was not in any way opposed to noting metaphors in the text, or recognizing a diversity of genres in Scripture. For instance, a commitment to the literal sense did not mean that readers approached poetic genres of Scripture as literal history. Moreover, the historical sense generally did not refer to the history *behind* the text or the text's historical origin. Rather, in its most basic sense, the literal or historical sense refers to the story given in the text, "not under or behind it."[32] In other words, "'history' refers . . . both to the event narrated and the narration of the event." Moreover, the historical sense does not force all biblical genres into "history"; attention to literary genre helps readers discern the historical sense.[33] Rather, the historical sense refers to what is portrayed in various genres by the text itself — the "letter" of the text.

It may seem vicious to blur history and the "narration of history." However, it is actually simply an implication of the view advocated above that the flow of history through time (a diachronic view of history) should not be viewed autonomously, that is, apart from divine action in the world. Some scholars claim that history should have "a significance and an intelligibility contained simply within itself," and that judgments about God's action in history are private judgments of faith. But as Brian Daley points out, "there is a certain tension, even a

---

31. On Origen's own terms, he grounds spiritual interpretation in the historical sense, and de Lubac gives an exposition and defense of this aspect of Origen. However, scholars such as R. P. C. Hanson offer a very different interpretation of Origen: Hanson, *Allegory and Event: A Study of the Sources and Significance of Origen's Interpretation of Scripture* (Louisville: Westminster John Knox, 2002), esp. pp. 82-83.

32. See Muller and Thompson, *Biblical Interpretation,* p. 339.

33. See Wood, *Spiritual Exegesis,* pp. 31-32.

contradiction, in such a view of 'salvation history.'" If "historical reality" is assumed to be objective apart from the narration of that history, then methodologically one is only permitted "'natural,' inner-worldly explanations of why or how things happen."[34] But history does not come to us objectively: it is always a historian's history, tied to the interests, preconceptions, and theological (or atheological) beliefs of the historian. For example, when speaking about the Jesus of history portrayed to us in the Gospels, we should not wish for an account of "the historical Jesus" in its place. All accounts of "the historical Jesus" are scholarly reconstructions — the "Jesus" of historians. Every historian of Jesus tells a story about Jesus that emerges, to some extent, from his or her own theological (or atheological) presuppositions. The Gospels tie the history of Jesus together with the narration of that history, which is a more truthful way of presenting the history of Jesus than to simply record events behind the text that then invite our own private interpretations. History and the narration of history must be blurred in Scripture because there is no such thing as history that is separated from the drama of God's action in the world, action that comes to us as the narrative of God's creating, upholding, and redeeming work with creation.

In light of this, the place of historical research in premodern exegesis both differs from and yet has continuity with contemporary historical-critical approaches. On the one hand, premodern authors did not identify the "literal" or "historical" sense with a reconstruction of the original meaning as it would have been understood in an ancient context. The historical meaning had to be understood in a canonical context: the word of God for the community of faith now receiving the text in relationship to other parts of the biblical canon. It is not simply the record of the religious community that originally produced the text.

Yet, on the other hand, premodern interpretation is not unconcerned with critical concerns related to the historical origins and critical issues surrounding the texts. That is why I avoid calling these interpreters "precritical." While premodern interpreters did not understand "historical or contextual issues as providing the final point of reference for the significance of the text," they were engaged with many critical biblical issues. While the humanism of Reformation-era exegesis dis-

---

34. Daley, "Is Patristic Exegesis Still Usable?" pp. 190-91.

played a renewed interest in the historical context of biblical writings, many earlier interpreters shared these interests as well. Muller and Thompson give some examples:

> Aquinas, for example, offers as much detail concerning the historical context of Romans as most Reformation interpreters of the text; Alcuin of York ponders in detail the situation that produced the Pastoral Epistles; virtually all precritical exegetes recognized what has come to be called the "synoptic problem"; and many of the older exegetes recognized the redacted character of the Pentateuch and of the historical books from Joshua through 2 Kings.[35]

Those seeking to retrieve a premodern understanding of the historical sense of Scripture need not jettison more recent critical scholarship on the Bible. On the other hand, it would be a mistake to think that modern historical-critical scholarship has been seeking after the "historical sense" as understood by premodern authors. Premodern exegetes do not think that a historical reconstruction of a text's origin — or even its meaning in the original ancient context — fully constitutes the historical sense. What, then, is a positive meaning of the "literal" or "historical" sense of Scripture?

The "Historical Sense," Allegory, and Typology: The Example of Hagar

To explore the particular way in which the literal sense of the Old Testament was historical, and how that relates to spiritual readings, let us look at an exegetical example. As noted above, Paul himself uses the language of "allegory" in speaking about the two wives of Abraham in Galatians 4: Sarah, who received God's promise of offspring for a great nation in Genesis 12, was a "free woman," according to Paul; Hagar, an Egyptian slave whom Sarah brought to Abraham because of Sarah's apparent barrenness, was "a slave woman." In Paul's allegory, the child of Sarah (Isaac) was "born through the promise," while "the child of the slave" (Ishmael) "was born according to the flesh." The allegory for Paul

---

35. Muller and Thompson, *Biblical Interpretation*, pp. 340-41.

is that the two women represent "two covenants": Hagar "corresponds to the present Jerusalem, for she is in slavery with her children"; Sarah "corresponds to the New Jerusalem above; she is free, and she is our mother." Paul uses this allegory to assure early Christians that they need not look to the synagogue to be children of the promise, but to Jesus Christ. "For freedom Christ has set us free. Stand firm, therefore, and do not submit again to a yoke of slavery" (Gal. 5:1).

Why present this argument in Galatians? For the book of Galatians, it is part of Paul's response to opponents who claimed that Jews must continue to follow the law and engage in synagogue worship to continue to be children of Abraham. Hence, contemporary commentators point out, Paul presents this allegory as part of an argument against the "Judaizers." Some commentators speculate that the Judaizers developed the Sarah-Hagar narrative such that they are "directly associated with Abraham and the God-ordained channels for the reception of the Abrahamic promise."[36] In contrast, Paul says that just as Ishmael "persecuted" the child born of the Spirit, "so it is now" that those who believe that the inheritance of the children of Abraham comes through obedience to the law persecute those who are free in Christ (Gal. 4:29).

Paul's point is a crucial one for Christian teaching: faith in Jesus Christ, not obedience to the Jewish law, brings gentiles into the fold of Abraham's children. But given Paul's allegory, has the literal sense of Genesis 16 and 21, which speak about Hagar and Sarah, been exhausted? In the church's reception of Genesis 16 and 21, that sometimes appeared to be the case. All major interpreters were aware of Paul's allegory, and sometimes the details of the literal sense simply fold into Paul's allegory. After all, this allegory has apostolic precedent.

But this story's reception by premodern interpreters is a complex one, for premodern interpreters often supplement Paul's allegory with other readings of the literal and allegorical Sarah and Hagar. Some interpreters, such as Augustine, show relatively little interest in the literal Hagar of Genesis 16 and 21, and work from Paul's allegory: they extend it to "false Christians" or schismatics in their own day. Other patristic authors, such as Didymus, combine Paul's allegory with an in-

---

36. See, for example, Richard N. Longenecker, *Galatians,* Word Biblical Commentary, 41 (Dallas: Word, 2002), p. 218.

terpretation of Philo, a Jewish allegorist, that Hagar is the subordinate but necessary "preliminary studies" in the law, preceding Sarah.[37] While offering a spiritual interpretation, Didymus pays a great deal of attention to the details of the Genesis narrative, continually returning to the literal Hagar and Sarah side by side with his allegorical reflections. "It is impossible to understand any of the spiritual or elevated doctrines apart from the shadow according to the letter," Didymus writes.[38] Didymus makes a special note that Hagar receives a vision of God in the wilderness in Genesis 16:13, lauding Hagar's virtue by evoking Matthew 5:8: "Blessed are the pure in heart, for they shall see God." The literal Hagar reemerges precisely as she is interpreted as foreshadowing the saints who receive a vision of God. Other interpreters, such as Maurus, later continue this line of interpretation, explicitly associating Hagar with "the church of the gentiles" and extolling Hagar's theophany as "an appearance to her [Hagar] of that object of contemplation longed for by everyone who aspires to love God with all of his heart."[39]

Luther continues this trajectory in referring to "saintly" Hagar, ostensibly defending a literal and historical sense of the text. In his commentary on Genesis 16, he says, "If anyone cares to look for allegories, let him do so. I am satisfied with this literal meaning which the historical account itself presents." But Luther interprets Hagar as a saintly precursor to Christian believers. Luther admits that Hagar is a negative symbol in Paul's allegory, which he affirms. Yet, "in Scripture even the saints frequently symbolize the ungodly." And Hagar, a sinner, is nevertheless "justified and sanctified by the Word of God" like Christian believers, and thus Hagar "symbolizes the ungodly without detriment to herself."[40] Luther goes on to give a very detailed exegesis of the Genesis narrative, in which he encourages his Christian reader deeply to identify with Hagar's trials and sufferings. Informed by this Christian identification with Hagar, Luther notes the deep tensions in the literal sense

---

37. John L. Thompson, *Writing the Wrongs: Women of the Old Testament Among Biblical Commentators from Philo Through the Reformation* (Oxford: Oxford University Press, 2001), p. 31.

38. Didymus, quoted in Thompson, *Writing the Wrongs,* p. 32.

39. Maurus, quoted in Thompson, *Writing the Wrongs,* pp. 50-51.

40. Martin Luther, *Luther's Works,* vol. 3: *Lectures on Genesis: Chapters 15-20,* ed. Jaroslav Pelikan (St. Louis: Concordia, 1961), pp. 70, 72.

of the Genesis story when Abraham exiles Hagar and Ishmael (much as recent feminist critics have done).[41] "If someone wanted to rant against Abraham at this point, he could make him the murderer of his son and wife. . . . Who would believe this if Moses had not recorded it?" For the Genesis 21 narrative is "surely a piteous description, which I can hardly read with dry eyes." Yet Hagar's humility and trust in God amid these trials are followed up by the theophany to Hagar, in which she is "enlightened with . . . the Holy Spirit, and from a slave woman she also becomes a mother of the church."[42]

PREMODERN READINGS of the Hagar narrative are undoubtedly theological, but in the examples above this is combined with an acute historical sensibility as well. As Thompson says, "precritical interpretation is thoroughly theological" in the sense that it asks "what is God doing among the characters in this story and what is God therefore doing in us?" But it is also historical, adding a diachronic perspective: the story is thus not simply absorbed into our new context, or even absorbed into Paul's own authoritative allegory in Galatians 4. It is striking that even with an apostolic precedent for an allegory, many commentators insist that the meaning of Hagar's narrative is not exhausted by Paul's allegory; it must still be read on the historical level of the text itself. As Luther says, there is a difference between who Hagar was (in Genesis) and what Hagar symbolizes (in Galatians).[43]

But this account may also clarify the sense in which the "letter" — or the "historical" sense — of the text tended to be understood. Premodern readers did not seek a reconstructed history outside of the text, a search for the "historical Hagar" in the ancient Near East, as some modern historical criticism has done. It was not historical in the sense that it shut down theological questions, or questions that apply directly to the reader's own community of faith. Each interpretation above is attentive to the question of how the Hagar account in Genesis 12–16 can be God's word to the receiving community. The literal readings of Hagar's narrative were historical in the sense that they referred

---

41. On this point, cf. Thompson, *Writing the Wrongs,* pp. 18-24, 87-92.

42. Luther, Commentary on Gen. 21:15-17, *Luther's Works,* 4: 46, 58.

43. John Thompson, "Using the Bible in the Midst of Suspicion and Depravity," 2004 essay, http://documents.fuller.edu/sot/faculty/thompson_john/Inaugural.pdf, pp. 5-7.

to the historical narrative in the text itself — a "realistic" or "history-like" narrative, to use the terms of Hans Frei.[44]

In the exegetical accounts above, we see how there is not an either/or relationship between an emphasis on the historical and spiritual senses. Indeed, for Didymus, Maurus, and Luther, it is the spiritual reading of Hagar as a figure of a Christian saint that drives their exegesis to consider the letter of the Genesis text in great detail. All three give a historical reading of Hagar that eludes the negative reading in Paul's allegory, not because they are suspicious of spiritual readings of Scripture but because they have a different spiritual reading of Genesis 12–16 that drives them back to the details of the text. It is precisely because Hagar is interpreted in light of Christ as a "saint" that the literal Hagar receives such close attention. For these commentators, reading Old Testament characters as shadows that find their fulfillment in Christ is not a way to obfuscate the Old Testament narrative, but it is an impetus to return to the literal narrative itself.

IN LIGHT OF this example, let us turn to terminology commonly used in speaking about how the Old Testament provides figures that are fulfilled in the New Testament: typology and allegory. Frequently, in its contemporary usage, "typology" refers to reading the Old Testament as containing "types," which means a "person, institution, or event prefiguring a later fulfillment in God's plan."[45] "Allegory," by contrast, is seen as an approach in which "the words, events, and characters . . . stand for something else; they speak for another reality, another realm of meaning. The trick, then, is to decode the true or extended meaning and translate the literal sense into its allegorical sense."[46] At first glance, it looks as though typology is a way of reading that values the diachronic flow of salvation history, while allegory is less concerned with salvation history: it decodes the text to uncover its true realm of meaning.

44. Hans W. Frei, *Eclipse of the Biblical Narrative: A Study in Eighteenth and Nineteenth Century Hermeneutics* (New Haven: Yale University Press, 1974), p. 10. Frei offers an important account of how an "eclipse" of this sense of the literal reading of Scripture began to be advocated in the eighteenth century.

45. Treier, *Introducing Theological Interpretation of Scripture: Recovering a Christian Practice* (Grand Rapids: Baker Academic, 2008), p. 45.

46. John O'Keefe and R. R. Reno, *Sanctified Vision: An Introduction to Early Christian Interpretation of the Bible* (Baltimore: Johns Hopkins University Press, 2005), p. 89.

This positive evaluation of typology and negative rendering of allegory is often reflected in textbook accounts of the history of exegesis.[47] As the story goes, allegorical interpretation was championed by a patristic school of exegesis known as the Alexandrian school, and a more historical and typological alternative was used by Antiochene theologians. Allegedly, the medieval period became more and more obsessed with allegories, showing little concern for the literal and historical sense of the text until the Reformers came to "save the day," doing so, according to the textbook, by recovering the Antiochene approach toward exegesis, eschewing allegory, and returning to the literal and historical sense.

What the textbooks do not usually provide is the agenda that underlies such a telling of history: the modern emphasis on the literal and historical sense is legitimated as an old tradition with patristic predecessors, with the Protestant Reformers continuing to extend this trajectory. At the highest evolutionary stage of development, therefore, is modern historical criticism, toward which the Antiochene school and the Reformers had been pointing, even if they did not fully adopt the thoroughly historical character of interpretation as modern scholars did during the Enlightenment. In this account, all legitimate interpretive roads lead to the Enlightenment.

However, more recent historical scholarship has called into question the "textbook" account on several fronts. The Reformers do, in fact, present a polemic against the allegories of medieval exegesis; but the polemic functions as something closer to a family quarrel than a rejection of a totally foreign allegorical approach toward exegesis. In many ways, medieval exegesis already represents a move toward emphasizing the historical sense of the text; thus the Reformation is an extension of this trajectory.[48] Moreover, as de Lubac points out, even patristic writers who seem most strongly allegorical, such as Origen, seek to ground their allegory in the historical sense.[49]

Patristic scholars have also called into question the sharp polarization of the Alexandrian and Antiochene schools of exegesis; for, in spite

---

47. See the examples and analysis in Muller and Thompson, *Biblical Interpretation,* pp. 343-45.

48. Muller and Thompson, *Biblical Interpretation,* p. 344.

49. De Lubac, *Medieval Exegesis,* 2: 45-50.

of their very real christological differences, they have a great deal in common in exegetical approach. These schools of thought were first and foremost distinguished by their christology during the fifth-century controversy leading up to Chalcedon, not for their diametrically opposed methods of scriptural interpretation.[50] Although there are some broad differences in their exegetical approaches, both schools of thought used historical, allegorical, and typological readings of the Old Testament.[51]

Rather than seeing typology and allegory as diametrically opposed methods of interpreting the Old Testament, we would probably do best to view them on a continuum based on the extent to which the "figure" draws on the historical sense of the biblical text. In a sense, typology and allegory are two types of "figural" reading, and sometimes the boundary between the two can be very thin. For example, is Luther's reading of Hagar as a Christian saint undergoing regeneration by the Holy Spirit a typology or an allegory? It pays close attention to the literal sense; and ostensibly, according to Luther, his interpretation is not allegorical. Yet, in the way that Luther reads the details of the Genesis text to have Christian symbolic significance, many contemporary advocates of typology would consider his exegesis to be quite allegorical.

However one uses the language of typology and allegory, it is important to recognize a real concern underlying the distinction: that the Old Testament should be read in light of Jesus Christ, but that its inherent richness as God's word can be missed if the text's diachronic history is eclipsed, that is, if the New Testament use of the Old is allowed to exhaust its meaning. Part of the issue here is christological: if Christ truly recapitulates the story of Adam and Israel, he fulfills it in a way that does not annihilate that earlier narrative, but reveals its true shape. In

50. Diverse scholars have questioned the polarizing of the Alexandrian and Antiochene schools of exegesis and the association of Antiochene exegesis with a trajectory of modern biblical criticism. These scholars include Frances Young, John H. O'Keefe, and Rowan Greer. One of the most significant works along this line is Frances Young, *Biblical Exegesis and the Formation of Christian Culture* (Cambridge, UK: Cambridge University Press, 1997).

51. Indeed, in our example above about Hagar and Sarah, all of the patristic writers give "spiritual readings," and it was actually Greek interpreters such as Didymus in Alexandria who gave a stronger rendering of the literal sense of the Hagar narrative. See Thompson, *Writing the Wrongs,* pp. 31-33.

other words, Christ as the perfect prophet, priest, and king does not annihilate or obscure the Old Testament narratives of prophets, priests,
and kings, but illuminates their proper end and fulfillment. As I noted
in the first section above, diachronic history does not exist autonomously from God, but as *participating* in God's providential acts
brought to fulfillment in Christ. On the other hand, we should not lose
sight of the diachronic history of salvation, the story of creation and of
Israel held forth to us as God's word in the Old Testament text.

Why Does Premodern Exegesis Matter for the Contemporary Interpretation of Scripture?

Let us return to the basic question of why contemporary interpreters of
Scripture should bother to read premodern exegetes. Drawing on the
work of several scholars in the history of exegesis, I would like to suggest four overall reasons.[52] The first two are primarily summaries of
material above, while the second two develop the material above a step
further.

1) Premodern exegetes can supplement the work of critical biblical
   scholarship by showing us how Scripture should be received from
   within a theological framework that believes God was and is active
   in the world.

   Christians should not assume that human history exists in an autonomous realm separated from God's work. Rather, human history participates in God's own providential activity, and we misunderstand history when we conceive of it as an immanent realm that is isolated from
divine action. Thus, while Christians can appreciate the linear aspects of
the "natural history" of textual origin provided in critical scholarship,
Christians must insist that a theological framework is indispensable for

---

52. These categories draw on yet modify the categories of Frances Young, "The
'Mind' of Scripture: Theological Readings of the Bible in the Fathers," *International Jour-
nal of Systematic Theology* 7, no. 2 (April 2005): 126-41; Brian Daley, "Is Patristic Exegesis
Still Usable?" and John L. Thompson, *Reading the Bible with the Dead: What You Can Learn
from the History of Exegesis That You Can't Learn from Exegesis Alone* (Grand Rapids:
Eerdmans, 2007).

understanding this history properly. A naturalistic reconstruction of textual history does not access an "original context" that defines the scope of the text. The original context is part of a history of God's own action that culminates in Christ. In addition, Christians should trust that God continues to be active in the world, working to restore and redeem his creation in Christ through the power of the Spirit. The very process of Christians "reading Scripture" is taken up into this divine drama of salvation: bringing death to the old self and life to those united to Jesus Christ by the Spirit's power.

2) Premodern exegetes help us see how the biblical canon is a unified book because of its narrative of God's self-revelation in creation and with Israel, culminating in Jesus Christ. Therefore, Christians should seek "the Word within the words" of the Bible to perceive its unity.[53]

Apart from a canonical framework, the Bible may appear to be a book of disconnected writings with voices vying against one another rather than speaking in harmonious accord.[54] However, premodern exegetes remind us that there is a reason that Christians read these divergent writings together, all in one book: because of the belief that the story of God's work in creation and in covenant with Israel finds its culmination in the life, death, and resurrection of Jesus Christ. Because of this, Israel's scriptures are received by the church as the "Old Testament," bearing witness to the new covenant in Christ even when the Old Testament writers would have been unaware of any such witness. In this way, faith in the unique identity of Jesus Christ — the eternal Word made flesh — gives the entire Scripture its unity, for it is to Jesus Christ that Scripture points. While readers should be attentive to the diachronic aspects of the history of God with his creation, Christian readers should also seek to see the ways in which the literal sense of the Old Testament can lead to types and allegories of realities shown forth in Jesus Christ.

53. Young, "The 'Mind' of Scripture," pp. 139-40.

54. While many and varied contemporary advocates of theological interpretation call for a retrieval of a patristic sense of canonical unity, there are a variety of construals about the details of what it means to read canonically. See Kevin Vanhoozer, *Reading Scripture with the Church,* 66-73.

3) With difficult Scripture passages, premodern exegetes show us that discerning "the Word within the words" is often not easy. Premodern exegetes model the way exegetical difficulties are not simply problems to be fixed, but mysteries of God's word to be discerned.

Premodern exegetes believed that all Scripture is God's word to the church in Christ; but they held that conviction with the awareness that it is not always easy to discern how it is true. How is a psalm that curses the psalmist's enemies bearing witness to Christ, who teaches love of enemies? How are the passages of rape, abuse, and violence in the Bible seen as the word of the God shown forth in the self-sacrificial love of Christ? Premodern exegetes struggle greatly with questions such as these, and even where we do not agree with their reflections, they have something to teach us about approaching the Bible as Scripture.

For premodern exegetes, discerning the meaning of difficult texts requires more than a good lexicon and a "Bible-background" commentary. It requires a life of prayer and worship before a holy and mysterious God. In describing patristic exegesis, Daley says that "holy things" are held before us in Scripture, and "the discovery of these holy things — which are Scripture's actual *content* and *meaning* — require of the reader a process of purification and an attitude of reverence that are not simply the product of academic learning, but belong to the life of worship and faith. The key to this attitude . . . seems to lie in the sense that it is God who speaks through the biblical author and text, and that our own engagement with the text is nothing less than a personal encounter with the Divine Mystery."[55]

In light of this, we can see how practices such as allegory need not be seen as a strategy of "erasing textual difficulty" but of "shifting to and preserving a certain sort of difficulty: that of seeing Christ, who may be difficult to see, in a place where we believe he must be present."[56] Thus, when Origen encounters the senseless death of Jephthah's daughter based on her father's rash oath (Judges 11), he seeks to discern how this relates to the mystery of Christ. When he calls

55. Daley, "Is Patristic Exegesis Still Usable?" pp. 203-4.
56. Jason Byassee, *Praise Seeking Understanding: Reading the Psalms with Augustine* (Grand Rapids: Eerdmans, 2007), p. 39.

her a martyr, he says she presents a sacrifice that prefigures the death of Jesus as the Lamb of God. Origen's account does not make the narrative of Jephthah's daughter neat and tidy, however, for he insists that martyrdom is not a visible triumph — but appears to be a senseless, terrible defeat. Jephthah's daughter's martyrdom, like Origen's father's martyrdom (and later his own), does not appear to be a glorious victory. As John Thompson observes of Origen's account, "the martyr's crown is visible only to faith. The true significance of these cruel deaths remains, for now, one of those secrets or mysteries known only to God."[57] Origen's spiritual reading of Jephthah's daughter does not soften a difficult text, but it contextualizes the silences and conundrums of the text within the larger mystery of God in Christ.

4) Reading premodern exegetes reminds us of the contextual location of all interpretations, as well as the sinfulness of all interpreters. Even when we disagree with premodern interpreters, it can help us become more self-aware and self-critical readers.

As we discovered in chapter 4, all interpretation of Scripture takes place within a particular context, and reading exegetes from various contexts can provide mutual enrichment and also call into question our idolatries. This point is particularly true for the history of interpretation and the reading of premodern exegetes. If we want to become aware of the shaping — sometimes idolatrous — force of modernity, we need to read premodern exegetes. Just as Americans who move to China for a year may discover the many ways in which they are distinctively American, reading premodern exegetes can reveal to us that many of our assumptions about the world are not "just the way things are" but have a distinctively modern perspective on the world. The discussion of the historical sense of the text above is a case in point: premodern authors do not assume that history is an autonomous realm that is accessible only by the "neutral" inquiries of historical methods, insulated from the possibility of God acting in and through history. Such a view of history is functionally Deistic, and we should reject it as a modern form of idolatry.

Yet at other times the historical distance that we have from premodern interpreters can make obvious a fact that we should keep in

57. Thompson, *Reading the Bible with the Dead,* p. 36.

mind as interpreters of Scripture: all exegetes are sinful, and not above a certain degree of suspicion. There is a paradox on this point. On the one hand, the Spirit has united believers to the living Christ in and through their reading of Scripture; so members of the church read as ones who belong to Christ. On the other hand, Christians are still sinners, and on this side of eternity we will continue to see the "old self" in scriptural interpretation as well as the "new creation" of the Spirit. This happens not only on an individual level, but also collectively, as Christians share many patterns in their reception of Scripture and rendering of particular passages.

The historical and social location of contemporary readers of Scripture tends to highlight two sins of premodern exegetes in particular: a frequent anti-Jewish polemic and patriarchal attitudes that sometimes belittle women, reducing them to narrow, stereotypical roles. While I believe that these examples should not make us jettison premodern exegesis, they should poignantly remind us that, while we should read the Bible together with the community of faith through time, that community is also a sinful community, and we are among them, as sinners. While we should be open about the sinfulness of premodern exegetes on these points, we should also seek to understand their positions on their own terms, not prematurely absorbing their views into totalizing categories such as "anti-Semitic" or "misogynist." Indeed, as strange as it may sound, renewed interest in premodern Christian exegetes has actually fueled interest in Jewish interpretation among many recent scholars, and the patristics, far from being simply "patriarchal," have been mined in profound ways by prominent Christian feminist scholars. These contemporary movements of retrieval do not simply accept anti-Jewish polemic or belittling comments about women; but they still find a great deal of value in these premodern Christian thinkers.

On the issue of anti-Jewish polemic, premodern Christian authors should not be understood as advocating a racial inferiority or other deficiency based on "blood," as recent anti-Semitism has done. On a theological level, premodern polemics are driven by an anti-Judaism that claims the inferiority of the law and the Temple as a way to be the people of God. On this particular point, premodern writers were right at least to realize that they would understand the Old Testament differently in light of Christ. Unfortunately, this theological point was often infused with cultural stereotypes that scapegoat and demonize Jews.

Contemporary Christians should openly confess the centrality of Christ, but we should recognize the depravity of our own community and mourn those times when a clear proclamation of Christ has been tarnished with the scapegoating of the Jewish community. To counteract this alienating tendency, the priority among Christians to seek to preserve the literal as well as spiritual senses can provide common ground for Christian and Jewish interpreters of the past.[58]

Indeed, the premodern exegete John Calvin attempted to recover a more robust historical sense of the Old Testament and was criticized by some as being "too Jewish" for his practice of drawing on Jewish patterns of interpretation and lexical insights as part of his distinctively Christian interpretation of the Old Testament.[59] Contemporary Christian scholars who are attentive to the history of exegesis have often engaged fruitfully with premodern Jewish interpretation.[60] Indeed, unlike historical-critical approaches that seek to bypass the differences in how Jewish and Christian communities receive Scripture, reading the history of interpretation highlights these distinctives explicitly. Although critical approaches may seek a "neutral" approach to the biblical documents as ancient literature, this can effectively obscure the centrality of postbiblical traditions for both communities of faith and should not be understood as genuine dialogue between Christian and Jewish communities.[61]

On a practical level, why should Christians read historical Jewish interpreters of the Bible? By reading alongside another community of

---

58. "Common ground" here does not suggest that Jewish and Christian renderings of the literal sense will be identical, but they will have enough in common to be partners in fruitful dialogue about the letter of the text.

59. This is not to say that Calvin's historical sense was a reading that was not christological, but it was one that gave a significant place to the diachronic history from within a christological framework. In the course of this, Calvin drew fruitfully from the insights of Jewish commentators. See David Puckett, *John Calvin's Exegesis of the Old Testament* (Louisville: Westminster John Knox, 1995), pp. 1-4, 52-81.

60. Significant examples include the scholarship of Brevard Childs in various works, and Gary A. Anderson, *The Genesis of Perfection: Adam and Eve in Jewish and Christian Imagination* (Louisville: Westminster John Knox, 2001).

61. For more on the limitations of critical approaches to the Bible by which Jews and Christians encounter each other in their particularity, see Jon Levenson, *The Hebrew Bible, the Old Testament, and Historical Criticism: Jews and Christians in Biblical Studies* (Louisville: Westminster John Knox, 1993), chap. 4.

faith — each with its own distinct theological and practical commitments — we learn more about areas of common ground, but we also learn what it means to be a distinctly Christian interpreter of Scripture. Before being exposed to Jewish biblical interpretation, many Christians assume that they are simply "interpreting what the Bible said." For example, many seminary students do not realize the distinctly Christian assumptions at work in interpreting the disobedience of Adam and Eve as the fall of all humanity until they are exposed to contrasting interpretations from Jewish interpreters. The point is not to rid oneself of distinctively Christian hermeneutical assumptions; rather, it is to become aware of them and to see the insights and differences that come out in Jewish interpretations of Scripture. As many past and present Christian interpreters of Scripture can testify, exposure to Jewish scriptural interpretation often provides fresh insights.

Moving on to the second "sin" of premodern interpreters mentioned above: How should we evaluate the male-oriented bias of premodern exegetes? Given the prejudices of many premodern authors about the roles and capacities of women, one might expect that contemporary women readers and feminist scholars would have ignored the premodern authors. But that is not the case: there has been considerable engagement and interest in premodern exegetes by women scholars. Why have feminist scholars and other female readers drawn deeply from the premodern exegetes despite their patriarchal assumptions?

First, though premodern male authors could certainly not be regarded as "feminists," many of them display profoundly humanistic intuitions. They show considerable empathy for and understanding of other human beings, particularly ones who suffer injustice or maltreatment. When it comes to the history of exegesis, John Thompson has shown how male premodern authors often parallel contemporary feminist critics in their empathy, concern, and admiration for women of the Bible, even women who appear to have marginalized roles, such as Hagar, Jephthah's daughter, and other victimized women in the Old Testament.[62] While the history of exegesis sometimes displays prejudice against women, it often has a broad humanism that has much in common with the concern for women among contemporary readers.

Second, feminist theologians have found that certain premodern

---

62. See Thompson, *Reading the Bible with the Dead,* chaps. 1–2.

thinkers have theological ideas — even ideas about gender — that can call into question contemporary forms of patriarchy. Part of this involves taking a step behind the patriarchy of the Enlightenment itself — and the ideal "man of reason" that the Enlightenment promulgated. Engaging premodern exegetes means the possibility of drawing on a broad diversity of scriptural interpretation that often eludes particular aspects of contemporary patriarchy. For example, thinkers such as Kathryn Tanner draw heavily on Alexandrian church fathers in giving an account of salvation that is centered in a Trinitarian way of participating in God rather than a guilt-oriented approach that can often be used against women in particular.[63] Patristics scholar Frances Young connects her own experience of being called to ordained ministry with the insights of desert monks and church fathers in their account of the mystery of God and encountering God in the wilderness.[64] Feminist theologian Sarah Coakley takes from Gregory of Nyssa's interpretation of the Song of Songs a theological contribution for thinking in a Christian way about gender theory.[65] These examples represent just a small sampling from a growing number of feminist scholars who have absorbed much from patristic writings for their work.

Third, though premodern women were influenced by patriarchal attitudes along with the men, there have been an increasing number of women's voices that have been discovered or reclaimed in recent years from premodern Christianity.[66] In particular, the desert mothers and medieval monastics have rich material that has both commonalities with and differences from male premodern authors. Increasingly, texts from premodern women are becoming available in English translation, and they are being included in anthologies on the history of exegesis.[67]

---

63. See Kathryn Tanner, *Jesus, Humanity, and the Trinity: A Brief Systematic Theology* (Minneapolis: Fortress Press, 2001).

64. See Frances Young, *Brokenness and Blessing: Towards a Biblical Spirituality* (Grand Rapids: Baker Academic, 2007), chap. 1.

65. See Sarah Coakley, *Re-thinking Gregory of Nyssa* (Oxford: Blackwell, 2003), pp. 1-13.

66. For a helpful anthology of women's voices in the history of Christian theology, see Amy G. Oden, *In Her Words: Women's Writings in the History of Christian Thought* (Nashville: Abingdon, 1994).

67. See Beverly Kienzle and Pamela J. Walker, eds., *Women Preachers and Prophets through Two Millennia of Christianity* (Berkeley: University of California Press, 1998).

IN THE END, we should read premodern exegetes in particular not because we always agree with their positions. Indeed, they often disagree with each another. We should not read them because they replace or make obsolete the insights that come from critical studies of the Bible. Premodern interpreters are fallible and limited, as are we. But they also reflect the work of the Spirit in the past, and they show great insight into how to interpret all of Scripture as God's own word in Christ.

Jason Byassee speaks of how his own discovery of premodern biblical interpreters grew out of "the experience of leading a congregation."

> As a preacher I spent a great deal of fruitless time seeking biblical commentaries to help me read Scripture well for the sake of the church. I have found modern commentaries helpful for certain things — in clarifying historical events or linguistic problems with greater confidence than ancient commentators could, for example. But I found ancient commentators more helpful in doing the most important thing that Christian preaching and teaching must do: drawing the church to Christ.[68]

In summary, we read premodern exegetes not to simply repeat or "submit" to the exegetical thoughts of earlier exegetes, but to see new possibilities by engaging the thought of brothers and sisters in the Lord who had a clear sense that all Scripture is God's word — even if God's word also contains much that is difficult to make sense of. As Thompson has pointed out, there is much that we can learn from the history of exegesis that we cannot learn simply from exegesis alone.[69]

Extended Exegetical Example:
How Can We Pray the Curses of the Psalms?

Historically, the Psalms have been the prayerbook of the Christian church. If you are well acquainted with Christian worship and prayer, you are likely to recognize that the Psalms constitute the backbone of Christian liturgy, songs, and hymns. But think for a moment about your own experience in reading the Psalms. Psalms present praise to God,

---

68. Byassee, *Praise Seeking Understanding*, p. 1.
69. See Thompson, *Reading with the Dead*, pp. 1-11.

celebrate with joy, and mourn with sorrow and lament. But many Psalms also do something else: they curse the psalmist's enemies.

If you are like many contemporary Christians, you have considerable doubt about how to appropriate these psalms. If you are choosing a psalm for worship, you may be likely to skip over the psalms that plead for the blood of the psalmist's enemies, as the lectionaries tend to do (Thompson, pp. 50-51). After the moving words of Psalm 139 in praise to God for knowing us as "fearfully and wonderfully made," most of us prefer to omit later verses in the psalm. "O that you would kill the wicked," the psalmist pleads, "do I not hate those who hate you, O Lord? And do I not loathe those who rise up against you? I hate them with perfect hatred; I count them as my enemies" (Ps. 139:19a, 21-22). Likewise, many of us do not know how to respond when the psalmist blesses those who kill the infants of the Babylonian captors. "Happy shall they be who take your little ones and dash them against the rock!" (Ps. 137:9) In many psalms, the anger is raw and the call for vengeance is clear (see Pss. 28:4-5; 58:6-10; 69:22-28; 79:10-13).

Our caution about repeating the curses in these psalms is well deserved: on that point we share a reluctance with premodern exegetes to turn the praying of the psalms into vindictive attacks on the enemies of the one who is praying. But many of us may be tempted to stop there. We don't know how to receive these psalms as Scripture, a word from God, so we skip over them. On that point premodern exegetes can offer insight. In the exegetical example below, we will look at Augustine and Calvin to see their appropriation of the curses in the psalms.

Premodern Exegetes Read Imprecatory Psalms Canonically and Christologically

In various ways, premodern exegetes make two significant moves that make possible the receiving of the psalms of cursing as God's word, a word given for our own prayer and worship. First of all, premodern exegetes read these curses in light of the overall Christian canon. All of Scripture is given to build up love of God and neighbor, and to form believers deeper into Christ's image by the Spirit. Thus, even though the curses of those psalms may seem to contradict Jesus' prohibiting of the cursing of enemies (Matt. 5:22) — indeed, his command to love one's enemies (Matt. 5:44; Luke 6:27) — they read these verses of the Gospels alongside those psalms, not against them. As Christians, it is not acceptable to bracket the words of Christ when we pray the Psalms; for Christ is the fulfillment of true humanity, the recapitulation of the true covenant partner. The Psalms find their fulfillment and culmination in Christ, whether or not the psalmist is looking forward to a messianic figure.

Yet, there are different ways in which premodern exegetes read the Psalms christologically. Augustine tends to see Christ as the primary subject of the Psalms, as the fulfillment of David's office, the one to whom many psalms are attributed. Sometimes the Psalms are seen to prophesy Christ; other times Christ is seen as the speaker of the Psalms, either as a representative of humanity or as the head of the church. When it comes to the imprecations in the Psalms, the "enemies" are not the enemies of David or Israel, but of Christ. Thus, the "little ones of Babylon" bashed against the rock in Psalm 137 are "newly born evil desires" that are dashed against the rock, who is Jesus Christ.[70] This allegorical reading relates the text to Christ so that the believers in Christ can curse the sin that threatens their own life of faith.

Calvin also gives a spiritual reading of the Psalms, but with a much stronger accent on the literal and historical sense. Hence, Calvin does not quickly pass over the attribution of a psalm to David, but he seeks to read the psalm in light of David and the history of Israel.[71] Calvin does not stop with a reading of a psalm in its Israelite context, however, for David is also a type of Christ, and believers in Christ must approach the psalm in light of Christ's own teaching. Thus, Calvin reads the curses of Psalm 137 as an indication of the punishments of Edom promised by God in Ezekiel, Jeremiah, and Obadiah. They are not simply the "enemies" of God's people, for "to pray for vengeance would have been unwarrantable, had not God promised it." One should not pray these psalms to take care of personal grudges, for Psalm 137 simply declares the mighty promises of God in Israel's history, while for "even our greatest enemies, we should wish their amendment and reformation." Cal-

---

70. See Thompson, *Reading with the Dead*, p. 57.

71. Whatever historical reconstruction one accepts regarding the composition of the Psalms, a canonical reader will still be attentive to the attribution of certain psalms to David. The literal-historical sense is not a reconstruction behind the text, but the story within the text.

vin's overall approach holds together Psalm 137 as a story about Israel, with the psalm giving a typology for the church. For the "Jerusalem" that is being cried out for is both the Jerusalem of Israel in exile and the church facing trials and persecutions.[72]

As Christians, We Are Called to Love Our Enemies, Not to Desire Their Destruction

Premodern interpreters have various ways of understanding Psalm 137's curses. But there is broad agreement that the psalm's curses should not be used as curses for our own enemy's destruction. This is not just an arbitrary softening of an ancient curse, but a direct result of reading these passages canonically and christologically. One historian of exegesis summarizes this point in this way: "Only Jesus is fit to lament and curse absolutely." This is a "universal apprehension among the teachers of the church . . . lest the Bible's curses be kidnapped to settle private scores."[73] Although believers are united to Christ in the church, it is Christ who is the only head, Christ who is the judge. Christ — not ourselves — is trusted to administer judgment justly.

For Augustine, this fits within an overall vision of the triune God who has shown love to his enemies in Christ. The very process of interpretation of Scripture should put believers in the school of transformation into ever-deeper love of enemies, deeper into the image of Christ that is shown not only in the Sermon on the Mount but in his life of love toward sinners. Jason Byassee describes the consequence of this for Augustine:

> Christians cannot curse, nor take joy in vengeance, nor even wish to see the wrongs against them avenged. When they come upon such sentiments in Scripture, these must be signs that God wishes for them to read deeper.[74]

Yet there were still times that Augustine used Psalm 137's curses in ways that contemporary readers will want to avoid. Augustine applies the curses prophetically to Christ and the church, such that the ene-

72. Calvin, CTS Comm. on Psalm 137:5, 7.
73. Thompson, *Reading with the Dead*, p. 69.
74. Byassee, *Praise Seeking Understanding*, p. 163.

mies of Christ are cursed. Frequently he frames Christ's enemies as sin, as in Psalm 137. But at times Augustine thinks he can discern the enemies of Christ's church — such as the Donatists. Even at this point, he does not apply the curses directly (only Christ can do that) — arguing that "we must not hate them" but seek their good through seeking their conversion (Byassee, pp. 158-59). Nevertheless, the Donatists saw Augustine's effort to seek their conversion and extend "love" with the psalm of cursing as a form of coercive violence.

In contrast, Calvin tended to be much more cautious about usurping the place of judgment, claiming that we cannot know who Christ's enemies are. In fact, it is his doctrine of predestination that supplements the psalms of cursing in a way that is a safeguard against abusing the curses of those psalms. For Calvin, it is axiomatic that with regard to other people, "we cannot distinguish between the elect and the reprobate." In our practical action toward others, therefore, we are always to assume that the person may be elect: that is, the Spirit could make today's hardened sinner into tomorrow's repentant believer. Thus "it is our duty to pray for all who trouble us; to desire the salvation of all; and even to care for the welfare of every individual."[75] Augustine and Calvin both seek to extend neighbor-love to enemies, and they interpret the Psalm 137's curses as having a prophetic dimension, applying to Christ and his church. But Calvin has a more emphatic caution about ascending to the judgment place of God.

In the end, premodern exegetes believe that we should utter those psalms — even with their curses — because they are part of God's transformative word through Scripture. Praying the imprecatory psalms reminds us that God cares for our suffering, and is a God of justice, even when we may never see that justice in our lifetime. Yet, in the words of Calvin, such psalms express the "sufferings" of God's people "in sighs and prayers," so as to "keep alive the hope of that deliverance which they despaired of."[76] The world around us does not look just, and God's people often face trials and persecutions. The curses of those psalms express the cry of God's people in such a setting.

In addition, if they are read canonically and christologically, the

---

75. Calvin, Comm. on Psalm 109:16, following Thompson's translation, in Thompson, *Reading with the Dead,* p. 66.

76. Calvin, CTS Comm. on Psalm 137:1.

curses in the Psalms do not speak against our calling toward enemy-love as disciples of Jesus. They express the fact that, on this side of eternity, the Christian life is a struggle that encounters opposition from without and within, even as it is "not against enemies of flesh and blood" (Eph. 6:12). Praying the curses in light of Christ as the only judge releases the church from the need to curse its own personal enemies, even though the cursing of enemies seems to be the instinctive response of sinners in a broken world.

For Further Reading

The Church's Bible Commentary Series (Eerdmans); Ancient Christian Commentary on Scripture (InterVarsity); Reformation Commentary on Scripture (InterVarsity).

Each of these is a multivolume series of biblical commentaries with rich selections from premodern exegetes in English translation. The Church's Bible and Ancient Christian Commentary on Scripture have selections from the patristic period, and the Reformation Commentary on Scripture from Reformation-era interpreters.

John O'Keefe and R. R. Reno, *Sanctified Vision: An Introduction to Early Christian Interpretation of the Bible* (Baltimore: Johns Hopkins University Press, 2005).

O'Keefe and Reno give an excellent thematic and theological introduction to early Christian biblical interpretation.

Hans W. Frei, *Eclipse of the Biblical Narrative: A Study in Eighteenth and Nineteenth Century Hermeneutics* (New Haven: Yale University Press, 1974).

Frei's book is a classic history of the "eclipse" of the Bible's narrative in favor of external, Enlightenment frames of reference in the eighteenth and nineteenth centuries.

John L. Thompson, *Reading the Bible with the Dead: What You Can Learn from the History of Exegesis that You Can't Learn from Exegesis Alone* (Grand Rapids: Eerdmans, 2007).

Thompson presents an accessible series of studies of how premodern exegetes have understood difficult parts of Scripture, passages that are violent, seem discriminatory, or are otherwise disturbing. These case studies lead to a strong cumulative case for reading Scripture together with premodern interpreters.

193

Brian Daley, "Is Patristic Exegesis Still Usable? Reflections on Early Christian Interpretation of the Psalms," *Communio* 29 (Spring 2002): 185-216; Frances Young, "The 'Mind' of Scripture: Theological Readings of the Bible in the Fathers," *International Journal of Systematic Theology* 7, no. 2 (April 2005).

These two articles present both a description of key features in patristic exegesis and a case delineating the continuing usefulness of patristic exegesis.

Jason Byassee, *Praise Seeking Understanding: Reading the Psalms with Augustine* (Grand Rapids: Eerdmans, 2007).

Byassee makes a case for how and why today's Christians should recover key aspects of ancient exegesis like those found in Augustine. Byassee is particularly helpful in pointing out the christological center of Augustine's exegesis (chap. 2), and a strategy for contemporary Christians to draw on ancient exegesis in a way that does not continue ancient polemics against the Jews (chap. 4).

CHAPTER 6

Scriptural Interpretation and Practices

Participation in the Triune Drama of Salvation

T HIS FINAL CHAPTER moves to an examination of the practices of
readers of Scripture. With that focus, I suspect that some readers
will exclaim, "Finally, here's the how-to approach to theological interpretation we've been waiting for." Others will be relieved that we have
now moved on from all of the God-talk and now we're going to explore
"our part" in theological interpretation.

However, if one accepts the view I propose for the theological interpretation of Scripture, neither of those directions would be appropriate
for a final chapter. If scriptural interpretation is not just about imple-
menting a method — like a scientific method — but involves discerning
a mystery in light of Jesus Christ, then a how-to approach won't do.
There are important elements of interpretation of Scripture that do involve the use of methods, particularly in linguistic and historical points
of analysis of the texts, their context, and our own context of reception.
But these constitute neither the starting nor the ending point for the
proper reception of Scripture as the church; therefore, attention to these
methods is not enough. Discerning the mystery of Christ in Scripture involves a life of prayer, worship, and Christian community, and even
these are not methods for interpreting Scripture that can be isolated and
repeated in a scientific sense of the word "method." Interpreting Scripture cannot be reduced to method or technique, because it is nothing
less than a part of our life of participation in Christ through the Spirit, a
means by which God nurtures our love of God and neighbor.

Moreover, it is not true that chapter 3 on revelation talks about "God's part," and this chapter now moves on to "our part" in theological interpretation. If one accepts the Trinitarian framework inherent in this book, no easy dichotomy between "God's part" and "our part" is possible. As interpreters of Scripture, we do have practices and commitments that inevitably shape our reading of Scripture. But that is not "our part." We do not own these practices in an autonomous sense; they are part of our participation in the work of the triune God. When we approach Scripture in prayer, wrestle with the text with honesty, and respond in obedience, we are empowered by the Holy Spirit, who enables us to live into our new life in Christ. When we approach Scripture with resistance, seek to assert our mastery over the text, and refuse to perform God's imperatives through the text, we are living in our "flesh" (to use Paul's term), which seeks autonomy from God. In the present time, both of these dynamics are at work in our practices of reading Scripture, for we have tasted the new life of the Spirit but still struggle with the sin of the flesh (cf. Rom. 7:14–8:11).

The proper starting point for thinking about our own practices in reading Scripture is not to look to ourselves, but to look to the saving work of the triune God. To the extent that our reading practices participate in the Spirit's work in conforming us to Jesus Christ as the Son of the Father, these practices should be valued as gifts from God. To the extent that our reading practices distract us from the Word in the words of Scripture — the Living Christ who comforts, judges, and restores his people through Scripture — we should move away from those practices. This is not a matter of approaching Scripture in a way that is liberal or conservative, seeker-sensitive or traditional. It's not a matter of one's stated doctrine of Scripture in a doctrinal statement. It is a question of profound discernment about the theology operative in practice: Have we come to use Scripture for our own purposes, or are we reading Scripture as part of the great triune drama of the gospel of Jesus Christ? There is no "interpretation machine" that Christians can put a biblical text into and receive out of it "the word of God." There is no foolproof method that a biblical exegete, locked in a library basement, can use to end up with a rightly construed interpretation. There is no unmediated way in which to encounter Scripture's guidance and critique of our culture. For Scripture is not an agent that critiques us; the Spirit is the agent who uses Scripture as an instrument for critique, guidance, and restoration. Hence, becoming better interpreters means more than mastering a set of ancient documents. Biblical interpretation for Christians involves nothing less than a worshipful consecration of our practical lives to participate in the triune God's work, so that we may be mastered by the living Christ who speaks through Scripture.

This chapter begins with a sketch of the Trinitarian drama of salvation that provides the context for our understanding of our own practices and the "practical wisdom" in reading Scripture as the church. Next, the chapter highlights the dramatic character of God's word by examining God's word as a powerful speech-action. Then, in order to clarify the reading practices that do and do not cohere with this Trinitarian vision of salvation, in the next few sections I will discuss specific reading practices and the operative theology within them. The first section examines well-intended reading practices that nevertheless point to a lesser story than the gospel of Jesus Christ. This is followed by three sections that explore ways in which reading practices participate in the Trinitarian drama of salvation: the practices of prayerfully reading Scripture as a spiritual discipline; the church's reception of Scripture in the ministry of word and sacrament; and scriptural reading practices displaying missional faithfulness. The chapter concludes with reflections on how the practices of theological interpretation included in this book are intrinsically tied to God's renewal of the church's life and ministry.

A Trinitarian Soteriology: Reading as Acting in the Drama

Those who have read the preceding chapters will recognize that reading as part of a Trinitarian theology of salvation is not new to this final chapter, but a key dimension of each chapter of the book so far. In the paragraphs below, I will highlight this important thread through the book and then expand on a few of its implications.

In chapter 1, I articulated an approach toward scriptural interpretation as part of a journey of faith seeking understanding, in which readers follow the path of Jesus Christ by the power of the Spirit, anticipating a face-to-face vision with the triune God. The chapter explores how the rule of faith is not a rigid straitjacket for interpreting Scripture but a functional rule for interpreting Scripture in a Trinitarian way.

Chapter 2 deals with the issues of general hermeneutics and the role for preunderstandings, tradition, and critical studies in engaging the Bible in particular. On the one hand, Christians should not be embarrassed about their ecclesiastical location in interpreting Scripture. We should celebrate the way in which the history, worship, and practice of belonging to the church shapes our interpretation. On the other hand, the Spirit speaks a word of transformation through Scripture, so we need to be open to surprise, wrestling with the scriptural text and drawing on critical studies of Scripture to enter into play with the text. The combination of these two dynamics is that the Spirit is always speaking a word to call the church to further transformation through Scripture, yet the church's tradition also reflects the Spirit's work in a people whom God has united to Jesus Christ.

The third chapter puts the triune drama of revelation at the forefront. In our operative theologies, we either have a theology grounded in the revelation of Jesus Christ or one that is based on the inherent, ostensibly "universal" capacities for human judgment. Second, we either have a Trinitarian theology of revelation or a Deistic one. Between the two either-or's is a continuum of positions on both sides, but every time we act and make decisions as Christians, we operate in one sphere or the other. In a Trinitarian account of revelation, human beings do not have the natural capacity to apprehend the truth, and a teacher does not draw out truth that resides within human reason. Instead, the moments in the history of Israel and Jesus Christ are decisive for the truth, and humans are blinded to the apprehension of truth apart from the Spirit's power. Revelation is the action of God in which humans are brought into the triune drama of salvation, united to Jesus Christ, the truth, by the indwelling power of the Spirit. Revelation brings not only knowledge of God but fellowship in and with the triune God, a saving fellowship that transforms believers ever deeper into Christ's image as Christ's body.

Chapters 4 and 5 develop dimensions of the Trinitarian soteriology that relate to culture and history in particular. Chapter 4 articulates a vision for how the Spirit produces a bounded diversity of scriptural interpretation through the Spirit's indigenizing work of the Word. Yet, it is the Word and not just any word that is indigenized, and it is the sovereign Spirit who uses Scripture to reshape our cultural idols into Christ's image. Chapter 5 continues this Trinitarian vision of God's saving work by speaking about how Christ's incarnation revolutionizes our notion of history, and how the Spirit uses Scripture to speak even beyond the intentions of the human authors of the Old Testament. In light of the incarnation, all of history participates in God's providential action, which finds its culmination in Christ. Thus does the Spirit testify to Christ through the whole of Scripture, both the Old and New Testaments. Moreover, Christians read Scripture as the bride of Christ, and yet still as sinners. As Christ's bride and body, we benefit by being attentive to the Spirit's use of Scripture in the church in the past, even as we recognize the sinful depravity of both those interpreters and ourselves.

Hence, in many ways this book has already been exploring reading practices in light of the triune drama of salvation. Many of the pieces have been explored, step by step, in earlier chapters. But for the purposes of this final chapter, let us point out some of the key overall dimensions of this vision.

Reading in the Trinitarian Drama of Salvation

What is the Bible to the church? Perhaps it is a religious document "owned" by a particular religious community, a sourcebook for its religious imagination? Whatever value such a suggestion may have, it misses the central Christian conviction of what the Bible is to the church. The Bible is the instrument of the triune God to shape believers into the image of Christ, in word and deed, by the power of the Spirit, transforming a sinful and alienated people into children of a loving Father.

The Bible should not be seen as the tool of the church; rather, it is the tool of the triune God, a key means through which the triune God has promised to act in the world. The Bible does not just deliver information about the triune God, but it mediates "God's communicative fellowship" by extending "Christ's active, communicative presence" by the Spirit's power.[1] Reading the Bible as the church is not about finding relevant principles for our life, but about the worshipful act of receiving the healing judgment and reforming love of the head of the church, Jesus Christ, who uses Scripture through the Spirit's power. Reading Scripture is not about self-improvement but about the mortification

---

1. John Webster, *Word and Church: Essays in Christian Dogmatics* (Edinburgh: T&T Clark, 2001), pp. 46, 36.

and coming to life of the self in Christ and his body, empowered by the Spirit to live lives of gratitude to the Father.

Kevin Vanhoozer highlights the distinctively Trinitarian character of the drama of salvation by using a theater analogy to describe the Trinitarian context of the church's reading and performance of Scripture. "The Father is the playwright and producer of the action; the Son is the climax and summation of the action. The Spirit, as the one who unites us to Christ, is the dresser who clothes us with Christ's righteousness, the prompter who helps us remember our biblical lines, and prop master who gives gifts (accessories) to each church member, equipping us to play our parts."[2] The triune God is the one who authors, initiates, empowers, and provides the "ends" for scriptural interpretation. Believers are active in the process of reading and performing Scripture, but only as ones who are gifted and indwelt by the Spirit, united to Christ as the climax of Scripture's drama of redemption, all in the context of the loving initiative of the Father, who sends the Son and the Spirit on our behalf.

Reading in the Trinitarian Drama of Salvation

The church reads Scripture from within a narrative framework. As I have observed in chapter 1, the rule of faith is a narrative emerging from Scripture that is also a lens through which to view Scripture. But this is not just a story about the past, or a fable of the imagination. This narrative is rooted in the action of God in history, culminating in the incarnation, life, death, and resurrection of Jesus Christ. Hence, we do not apply principles from a story to our lives so much as we enter into the ongoing drama being played out by God's work in the world around us. We are actors in the drama of creation, fall, and redemption in Christ, actors and not merely spectators of the triune God's work in the world.

Drama and performance metaphors have been used by various

---

2. Kevin Vanhoozer, *The Drama of Doctrine: A Canonical-Linguistic Approach to Christian Theology* (Louisville: Westminster John Knox, 2005), p. 448. Vanhoozer is adapting the work of Hans Urs Von Balthasar in this configuration of a drama as the context for scriptural interpretation.

theologians in the last century to describe the relationship of the community of faith, Scripture, and God's action.[3] Sometimes it is used in a way that suggests that Scripture is basically a script to be used as a tool of the Christian community in its performance. But if Scripture is the church's tool rather than God's instrument of transformation, then one can lose sight of the centrality of divine action in the Trinitarian drama described above. In ourselves, we are not the central actors in God's inbreaking kingdom; we are members of the body of Jesus Christ, who is central in the drama's action. Insofar as we act in this drama at all, it is only as those united to Jesus Christ and filled with the Holy Spirit. When we act in sin, which we will continue to do on this side of the *eschaton,* we are moving away from the communicative fellowship of the triune drama.

The image of Christian readers of Scripture participating in the triune drama has several distinct virtues. It reminds us that knowledge of God is not simply a matter of mental assent, but of active participation in a world in which the triune God is active in saving, judging, and redeeming. As such, scriptural interpretation should fire our imagination about the world (as we see it through the lens of Scripture), showing the significance of our daily action. For knowing God through Scripture is not mainly about marking the correct answer on a theology exam, but acting in a way that is a faithful performance of the canon's gospel. For, as Vanhoozer points out from the context of theater, "to interpret a script is to *act,* and to act is to *interpret.*"[4] As readers and performers of Scripture, we live our lives before the face of God *(coram deo)* through a constant reengagement with the authoritative script.

The emphasis on practice in the drama metaphor should not be misunderstood as a pragmatism that is governed by expediency, or by

---

3. One of the most significant treatments is in Hans Urs von Balthasar's five-volume work *Theo-drama: Theological Dramatic Theory* (San Francisco: Ignatius Press, 1988-98), which gives a vision of Christian theology that is "full of dramatic tension, both in form and content" (1: 125). See also Trevor A. Hart and Steven R. Guthrie, eds., *Faithful Performances: Enacting Christian Tradition* (Burlington, VT: Ashgate, 2007); Frances M. Young, *Virtuoso Theology: The Bible and Interpretation* (Cleveland: Pilgrim, 1993); N. T. Wright, *The Last Word: Beyond the Bible Wars to a New Understanding of the Authority of Scripture* (San Francisco: Harper, 2005).

4. These reasons are adapted from Vanhoozer, *Drama of Doctrine,* pp. 79-81 (italics in original).

what is clever or catchy. Rather, it is best understood as enacting a form of practical reason. "Practical reason" (or *phronesis,* in a term Aristotle used regarding ethics and Gadamer used regarding hermeneutics) refers to a form of reason that is not simply the implementation of a regularized method to get a correct outcome. Rather, it is a form of reason that operates in the realm of wisdom and virtue. *Phronesis* is a form of knowledge that means knowing how to respond with wisdom in the new concrete situation that we find ourselves in on a practical level each day.[5] It is not a scientific form of knowledge and perception; but it is also not in an "anything goes" realm. As participants in the triune drama of salvation, we need to *"improvise judgments"* about how to respond to new situations *"that are nevertheless consistent with our canonical script."*[6] As Samuel Wells points out, improvising from the Bible does not involve being "original" or "clever," as if one created the overall drama in which one acts. Nor does it involve mere repetition of the script without awareness of new circumstances. Instead, improvisation is a form of practical reason and "abiding faithfulness" that involves performing the Bible in a way that has boundaries from Scripture and tradition, but continues to act as the church in new contexts.[7]

In order to sharpen our practical knowledge — wisdom — about the performance of Scripture in the triune drama, I will deal in the following sections with specific examples and practices of reading Scripture. Ultimately, however, the drama metaphor indicates to us that even the final section of this book cannot be a how-to manual. Performing the canonical script draws on the wisdom necessary to respond to new and unforeseen situations. The metaphor of drama (and what is related to practical wisdom) is one of the most vigorously discussed subjects in recent scholarly work on the theological hermeneutics of Scripture.[8] But even becoming an "expert" on this literature does not make one an expert in theological interpretation, because reading Scripture for the

5. Hans Georg Gadamer, *Truth and Method,* 2nd ed., trans. Joel Weinsheimer and Donald G. Marshall (New York: Continuum, 1993), p. 21.

6. Vanhoozer, *Drama of Doctrine,* p. 335 (italics in original).

7. Samuel Wells, *Improvisation: The Drama of Christian Ethics* (Grand Rapids: Brazos, 2004), pp. 65-69.

8. For example, see Daniel Treier, *Virtue and the Voice of God: Toward Theology as Wisdom* (Grand Rapids: Eerdmans, 2006); Vanhoozer, *Drama of Doctrine,* chap. 10; Hart and Guthrie, *Faithful Performances.*

Christian involves nothing less than acting in our Christ-formed identity by the Spirit's power, in service to the Father. No technique — nor academic discourse — can make that happen.

Reading in the Trinitarian Drama of Salvation

We are seeking to read Scripture as part of the journey of salvation, of healing, of redemption in Christ by the Spirit's power. Yet there are many other ends toward which people can, and do, read Scripture. Some read Scripture in order to find self-help principles; others read it for how to succeed in daily life; still others read Scripture as part of a quest to find Paul's theology or the theology of the Gospel of John. While Christians should be interested in the theology of Paul and of John's Gospel, even this should not be confused with the proper goal of interpreting Scripture, which is not simply the discovery of a meaning but a means in the process of transformation in Christ, as the living Christ speaks words of comfort, rebuke, and healing through the Spirit's power. Ultimately, Christians should not read Scripture in order to master the biblical text, or even to develop a set of theological concepts. Rather, reading Scripture is about being mastered by Jesus Christ through a biblical text that functionally stands over us as the word of God, not under us as a word we can control, rearrange, and use for our own purposes. Reading the Bible as Scripture involves nothing less than entering into the triune God's own communicative fellowship.

Because reading the Bible takes place in the economy of salvation, it is intrinsically connected to our identity as disciples of Jesus Christ. This does not mean that we interpret Scripture in light of a "Jesus and me" spirituality. But as Stephen Fowl and Gregory Jones have pointed out in *Reading in Communion,* we read as followers of Jesus incorporated into a community "set on a journey of becoming friends of God and bearing witness to the good news of God's inbreaking kingdom" in Jesus Christ. As we read Scripture, we "engage in the process of unlearning the ways of the 'world' and learning how to pattern our lives in Jesus Christ" by the Spirit. Thus, when we seek to discern how every page of Scripture finds its fulfillment in Christ, we are not simply engaging in theological speculation. Wrestling with how a psalm of cursing or a conquest of Canaan relates to Jesus Christ is an imperative for the

Christian because we need to see how Jesus Christ relates to our world of cursing and violence. We need to see the pattern of Jesus Christ's life and teaching where it is hard to see. This is not simply a task of perception, nor of overcoming the historical gap between an ancient text and our contemporary context. As Fowl and Jones note, the "moral discontinuities between Scripture and us" demonstrated in our action are among the most important "gaps" to be bridged in interpretation.[9] Moreover, following Jesus as a community of disciples is impossible without the Spirit. Neither the perception of the pattern of Jesus nor the learning of the moral ways of Jesus happen by our own power, but only through the Spirit who initiates and empowers our identity as children of the Father.

Reading Scripture as disciples of Jesus, who declares the inbreaking of God's kingdom, is also an eschatological act. We do not receive God's word as something we can circumscribe and repackage, but as a word from God's future new creation being received into the present. The supreme eschatological event in history — the resurrection of Jesus Christ — provides the standpoint from which all Scripture should be viewed, for we have been united to Christ not only in his death but also in his resurrection and ascension, being "seated at the right hand of God" with Jesus Christ (Col. 3:1).[10] We read Scripture to discern through the Spirit the manifestations of Christ's reign in the world around us. The kingdom is amidst us, and through Scripture we can come to discern "parables of the kingdom" in unlikely places, even outside the visible church.[11]

However, reading Scripture as an eschatological act also requires the recognition of the partial character of our knowledge, "for now we see in a mirror, dimly, but then we will see face to face" (1 Cor. 13:12). We read not only as the new creation of the Spirit, united to Christ, but as ones who continue to live in a fallen age of darkness, filled with structural and personal sin. We read with trust that we will encounter the living Christ as we read Scripture, but also some suspicion of our own

---

9. Stephen E. Fowl and L. Gregory Jones, *Reading in Communion: Scripture and Ethics in Christian Life* (Grand Rapids: Eerdmans, 1991), pp. 70-71, 61.

10. See Richard Hays, "Reading Scripture in Light of the Resurrection," in *The Art of Reading Scripture,* ed. Ellen Davis and Richard Hays (Grand Rapids: Eerdmans, 2003), pp. 216-38.

11. See the section on secular parables and "lesser lights" in chap. 3.

fallen tendencies to manipulate and control the reading process for our own autonomous purposes. Scripture is not "us" in disguise. It gives us words of life — but words that as sinners we resist, distort, and subvert. The kingdom is amongst us, but until the consummation of Christ's kingdom, his disciples will continue to struggle with sin. Whether through active disobedience or slothful inaction, Christians continue to read Scripture with an incomplete recognition of the all-encompassing reign of God.

However, while our continued fallenness should give us caution and even suspicion about the possible self-serving ends of our scriptural interpretation in the Christian community, we should remember Paul's imperative to live into our new eschatological identity. Our union with Christ is both a fact (an indicative) and a command (an imperative) for Paul. For if in baptism "we have been united with [Christ] in a death like his, we will certainly be united with him in a resurrection like his" (Rom. 6:5). This indicative leads to an imperative. "The death he died, he died to sin, once for all; but the life he lives, he lives to God. So you also must consider yourselves dead to sin and alive to God in Christ Jesus" (Rom. 6:10-11). Because you who are baptized are united to Christ, you are to "consider yourselves" in light of your new identity and "not let sin exercise dominion in your mortal bodies" (Rom. 6:12). Reading Scripture is an act of trust in the God who has united us to Christ and filled us with the Spirit, even as this is balanced with a suspicion of the continued sin of all who live in this "now but not yet" overlapping of the ages.

Finally, reading Scripture is also a covenantal act: we read as participants in the covenantal drama of redemption. The notion of covenant is one of the most widely used images for God's saving relationship with creation in Scripture. The Old Testament tells us of multiple covenants that God makes with creation and his people: with Noah (Gen. 9), Abraham (Gen. 17), Moses and the people of Israel (Exod. 6), and David (2 Sam. 2:7). God's covenantal acts are central in the drama of salvation, and these acts find their culmination in the person of Jesus Christ.[12] Christians encounter the covenanting God through the Spirit's voice in Scripture, who incorporates believers into the covenant in Christ. Christians reading Scripture are not reading someone else's mail or

---

12. This account follows the direction of Vanhoozer, *Drama of Doctrine*, pp. 135ff.

simply trying to glean true propositions about God. Instead, we read as those who are united to God in covenant through the person and work of Christ. Our covenantal union with God means that we read Scripture in fellowship with God, but also with covenant obligations toward God. To put it differently, we read Scripture as a "love letter," as Kierkegaard puts it: as the bride of Christ, but also as servants of the master.[13] Both sides of this are held together in Christ, the key to Scripture, who is also both the Lord and the servant of the covenant. Reading Scripture as those who are in Christ, we see how Scripture sets forth a playbook for how to be a covenant people. Scripture as a covenantal book records the "dialogical action" and the "plot" of the divine drama and "prescribes our roles" for participating in it as God's covenant people.[14]

The Power of God: God's Word as Action

In light of the vision above about the way in which we read Scripture within the triune drama of salvation, we can move onto an old theological insight that has some new exponents: God's word received through the instrument of Scripture does not just give information about God, but it mediates the powerful *action* of God. An early twentieth-century Christian dogmatician put it this way: God "is always present in his word," such that the word "is never separate from God, from Christ, from the Holy Spirit." Thus the word of God performs actions in God's own power: "The word that proceeds from the mouth of God is indeed always a power accomplishing that for which God sends it forth."[15] God's word creates, upholds, sustains, and redeems in Christ through the Spirit.

In and through Scripture, God promises, commands, beckons, and admonishes. All of these things involve more than just giving informa-

---

13. "Think of a lover who has now received a letter from his beloved — as precious as this letter is to the lover, just so precious to thee, I assume, is God's word. In the way the lover reads this letter . . . dost thou read God's word and conceive that God's word ought to be read." Søren Kierkegaard, *For Self-Examination and Judge for Yourself,* trans. Walter Lowrie (Princeton, NJ: Princeton University Press, 1941), p. 51.

14. Vanhoozer, *Drama of Doctrine,* p. 145.

15. Bavinck, *Reformed Dogmatics,* vol. 1, *Prolegomena,* trans. John Vriend (Grand Rapids: Baker Academic, 2003), pp. 459, 458.

tion about God, though they are, in fact, part of divine revelation in Scripture. When promising a covenantal relationship to Abram, God says, "I will make you into a great nation, and I will bless you" (Gen. 12:2a). God makes promises to Abram, and these promises extend beyond simply giving information to Abram and to others included in God's covenant people. Christian readers should not be content with a reading that simply says, "God is the sort of God who makes covenant with Abram and his people." That statement does not go far enough. The state of affairs between God and Abram has changed because of God's words, just as is true when words are spoken at a wedding — words to declare that a couple is now "husband and wife." God *promises* and *makes covenant* with Abram: it is an action. And if readers see themselves as within Abram's covenant, God promises and makes covenant with readers by means of the text.

What difference does this make? If all of God's actions of speech are translated into simply true information about God, then we respond differently to this biblical text than we do if God *acts* through his speech. The statement "God is a God who makes promises to Abram and his descendents" keeps God's word at arm's length. "We go to church, and they tell us about God," a parishioner might think. "It is reassuring to know that God is the kind of God who makes promises to people. That's good, because I think it's good to make promises." But if, through the action of God's speech, God changes the state of affairs (i.e., God makes promises to us), then we must consider how to respond. How am I to see my life, my marriage, and my workplace in light of the fact that the God of Israel makes promises to me and my faith community? How am I to live now, as one whom God actively blesses (Gen. 12:2a) and promises that "all peoples on earth will be blessed through you" (Gen. 12:3b)? How do my actions toward other peoples, nations, and cultures live into God's promise or deny it? God promises, God blesses, and in the midst of this God calls us to participate in his action of blessing the peoples of the earth.

Word-actions such as promising, commanding, asking, and beckoning accomplish what speech-act theorists call "illocutionary acts."[16]

---

16. The prefix "il-" in "illocutionary act" has the sense of "in." Hence, an illocutionary act is an action of promising, commanding, or asking *in* or *through* the locution (the speaking of words). Speech-act theorists also talk about a "perlocutionary act," which is

These acts involve the communication of knowledge, but they are not reducible to the communication of knowledge or information. A question tells us certain things about the questioner. But a question is more than that: it implicates our response; it brings us into a new state of affairs. There is something wrong if we respond to a question or command by thinking, "That's interesting, a person is asking me a question or is commanding something." But that is exactly how humans often respond to God's word.

Moving from a one-dimensional to a three-dimensional reception of God's word is part of entering into the Spirit's work of being renewed in Christ. In Matthew's Gospel, Jesus offers the parable of the sower to bring up the various responses to the word of God's kingdom. Jesus quotes Isaiah to the effect that some will hear, but never understand; they will see, but never perceive (Matt 13:14). But Jesus measures hearing and seeing by the *response* to the seed of the word: the fertile soil bears fruit and "produces a crop" (Matt. 13:23). A proper response to God's word is not just about receiving information that is transmitted, but about perceiving the powerful action of God in that speech and responding by the Spirit. Apart from the Spirit, Jonathan Edwards says, we receive God's word as an abstract word, as in reading a dictionary entry about "honey." But through the Spirit we gain a fuller reception of the word; we taste the sweetness of honey so that we respond to the word with our affections and delight.[17]

In some ways, our tendency to flatten God's word into abstractions is like being actors in a drama who receive information by way of computer, not the action conveyed through God's speech. Ultimately, it points to an inability to enter into the new state of affairs brought about via God's word, to be actors in a loving relationship with God.

Our situation of translating the action of God's word into mere in-

---

an act performed *by* saying something. For more on speech-act theory, see John L. Austin, *How to Do Things with Words,* 2nd ed. (Cambridge, MA: Harvard University Press, 1975). For two significant but differing ways of using speech-act theory for the theological hermeneutics of Scripture, see Nicholas Wolterstorff, *Divine Discourse: Philosophical Reflections on the Claim That God Speaks* (Cambridge, UK: Cambridge University Press, 1995), and Vanhoozer, *Drama of Doctrine.*

17. See Jonathan Edwards, "A Treatise Concerning Religious Affections," in *A Jonathan Edwards Reader,* ed. John E. Smith et al. (New Haven: Yale University Press, 1995), pp. 160-61.

formation is similar to the predicament of Lars in the film *Lars and the Real Girl* (2007). Lars, a twenty-seven-year-old man living in the garage-apartment of his brother, has lost the ability to give and receive love from another human being. He has experienced great trauma in his childhood, and he is unable to process illocutionary acts, such as being asked out on a date or being promised the nourishment and fellowship of a warm meal. To Lars, these actions simply portray information rather than bringing him into a new state of affairs requiring his response. As such, Lars sees these actions as little more than distractions from the lonely reality he experiences. Unable to be responsive to acts of love, Lars eventually buys a life-size, plastic "girlfriend" online. Here is a companion who can mirror his own hurts, needs, and desires without bothering him with those illocutionary acts that call for a response.

As part of his delusion, Lars believes that his plastic girlfriend, named Bianca, is a real girl. The small community around Lars decides to go along with it, greeting Bianca as Lars brings her to parties, church, and various events. But eventually, this action of the community begins to corrode Lars's own delusion. Lars has his first fight with Bianca when a member of the community takes Bianca out for an evening of volunteering at the hospital. Even though Bianca cannot speak, her "action" of leaving Lars for the evening shakes up his world: he is required to give a *response* with some action of his own — not just inserting words into Bianca's mouth. As the story ends, Lars is finally able to receive healing to the point that he can respond to the illocutionary action of a "real girl," someone who has been interested in a relationship with him all along. Finally, Lars is able to receive and respond to her speech-actions of asking questions and comforting as something more than abstract information to be ignored. When she asks something, he is implicated, and he can respond. When she offers words of comfort, Lars can act as one who needs to be comforted and has received, through this speech-act, a word of comfort. Lars comes to experience the fact that words do not just present information; they change the state of the world he inhabits.

As readers of Scripture, "we were dead through our trespasses," but God "made us alive together with Christ" (Eph. 2:5). But while we taste the eschatological reality of life in Christ, we still struggle with the deadening effect of sin. In our sin, we still often hear God's word through Scripture in a way that is one-dimensional — an abstract, mildly interesting word about God. But we do not receive it as a word that announces a new state of affairs, implicating our lives and action through God's promising, asking, electing, and commanding action. Ultimately, since Christians are united to the true, active humanity of Christ, reading Scripture "in Christ" will always be an active affair. Reading Scripture as participating in Christ the triune actor, we participate by responding to the new reality caused by the illocutionary acts of God's word, empowered by the Spirit to show the Spirit's own fruit in response to the word. The translation of God's word in Scripture into abstract information is not simply bad hermeneutics; it is a sinful refusal to participate in the active life of union with Christ.

Acting in Lesser Dramas: Reading Practices That (Unintentionally) Tell Lesser Stories than the Gospel

Before examining reading practices that participate in the triune drama of salvation, we should consider for a few moments some of the temptations we need to overcome. The temptations are legion, but because we are dealing in an area of practical wisdom, dealing with specific examples can help sharpen our thinking for situations we are yet to encounter. These examples focus on how Scripture is preached and taught, but they also apply to the ways in which Christians approach Scripture in other contexts.

In order to make Scripture "relevant," we tend to make ourselves the primary focus of scriptural interpretation, dislocating the centrality of the triune God and his saving work. If we assume that teaching or preaching about God will seem irrelevant to a congregation, it is tempting to change the subject to a source of endless fascination: the hearers themselves. The hearers are concerned with how to pay the bills, how to fit in at school, how to have a better marriage. God will take care of God. Why not focus directly on ourselves in the teaching and preaching of Scripture?

For example, one pastor decided to preach a sermon addressing a question that everyone faces: how to deal with criticism. He chose to preach on Romans 8:1-4, which begins, "There is therefore now no condemnation for those who are in Christ Jesus," and continues by contrasting "the law of the Spirit" with "the law of sin and death." The pastor said that we are called to walk according to the Spirit, which means we should reject the legalistic demands of others when they criticize us. We should be more like Paul, who was grounded in his acceptance by God (from whom there is "no condemnation"): we, too, can be empowered to listen to legitimate criticism and to ignore condemning, legalistic criticism. We should deal with criticism by sorting out the legalistic from the constructive, and we should make sure to leave the legalistic behind. The preacher mentioned Christ and the Spirit only in passing, because the real point of his interpretation of the Romans text was to glean advice about how we should deal with criticism.

In setting up Paul as a model for how to deal with criticism by way of this text, the pastor obscured the subject matter *(sache)* of the text: the significance of God's action in Jesus Christ and the Holy Spirit. This is the subject that animates Paul's text. The pastor assumed that that subject was abstract, thus not essential in forming the actual content of his message. However, the pastor could probably have reached his same practical insights concerning outside criticism by preaching on a selection from Greek mythology — or any number of texts. The practical insights he wanted to convey were nearly oblivious to the divine drama mediated by the biblical text.

The scandalous part of this approach is that it fails to realize that leading hearers to see and experience the triune drama of salvation through the biblical text is one of the most practical things a teacher or preacher can do. To put it bluntly, preaching or teaching about the triune God's action in the world *is* to preach about the practical lives of Christians. Why? Because believers are filled with the Holy Spirit and are being transformed into Christ's image, empowered to live in gratitude to the Father. This is good news for all parts of life: for Christians struggling with criticism, with finances, with family trouble, with suffering and injustice in a broken world. When read with a hermeneutic of a Trinitarian theology of salvation (as I have discussed in preceding chapters), Scripture becomes a practical book for discerning the saving work of the Trinity in the messiness and ambiguities of life. For Christ is the fulfillment of God's creational and covenantal promises, and our union with the living Christ opens our eyes to the new world of the kingdom.

Another temptation is that we, desiring "new" or "expert" insights, reduce the interpretation of Scripture to the conveying of historical information. Research about the history "behind the text" is an important part of the overall task of interpretation (see chapter 2), but historical reconstruction should not be the ending point for the preaching and teaching of Scripture in the church. It is not unusual for modern readers to focus more on historical background and reconstructions than on the realities mediated by the text itself. But when extrabiblical material moves the hearer away from engaging the actual text of Scripture rather than deeper into such an engagement, then preachers and teachers begin to tell a lesser story than the gospel of the triune God's saving work in the world.

For example, consider a sermon in which the preacher sought to use behind-the-text history to give a fresh reading of Jesus' conversation with the two thieves on the cross in Luke 23:39-43. Although Luke's text simply refers to the other two men being crucified along with Jesus as "criminals," the preacher said that some commentators believe that these criminals were probably Zealots, members of a revolutionary Jewish group violently protesting Roman rule. Her sermon then proceeded to focus on a historical account of the rise of the Zealots: it speculated about how we might draw lessons from the experience of the Zealots and their effort to overthrow Roman rule. The Zealots, she said, were mistaken in that they saw God's kingdom as an earthly kingdom and sought to bring it about by violent, earthly means. We should remember that the kingdom of Christ was not brought about by the sword; Jesus did not initiate an earthly kingdom. Rather than using historical inquiry to bring insight into the Lukan text, the preacher used the biblical text as a steppingstone to portray a history behind the text, which became the real subject matter from which she drew the imperatives of her sermon.

In an effort to give a "fresh" reading of the text, this preacher obscured the narrative of the Lukan text. The sermon itself became wholly contingent on an extrabiblical judgment that "the criminals were *probably* Zealots." In fact, some commentators claim this, but others conclude that these criminals were not Zealots. Instead of respecting the narrative within the text (and using extrabiblical information to move deeper into that text), this sermon focused on historical information as an end in itself; then it drew applications from its own reconstructed history. But the biblical text is not just one among many sources for reconstructing a story that then functions as a means of grace. The word of God comes *through* the biblical text. Reading Scripture is about dis-

cerning a mystery, the mystery of the triune God. It should not be reduced to conveying historical information from which we draw our own
application.

Instead of reading in a way that is receptive to the action of God's
word through Scripture, some read to extract *doctrinal propositions* to
fit a theological blueprint. From chapter 1, I have sought to differenti-
ate my account of theological interpretation from an alternative that
misconstrues the task, that is, the alternative of reading Scripture in
order to extract doctrinal propositions, which turns Scripture into a
set of blocks to fit into a blueprint of a "systematic theology." As I have
noted earlier, God's revelation through Scripture is not reducible to
propositional content. While we should not seek to interpret Scripture from a theology-free standpoint, we should be clear that Scripture stands in judgment over the church's theology as the word of the
living Christ, the only head of the church, spoken through the Spirit.
For some Christians, it is tempting, says R. R. Reno, "to dwell among
the concepts of election and incarnation . . . as if they have a substan-
tial, superluminous truth resident within themselves." But "this failure to see that the purpose of doctrine and theology is to maximize the
penetration of the mind into the world of Scripture, is what we must
overcome."[18]

We interpret Scripture in light of God's electing activity and the incarnation of the Word made flesh. But that does not mean that doctrinal concepts give us an improved version of the Bible, clarifying what
is messy and unclear in the biblical canon. We continually return to
Scripture — not to our theology textbooks — because Scripture itself is
the Spirit's instrument to transform God's people into the image of
Christ. This rule of faith is a path, a journey, not a list of doctrinal propositions with which to satiate our desire for God and occlude our need
for transformation. God acts through Scripture as a means of grace.
God does not simply deliver doctrinal information that we then can organize and use for our own purposes.

18. R. R. Reno, "Theology and Biblical Interpretation," in *Sharper than a Two-Edged
Sword: Preaching, Teaching, and Living the Bible,* ed. Michael Root and James J. Buckley
(Grand Rapids: Eerdmans, 2008), p. 20.

Participating in the Drama, Part I:
Reading Scripture as a Spiritual Discipline

For Christians, Scripture is not the kind of book we should simply skim or read for content. The psalmist says: "I treasure your word in my heart . . . O LORD; teach me your statutes. With my lips I declare all the ordinances of your mouth. I delight in the way of your decrees as much as in all riches. I will meditate on your precepts, and fix my eyes on your ways. I will delight in your statutes; I will not forget your word" (Ps. 119:11-16). For the people of God, the words of Scripture are life-giving words to be treasured, delighted in, meditated on, proclaimed, and remembered. They require attention, the attention of fixing our eyes on the word and work of God, the attention of delighting in and remembering God's word both "day and night" (Ps. 1:2).

In the New Testament we continue to see how Scripture is a book that we should remember and chew on rather than skim. When tempted by Satan, Jesus responds with Scripture that he has memorized (Matt. 4:1-11). When Paul exhorts readers of Ephesians to "be strong in the Lord and in the strength of his power," he tells us that "the word of God" is "the sword of the Spirit" (Eph. 6:10, 17). The book of Colossians admonishes believers to "let the word of Christ dwell in you richly." It does not say that you should merely know what the word of Christ says — but you should let it "dwell in you" (Col. 3:16). The Gospel of John shows the Trinitarian dynamic of this dwelling, for the Spirit sent to believers will "glorify" Christ, and "will take what is mine and declare it to you" (John 16:14). Together with the Old Testament, the New Testament affirms that Scripture is to be chewed, delighted in, wrestled with, and meditated on day and night. As the *Book of Common Prayer* declares, we should pray to "hear" the Holy Scriptures, and "read, mark, learn, and inwardly digest them."[19] We are called to feed on Scripture, to allow Scripture to dwell in us. This practice has a Trinitarian shape for us as Christians, such that if we belong to Jesus Christ, God's word in Christ dwells in us through the Spirit's mediation. "Knowing Scripture" is for the Christian a matter of spiritual survival, a matter of participating in the Spirit's new creation in Christ.

19. Episcopal Church, *The Book of Common Prayer* (New York: Church Hymnal Corp., 1979), p. 184.

Why do we meditate on Scripture in a way that is, ultimately, different from how we treat other books? Because as God's chosen means for communicating his triune presence, the biblical canon is different from any other book. With a canonical account of reading, "things to be read" are "divided into two basic categories: the canon, the reading of which is essential and primary; and everything else. The canon is deep and inexhaustible; everything else, while useful, is shallow and can be used up. Everything noncanonical (nonscriptural) is to be read in the light of what is canonical."[20] The Christian canon of Scripture is a book in a different category from other books, and it requires different ways of reading than do other books, since it is an inexhaustible fountain delivering God's transforming grace in Christ.

Because of the inexhaustible richness of the biblical canon, meditation and memorization has been combined with prayer for Christians in the past as a way to feed on Scripture. Consider the words of John Cassian (ca. 360-435), who combines an emphasis on Scripture memorization with a focused practice of prayer.

> Hence the successive books of the Holy Scripture must be diligently committed to memory and ceaselessly reviewed. This continual meditation will bestow on us double fruit. First, inasmuch as the mind's attention is occupied with reading and with preparing to read, it cannot be taken captive in the entrapments of harmful thoughts. Then, the things that we have not been able to understand because our mind was busy at the time, things that we have gone through repeatedly and are laboring to memorize, we shall see more clearly afterward when we are free from every seductive deed and sight, and especially when we are silently meditating at night.[21]

For all Christians, Scripture memorization and praying with Scripture are ways to enter into the Spirit's work, to move one's mind from the

---

20. Paul J. Griffiths, "Reading as a Spiritual Discipline," in *The Scope of Our Art: The Vocation of the Theological Teacher,* ed. L. Gregory Jones and Stephanie Paulsell (Grand Rapids: Eerdmans, 2002), p. 45. Griffiths is summarizing a view expressed by Hugh of St. Victor (1096-1141), one that has much in common with other premodern approaches to the Christian canon.

21. Quoted in Richard Lischer, *The Company of Preachers* (Grand Rapids: Eerdmans, 2002), p. 187.

head-spinning stream of words around us and focus on God's word in Scripture. For Christian preachers and teachers in particular, prayerful memorization of and meditation on Scripture can provide the space to hear the particular texture, logic, and flow of a biblical text that God has taken up for his own purposes. Since God uses Scripture as an instrument of grace, memorization is a way to patiently and humbly allow the words of Scripture to be chewed and digested, incorporated into our lives by the Spirit's power.

Ultimately, approaching Scripture with prayerful meditation is not so much an exegetical method as a disposition appropriate to Scripture because Scripture is the instrument of God's communicative fellowship. Prayerful meditation is not, in itself, an argument for legitimate exegesis. When discussing the exegetical merits of a particular interpretation, it is not sufficient to say, "I prayed about it." Christians who pray are still fallible; Christians who pray can still be sloppy and self-deceiving readers; Christians who pray are still sinners. Nevertheless, Scripture is properly approached with a sense that it is God's food for us to be "eaten, chewed, gnawed, [and] received in unhurried delight."[22] The time-honored practice of the *lectio divina* is one significant way that Christians can slow down and feed on the nourishment of Scripture.[23] The reading of Scripture in the practice of the daily office of communal prayer is another way for Christians meditatively to let the words of Scripture soak in. Without this prayerful and meditative dimension in our reading, we can quickly reduce Scripture to "information, mere tools and data" to be used for our own purposes. In such cases, "we silence the living voice and reduce words to what we can use for convenience and profit."[24] The disposition and practice of prayerful meditation on Scripture is a way to allow for a pause of silence before hearing the word of God, a way of seeking to participate in the Spirit's work, who speaks a word beyond our own scheming and manipulation.

22. Eugene Peterson, *Eat This Book: A Conversation in the Art of Spiritual Reading* (Grand Rapids: Eerdmans, 2006), p. 11.

23. For an accessible introduction to the *lectio divina*, see Peterson, *Eat This Book*, pp. 90-117.

24. Peterson, *Eat This Book*, p. 11.

Participating in the Drama, Part II:
Scripture and the Ministry of Word and Sacrament

A humble reception and worshipful embrace of God's word is paradigmatic to the identity of the people of God. From God's word to Adam and Eve in the Garden to God's promise to Abram, to God's law given to Israel through Moses — God's word is a fellowship-creating act that calls forth a human response. Ultimately, Christians have fellowship with God through the sending of the fellowship-creating Word, "made flesh for us and our salvation" (Nicene Creed). As a people who are made one by the Spirit in Christ's body, we gather to celebrate and enact the new life of the Spirit by hearing, touching, tasting, and singing about the mighty acts of the God of Israel made known to us in Christ. Scripture is our precious means for discerning the triune drama of salvation, and in worship we enter into this drama in remembrance, in communion with God and others, and in the hope for God's coming new creation.

The proclamation of Scripture and the sacraments are considered "means of grace" by many Christians because of their special role in the economy of salvation: both word and sacrament hold forth the heart of the gospel through creaturely means (through human proclamation and the elements of water, bread, and wine). The New Testament uses a variety of images to speak about the meaning of baptism, including images of cleansing, new life, and the gift of the Spirit. But one of the most all-encompassing images for this act of initiation into the church is that of "union with Christ."[25] In baptism, a person is united to the death and resurrection of Jesus Christ by the Spirit's power, and baptism then presents a vocation for lifelong growth into this identity in Christ, living by the Spirit rather than the old self (Rom. 6:1-14). Just as baptism is initiation into a life of union with Christ, the Lord's Supper is a participation in Christ, a continued nourishment in this salvific life through communion with Jesus Christ and his body, the church, by the Spirit's power. Both sacraments involve a scripturally mediated remembrance of God's mighty works that culminate in Christ, communion with God and others through Christ by the Spirit, and hope for the final consum-

25. James Brownson, *The Promise of Baptism* (Grand Rapids: Eerdmans, 2007), pp. 54-59.

mation of God's promises when creatures will celebrate complete communion with God, as the Lamb of God feasts with his bride.

The proclamation of Scripture functions in a similar way to how the sacraments function as the means by which those who are united to Christ by the Spirit remember, commune, and hope together. Preaching is not the proclamation of a human effort to find God but the proclamation of the revelatory history that we access through Scripture. Preaching proclaims the great drama of creation, fall, and redemption. Preaching tells the great story of the way the triune God incorporates sinners into the divine life through the forgiveness and renewal provided in the incarnation, life, cross, and resurrection of Christ. And preaching does this in a way that enacts the church's own identity: presenting the word of the living head to the body of Christ, so that it can grow in its life in the Spirit, in service to the Father. Preaching is, in some sense, "about Scripture," but it must simultaneously be about Jesus Christ, whose presence animates the worship of Christians through the Spirit's power.

As a result, Christian preaching should approach Scripture as a unified canon held together in its witness and fulfillment in Jesus Christ, not simply as a collection of varied, individual "texts."[26] Seminaries tend to train students to treat Scripture as a set of texts: each scriptural text is understood in its immediate literary and ancient historical context. While these contextual concerns are valuable, preachers need to be very clear about the canonical function of all biblical texts, particularly when it comes to Christian worship.[27] Preaching on atomized, individualized texts does not necessarily lead the hearers to focus on the gospel of Christ and the Spirit's transforming work. In a word, such an approach does not make disciples. In desperation, many pastors trained to deal with texts try to hold the congregation's attention by of-

26. Here I am indebted to a paper by Michael Pasquarello III, "Redeeming the Time: Homiletic Theology for a Pilgrim People," Institute of Christian Worship, January 2008.

27. As Richard Hays says, while theological exegesis should attend to *"the literary wholeness of individual scriptural witnesses"* and to the distinct voices in the scriptural witness, theological exegesis "can never be content only to describe the theological perspectives of the individual authors; instead, it always presses forward to *the synthetic question of canonical coherence,*" which asks "how any particular text fits into the larger biblical story of God's gracious action." Hays, "Reading the Bible with Eyes of Faith," in Root and Buckley, *Sharper than a Two-Edged Sword,* p. 91.

fering "flattened, trivialized truth by taking categories of biblical faith and representing them in manageable shapes without the material substance of the Word, Christ himself." When preaching and worship is centered on atomized texts, the congregation does not encounter the incarnate Word through the words of Scripture, but "discrete abstract topics packaged and transmitted" in a way that "reduce[s] the mystery of God to problems and solutions" on a self-help level, which displaces the need to find one's identity in Christ through the Spirit.[28] Preaching on atomized texts rather than the canon is not preaching the gospel of Jesus Christ.

The centrality of a christological-pneumatological account of the canon applies to the task of Christian formation and education as well. One widely used set of church Bible studies puts "text" over "canon" in this way. In describing the approach of its studies based on books of the Bible, it says: "Scripture should be allowed to speak for itself. If the Bible is understood on its own terms, it will convey its own truth. Biblical understanding should be a prelude to theological belief. The Bible should inform theology, not theology the Bible."[29]

On the one hand, this account shows some canonical intuitions: it speaks of Scripture and the Bible as a unified book, with a unified witness. But it is with this admission that there lies a problem. For Christians, the extremely diverse collection of books and genres in the Bible find their canonical unity only in relationship to their witness to Jesus Christ. But that *is* a claim from theology, a claim that the study series contends should never precede "biblical understanding." The question is: *What kind* of biblical understanding are we seeking? Presumably, if one consistently follows the viewpoint of this series, Old Testament texts should not be understood in the light of Jesus Christ, but exclusively with regard to their historical-literary context. But then we have lost a unified Scripture, as well as the indispensable sense that the function of all Scripture should be to form believers deeper into Christ's image by the Spirit's power. Christian formation and education need to be clear that they are not simply transmitting information or God's word

28. Pasquarello, "Redeeming the Time," p. 1-2.

29. The Kerygma Program, *Theology,* http://www.kerygma.com/mainpages/theology .htm.

in some generic form, but that we seek the Word through the word of God in Scripture.

Why are worship, Christian education, and the overall ministry of the word and sacrament so important? Ultimately, it is because the church, in these acts, holds forth the gospel of the triune drama of salvation to us — and to the world. Liturgy, preaching, and the sacraments all bear worshipful witness to the world-altering reality of the living Christ, as a community filled with a transforming Spirit. All of these ministries should be held together in their purpose and function. In these acts of Christian worship, believers taste the kingdom through their encounter with the living Christ, by means of the life-giving Spirit, who shows us our adopted identity as children of the Father. Worship tells us who we are as the church: the bride of Christ, citizens in a new kingdom. And it forms us deeper and deeper into the gospel, a gospel that is all about Christ and all about the Trinity.

The question for many pastors, worship leaders, and educators is how to reorient the ministries of the church back toward the triune gospel of God. This immediately raises questions about how worship, preaching, and education are organized. A lectionary approach can bring a congregation on a journey through the life of Christ in each given year. This can be an excellent way for congregations to grow deeper into their identity as Christ's bride. Another approach, which became prominent in the Reformation, is a *lectio continua* approach: this involves preaching and teaching continuously through a particular book of the Bible. While the *lectio continua* approach has the advantages of encouraging a congregation to dig deep into a particular book of Scripture, it has the disadvantages of not having the canonical variety of passages found in the lectionary, and it does not have the lectionary's structure based on the life of Christ.

Ultimately, congregations can move more deeply into acting in the triune drama of God by using the lectionary, the *lectio continua,* a combination of the two, or another approach for organizing the use of Scripture in worship and education. It is key to use whatever approach we adopt in a way that is self-consciously canonical and that self-consciously interprets Scripture as a way to discern the mystery of the Word in the words — as we are transformed through Scripture into our true identity as the body of Christ, by the Spirit's power. If there is no organized way of using Scripture in worship and education, then there is the tendency for leaders to play to their favorite themes and texts, making their own interests master over the scriptural canon. On the other hand, there is not a single surefire way to use Scripture in worship that automatically leads to fidelity to the gospel.

The ministry of word and sacrament is at the heart of the church's identity because the triune drama of God is *"really present* in the life of the church, and the liturgy helps us to see, taste, imagine, and *live* it."[30] Our lives are not our own, but belong to the living Christ and the Holy Spirit; in our worshipful celebration of the sacraments, we speak, hear, taste, and feel the source and identity of our true life. Worship is not constituted by a set of personal preferences resulting in a "traditional" or "contemporary" style.[31] It is constituted by the divine drama of salvation in which we are caught up in Christ, by the Spirit, in gratitude to the Father.[32]

Participating in the Drama, Part III: Scripture and Mission

Christians should not merely celebrate the individualized benefits of being in Christ and in the Spirit in worship. Rather, the Christ-centered focus of Christian worship forms a community to live as witnesses to Jesus Christ, the signs of God's kingdom, in the world. The service of word and sacrament begins with a gathering and ends with a sending, because worship is a place where church, kingdom, and world become intimately intertwined, in which creation itself is taken into the triune work of God, the church tastes the future kingdom, and believers are

30. Vanhoozer, *Drama of Doctrine,* p. 410 (italics in original).

31. The sharp separation between "contemporary" and "traditional" worship is suspect, in my view. All worship is traditional. The question is, what traditions are operative? Likewise, all worship has novel dimensions, even if it is a contemporary preference for what is "old." In a similar way, all worship is liturgical. The question is, what *kind* of liturgy is operative? A Pentecostal or Baptist church has just as much of a script (though unwritten) as more high-church liturgies, and high-church liturgical services have an irreducible dimension of spontaneity in their execution. For the purposes of this book, the key question for worship and liturgy is whether they *function* in such a way that participates in the triune drama of the gospel.

32. For more on this point, see Simon Chan, *Liturgical Theology: The Church as Worshiping Community* (Downers Grove, IL: InterVarsity, 2006), pp. 39-40.

empowered by the Spirit to live as "aliens and exiles" in the broader culture (1 Pet. 2:11).

As Darrell Guder argues, it is a fatal flaw for the church to separate the benefits believers have in Christ from their calling to be signs of the kingdom in the world.[33] Churches have tended to reduce the outreach ministries to a conception of the gospel based on either "individual salvation" or "social justice." Along with this, churches have tended to assume that worship and formation — and the ministry of word and sacrament — are internal activities for the church. Therefore, external activities are narrowly relegated to the activities of evangelism or social justice.[34]

On both sides of this internal/external dichotomy, we tend to exercise control over the purpose of Scripture in a way that is not centered in Jesus Christ. We assume that Scripture is present as an instrument for our programs — or our church's mission. But here's the problem: we don't establish or build the kingdom with our church programs. "The Kingdom of God is God's work, God's promise, and we receive it, enter it, respond to it." The kingdom is not present to serve the church; rather, the church is called to be a sign of the kingdom. In other words, the church lives under the sovereign Word, the living Christ, who is always calling the church to a "continuing conversion."[35] This conversion does not simply involve inviting outsiders to get in on personal salvation, or, on the other side, doing good in a social-justice sphere. It involves becoming a welcoming community of witnesses to Jesus Christ, a community that lives as pressing "toward the goal for the prize of the heavenly call of God in Christ Jesus" (Phil. 3:14).

The Christian's calling and identity in Christ are closely linked. Christians are called to be witnesses in the world to Jesus Christ, proclaiming in word and deed the message of Christ's gospel. The Christian calling is such because, in their identity, believers participate in

33. See Darrell L. Guder, *The Continuing Conversion of the Church* (Grand Rapids: Eerdmans, 2000), pp. 20-131.

34. While much of the "missional church" literature seeks to overcome the dichotomizing between an internal and outward focus of church ministries, some authors fail to see how the ministry of word and sacrament is not just something that happens in a particular place, but that it is an instrument for shaping a people sent by God in mission into the world.

35. Guder, *Continuing Conversion*, p. 125.

the sending of the Son from the Father to the world in love. Christians are united to Jesus Christ; the mission and sending of believers is derivative (though not identical) to that of Jesus Christ.[36] In the midst of this, Scripture is the means by which the living Christ instructs, builds up, and continually converts the church to be a people of his mission and his way by the Spirit's enabling power.

Thus, when we speak of the "end," or goal, of Scripture as being the conforming of a people to the image of Christ by the Spirit, we should not construe this as an internal matter — that is, purely in pietistic terms. The living Christ is king, and believers belong to him by the Spirit. This is the same Christ who was "sent into the world" to show God's love (John 3:16). This is the same Christ who fulfills the Abrahamic covenant, which brings God's blessing to the nations. That believers belong to God is secure: for just as the Father says, "You are my Son, the Beloved; with you I am well pleased" (Mark 1:11), so also those who belong to Christ are children of God by the Spirit (Rom. 8). But this *belonging* to Christ is not simply a static identity; it is also a journey of transformation, of entering more and more into our Christ-formed identity by the Spirit. This process involves the entirety of the Christian life: how believers act ethically, how they vote, how they relate to non-Christians, how they relate to the poor and others in need. All of these actions have ultimately one criterion: Jesus Christ. But we discern this criterion about how to participate in Christ *through Scripture,* by the Spirit's power, for Scripture is the authoritative witness to Jesus Christ and thus the authoritative word for the church's life and witness.

At the heart of this journey and transformation — not on the periphery — is the communal act of worship, centered in the act of discerning, celebrating, and tasting the Word together through God's word in Scripture.[37] There is no activity more missional than Christ-centered, Spirit-empowered worship, which speaks, hears, smells, and tastes the great drama of the gospel. Christian leaders who are concerned about outreach and church growth may be tempted to use the

36. Although believers participate, in a certain sense, in the sending of the Son as ones united to Christ, it is always as those subordinate to the lordship of Christ. The mission of Jesus Christ involves being mediator between God and humanity — acting as prophet, priest, and king. The mission of the church is not to take over these offices but to participate in them in a way that testifies to the sole lordship of Jesus Christ.

37. See Chan, *Liturgical Theology,* pp. 21-61.

Bible for making the church look more attractive to outsiders, or to convince insiders to give outreach a try. But what this insider/outsider approach obscures is that we are not so much called to make outsiders into insiders, but to *be* a people who witness with our lives that we are not our own but belong to Jesus Christ and his way, by the Spirit's power. When Scripture is performed as a script for participating in Christ by the power of the Spirit, then worship becomes a key way in which the Spirit shapes God's people for mission in the world.

Conclusion: The Theological Interpretation of Scripture and the Renewal of the Church

What is the "theological interpretation of Scripture"? Is it yet another academic trend? Why should pastors and other church leaders care about the theological interpretation of Scripture?

The theological interpretation of Scripture is, in many ways, simply the church's attempt to read Scripture again after the hubris and polarities of the Enlightenment have begun to fade. In comparison with theories of the interpretation of Scripture that see its beginning and end in historical-critical judgments (both liberal and conservative), the church through the centuries has had a remarkable amount of clarity about an alternative way: that we should read all of Scripture within a theological framework, a rule of faith that assumes that God's promises and purposes culminate in the incarnation, life, death, and resurrection of Jesus Christ. Christians have no other place from which to read Scripture than as those who are united to Christ by the Spirit. While there are important practices of reading that apply to nonbiblical books as well as to Scripture, ultimately we should not read Scripture as we read other books. We should read it in prayer, memorize it, speak and sing it with the congregation in worship — worship that delights in telling and tasting the story of God's saving work in Christ, accessed through Scripture. We should come to Scripture, as we do to worship, with an expectation of meeting the mysterious triune God, with the prayer that we would grow in our love of God and our neighbor — becoming more like Jesus Christ. Scripture is a divinely authorized instrument that the Spirit uses to make Jesus Christ present to us. It is the means for discerning the inbreaking kingdom of God in the world around us. It is the God-ordained set of writings to be used as a script for our action, which witnesses to the gospel of Jesus Christ in word and deed.

As I have noted repeatedly, recovering the theological interpretation of Scripture does not mean the rejection of historical-critical studies of Scripture. Such studies are indispensable for clarifying linguistic, contextual, and other historical dimensions of the biblical text. Yet, if one embraces the practice of theological interpretation articulated in this book, one must recontextualize historical-critical studies themselves. They provide neither the first nor final word on how Christians should interpret Scripture. While the interest in history displayed in these approaches is an asset, one must ultimately ask, "Whose history?" and "What sense of history?" For the Christian, history is a theater of divine action, and the supreme historical event that should illuminate all historical interpretation is the incarnation of the Word in Jesus Christ.

While we have much to retrieve and recover from premodern exegetes, our current historical moment is not one in which we should wish for time travel to a premodern age. Instead, our age is one in which the hegemony of the modern assumptions operative in many historical-critical approaches — with their polarizing of biblical interpretation from theology — is being challenged. As I argued in chapters 1 and 2, there is a sense in which theology is inescapable. All of our actions carry a lived ontology and theology that betray assumptions about the world, providence, and the nature of reality. It is both impossible and ultimately undesirable to escape the theological assumptions inherent in our horizons when we interpret the Bible.

The resulting "postcritical" picture is one in which interpretation is ultimately much more difficult and messy than even most historical-critics realized: the ideal exegete not only uses a broad range of tools and methods, but the ideal Christian exegete lives a life of discipleship in community, approaches Scripture with humility and a measure of suspicion about sinful interpreters (like herself), and seeks nothing less than an encounter with the mysterious triune God via the reading of Scripture. These dynamics, in which the nature of salvation and the church are implicated, are not peripheral add-ons to the foundational work of the historical critics who discern the text's meaning. They are constitutive of the joyful struggle of discerning from Scripture the script for entering into the triune drama of salvation.

At the heart of all of this is a theology of revelation, which is just as inescapable for Christians as is theology itself. Whenever Christians interpret Scripture, or speak about the inspiration or canon of Scripture, a theology of revelation is operative. There is no way to opt out. (Sometimes we may pride ourselves on being above holding a particular position on revelation, but our action will inevitably betray the facade.) Either Scripture is an external word of God, emerging from a particular history in Israel and Jesus Christ, or it is a word that contains truth only to the extent that it conforms to "universal" human categories, whether the criterion be one such as natural reason or the extent to which the text of Scripture is "humanizing." In addition, on an operative level we assume that either humans can recognize the truth when they encounter it, or that they are blinded by sin and can only recognize the truth if the teacher provides the eyes for apprehension. Concretely, this second either-or is between a Deistic operative theology and a Trinitarian one, in which the Spirit opens the eyes of the blind to apprehend truth in Jesus Christ himself, the Word of the Father.

This Trinitarian theology of revelation is also a Trinitarian theology of salvation: for when we encounter God in revelation, we do not just receive true information about God; we enter into the saving, communicative fellowship of the triune God. Again and again, we are faced with the question of whether our operative theology seeks to deny or marginalize the saving work of God in Christ, or participates in God's work through the Spirit. When we consider the contextual location of all interpretation of Scripture, we are tempted to reduce scriptural interpretation to a merely human act that sets one mode of culturally informed interpretation against another. But if we believe that Scripture is the instrument of the triune God for transforming us into Christ's image, then we must avoid such reductionism — both in theory and practice. We should be open and attentive to the Spirit's diverse work in indigenizing the gospel into cultures around the world in the process of Bible interpretation. But we must also seek to discern the bounded character of the Spirit's work as well, for the Spirit testifies to none other than the spacious yet very particular person of the church's living lord, Jesus Christ.

Why does all of this matter? Why is it worth the work of examining our own operative theology, thinking about the theological assumptions we bring to Scripture, and thinking about Trinitarian theology? It matters first and foremost because of God: God has chosen the widely divergent books and genres of Scripture to be one canonical book for the church — God's word to us — because by using the means of Scripture, God brings us into a life-giving fellowship with himself. For believers who are filled with the Holy Spirit and united to Christ, Scripture is not just a rule book; it is the fountain through which we receive the living water of Jesus Christ, the tool of the Spirit in mediating our Lord to us. Through our practices of reading Scripture, we seek to obey God by entering into the drama of God's work: reading as adopted children of the Father, reading as servants of the kingdom's king, Jesus Christ, and reading as vessels of the Spirit's own work. As we work through our practices of reading Scripture, the Spirit can enable us to discover more and more about what it means to receive Scripture as the church, that is, reading as the bride of Christ, the Spirit's living temple, God's covenant people.

Finally, through our practices of reading Scripture, we can participate in God's work of renewing the church today. We do not do this by using Scripture for our own ends, or using Scripture as something to authorize and legitimate our bright ideas about church growth, or soul saving, or society healing, or any other plan of our own. Our reading of Scripture can be part of church renewal because church renewal is not about flexing our muscles or adopting a new technique. Church renewal is about God: it is about discerning and participating in the work of the God who has been made known in Jesus Christ through the Holy Spirit, the God who is alive and active in the world today. May the church rediscover the delightful yet difficult process of reading Scripture as part of its own journey of dying and rising with Christ, by the Spirit's power, to the glory of the Father.

For Further Reading

Michael Pasquarello III, *Christian Preaching: A Trinitarian Theology of Proclamation* (Grand Rapids: Baker Academic, 2006).

Pasquarello gives a thoroughly Trinitarian portrait of the preaching task that complements the vision of preaching outlined in this chapter.

Eugene Peterson, *Eat this Book: A Conversation in the Art of Spiritual Reading* (Grand Rapids: Eerdmans, 2006).

Peterson provides an accessible and provocative portrait of feeding on Scripture in a meditative and prayerful way.

Darrell L. Guder, *The Continuing Conversion of the Church* (Grand Rapids: Eerdmans, 2000).

Guder offers a helpful account of the way God uses Scripture as a means to continually reshape the church for mission in the world.

Kevin Vanhoozer, *The Drama of Doctrine: A Canonical-Linguistic Approach to Christian Theology* (Louisville: Westminster John Knox, 2005).

Vanhoozer's significant work draws on speech-act theory and the metaphor of drama to give a vision for revitalizing theology and biblical interpretation in the church.

Joel B. Green, general editor, The Two Horizons New Testament Commentary (Grand Rapids: Eerdmans, ongoing); R. R. Reno, general editor, Brazos Theological Commentary on the Bible (Grand Rapids: Brazos, ongoing).

The above biblical commentary series seek to bridge the gap between theology and biblical studies, recovering the Bible as the church's Scripture. Both seek to put key features of a theological hermeneutic into practice in the act of interpreting Scripture.

Index of Names and Subjects

Index of Scripture References

2:21-22	133	**1 Thessalonians**		8:5	19
4:3-6	117	2:13	92	10:1	19
6:10	214			12:1	48
6:12	193	**2 Thessalonians**			
6:14-17	24	2:15	20	**1 Peter**	
6:17	214			2:11	222
		1 Timothy		3:21-22	164
Philippians		2:5-6	79		
2:4-11	82	4:16	14	**2 Peter**	
2:9-11	49			1:19	91
3:14	222	**2 Timothy**		3:15-16	92
		3	92		
Colossians		3:10–4:5	92	**1 John**	
1:1	89	3:16	16	2:4	125
1:3-5	2	3:16-17	91	2:22	125
1:5	89	4:3-4	15	4:3	14
1:15	134				
1:15-20	166-67	**Hebrews**		**Revelation**	
1:16	34	1:1-2	164	5:9	82
1:17	34	1:5-13	165	7:9	82
2:17	19	2:17	112	11:9	82
3:1	204	4:12	2, 123	14:6	82
3:3	88	4:15	112	19:17	27
3:16	214	8:1-7	157